AUSTRALIAN GUIDE TO LEGAL CITATION

Third Edition

Melbourne University Law Review Association Inc
in collaboration with
Melbourne Journal of International Law Inc
Melbourne
2010

Published and distributed by
the Melbourne University Law Review Association Inc
in collaboration with the Melbourne Journal of International Law Inc

National Library of Australia Cataloguing-in-Publication entry

Australian guide to legal citation / Melbourne University Law Review Association Inc., Melbourne Journal of International Law Inc.

3rd ed.
ISBN 9780646527390 (pbk.).
Bibliography.
Includes index.

Citation of legal authorities - Australia - Handbooks, manuals, etc.

Melbourne University Law Review Association
Melbourne Journal of International Law

808.06634

First edition	1998
Second edition	2002
Third edition	2010
Reprinted	2010, 2011 (with minor corrections), 2012 (with minor corrections)

Published by:

Melbourne University Law Review Association Inc
Reg No A0017345F · ABN 21 447 204 764

Melbourne University Law Review
Melbourne Law School
The University of Melbourne
Victoria 3010 Australia

Telephone: (+61 3) 8344 6593
Facsimile: (+61 3) 9347 8087
Email: <law-mulr@unimelb.edu.au>
Internet: <http://www.law.unimelb.edu.au/mulr>

Melbourne Journal of International Law Inc
Reg No A0046334D · ABN 86 930 725 641

Melbourne Journal of International Law
Melbourne Law School
The University of Melbourne
Victoria 3010 Australia

Telephone: (+61 3) 8344 7913
Facsimile: (+61 3) 8344 9774
Email: <law-mjil@unimelb.edu.au>
Internet: <http://www.law.unimelb.edu.au/mjil>

The *Australian Guide to Legal Citation* has been adopted by:

Adelaide Law Review
Alternative Law Journal
Australasian Journal of Natural Resource Law and Policy
Australia and New Zealand Maritime Law Journal
Australian Indigenous Law Review
Australian International Law Journal
Australian Law Librarian
Bond Law Review
Constitutional Law and Policy Review
Deakin Law Review
eLaw Journal: Murdoch University Electronic Journal of Law
Elder Law Review
Federal Law Review
Flinders Law Journal
Indigenous Law Bulletin
James Cook University Law Review
Journal of Applied Law and Policy
Journal of the Australasian Law Teachers Association
Journal of the Australasian Tax Teachers Association
Journal Jurisprudence
Journal of Law and Financial Management
Journal of Law, Information and Science
Journal of Social Security and Workers Compensation
Legal Education Review
Legal Issues in Business
Media and Arts Law Review
Melbourne Journal of International Law
Melbourne University Law Review
Monash University Law Review
New Zealand Armed Forces Law Review
Newcastle Law Review
Proctor
Public Space: The Journal of Law and Social Justice
Queensland University of Technology Law and Justice Journal
Revenue Law Journal
Sports Law eJournal
Sydney Law Review
University of New England Law Journal
University of New South Wales Law Journal
University of Notre Dame Australia Law Review
University of Tasmania Law Review
University of Western Sydney Law Review

The Melbourne University Law Review Association and
the Melbourne Journal of International Law
gratefully acknowledge the generous support of the sponsors of
the third edition of the *Australian Guide to Legal Citation*.

abl
Arnold Bloch Leibler
Lawyers and Advisers

HERBERT
SMITH
FREEHILLS

KING&WOOD
MALLESONS

Foreword to the Third Edition

The third edition of the *Australian Guide to Legal Citation* ('*Guide*') deserves celebration. The *Guide* is the successor to the *Melbourne University Law Review Style Guide*, the bane and *vade mecum* of student editors for many years. The first edition of the *Guide* appeared in 1998 and the second in 2002. This third edition is considerably longer and more detailed than its predecessors, offering guidance on the citation of new sources of law.

Until I worked on the *Melbourne University Law Review* as a student in the 1970s, I was oblivious to the delights, agonies and obsessions of editorial style and citation methods. That experience imparted enduring respect for well-tempered punctuation as well as accurate and judicious footnoting.

It is easy to dismiss rules of punctuation and legal citation as the province of pedants and to imply that attention to such matters privileges style over substance. Punctuation, however, can be critical to meaning and clarity. Lynne Truss acknowledges this significance in her charming meditation on punctuation, *Eats, Shoots and Leaves*, which she dedicates:

> To the memory of the striking Bolshevik printers of St Petersburg who, in 1905, demanded to be paid the same rate for punctuation marks as for letters, and thereby directly precipitated the first Russian Revolution.[1]

As for citation, scholars have a responsibility to acknowledge the sources of their information and ideas carefully so that they can be readily traced by their readers. In this sense, citation practices are akin to musical scales — technical exercises that ground scholarly sonatas.

The third edition expands and updates earlier versions of the *Guide*. Now legal scholars have a stern but reliable guide to the vexing issue of the use of ellipses in quotations, or the citation of parties' submissions in court cases. The distinction between em- and en-dashes is helpfully explicated. One particularly welcome change from earlier editions is the inclusion of examples for almost all rules. The third edition also contains a number of tables that present complex rules in a simple and accessible manner.

This volume mirrors the increasing significance of both comparative and international law in Australian legal scholarship. The earlier single chapter on the citation of international materials has now become seven chapters. The international section (Part IV) devotes considerable attention to treaties and the documents generated by international institutions. It includes an entirely new chapter on the citation of documents from international criminal tribunals, reflecting the astonishing growth in the law in this area over the past decade.

1 Lynne Truss, *Eats, Shoots and Leaves: The Zero Tolerance Approach to Punctuation* (Profile Books, 2003) v.

Part V introduces rules for citing legal materials from China, France, Germany, Malaysia, Singapore and South Africa and contains extensive revisions of rules relating to the United Kingdom and the United States. Such guidelines will enhance the accessibility of foreign legal sources and thus gently erode Australian legal parochialism.

The third edition is the product of intense and detailed work. It is meticulous without being stultifying. The authors are respectful sticklers working on behalf of readers everywhere and all Australian legal scholars will benefit from the careful scrutiny and sensibility of the three generations of the *Guide*'s authors.

Sticklers unite! Like the printers of St Petersburg, the authors of this *Guide* take the conventions of language and research seriously. May this compendium repay their hard work by encouraging precision in prose and clarity in citation.

Hilary Charlesworth
Professor of Law and ARC Federation Fellow
The Australian National University
Melbourne University Law Review Editor 1979
January 2010

Foreword to the First Edition

Many publishers and some publications have their own Style Guides. For years, the editors of the *Melbourne University Law Review* referred to the Style Guide published by the *Review*'s constituent body to solve problems of how to cite materials referred to in the articles and notes appearing in each issue. Now the Melbourne University Law Review Association has produced an *Australian Guide to Legal Citation*.

The project is ambitious. As its Preface says, the *Guide* 'attempts to set down and clarify citation customs where they exist, and to determine the best practice where no particular custom has been established'. In so doing the Association seeks to emulate other, long established and authoritative citation guides published by university law reviews. Of these, the 'Bluebook' is, perhaps, the best known. Published by a group of law reviews led by the *Harvard Law Review*, *The Bluebook: A Uniform System of Citation* has become the standard work in the field in the United States and has now passed through many editions. Other university law reviews have entered the field, for example, the *University of Chicago Manual of Legal Citation* and, in Canada, the *Canadian Guide to Uniform Legal Citation* published by the *McGill Law Journal*.

Not all such works attract only praise. Judge Posner has written of the Bluebook that it 'creates an atmosphere of formality and redundancy in which the drab, Latinate, plethoric, euphemistic style of law reviews and judicial opinions flourishes'.[1] But this *Guide* is not, and does not pretend to be a guide to legal style any more than it is a guide to substantive law. The *Guide* is concerned only with how sources may be identified. Its principles require that they be identified clearly and accurately, simply and efficiently, and with due sensitivity. The way in which the material from those sources is then used and presented is for the author to choose.

It is for the author to develop a style that will engage the reader. Every reader will, no doubt, wish that the style chosen is not 'drab, Latinate, plethoric [or] euphemistic'. If it is the fault will lie with the author not the *Guide*.

Justice K M Hayne
Justice of the High Court of Australia
Melbourne University Law Review Editor 1966
Melbourne
19 March 1998

1 Richard Posner, 'Goodbye to the Bluebook' (1986) 53 *University of Chicago Law Review* 1343, 1349.

Preface to the Third Edition

The third edition of the *Australian Guide to Legal Citation* is the product of collaboration between the Melbourne University Law Review Association and the Melbourne Journal of International Law. This edition marks the first time that the Review and the Journal have worked together on the *AGLC*. This collaboration has made this edition a more comprehensive, thorough and rigorous citation guide. As in previous editions, the *AGLC* aims to codify and clarify Australian citation customs where they are settled and suggests best practice where no settled custom exists.

History of the *AGLC*

The *AGLC* was first published by the Melbourne University Law Review Association in 1998. The second edition, marking a significant revision and expansion of the *AGLC*, was published in 2002. Since its first publication, the *AGLC* has become the authoritative legal citation guide within Australia, used by practitioners, law students and academics alike. It is currently prescribed by law schools and law journals around Australia as their official legal citation guide, the list of law journals who have adopted the *AGLC* reflecting the enthusiasm with which it has been received.

The Third Edition

The third edition of the *AGLC* marks a comprehensive restructure and revision. For ease of use, the *AGLC* has been divided into six Parts, separated by tabs, to allow readers to reach relevant rules quickly. For ease of reference, tables have also been included where lists of information were previously provided. All examples from the second edition have been replaced, and further examples to illustrate the possible permutations under each rule have been added. This, along with the 14 new chapters included, is the main reason for the increased length of the third edition.

Importantly, the general rules chapter has been expanded and reordered to improve the flow and clarity of rules generally applicable. This has also allowed the removal of repetition from later chapters. The Australian cases and legislation chapters have been carefully updated in order to ensure that the *AGLC* remains comprehensive and current for Australian materials. A particularly significant change has been the vastly expanded and updated international law section (now Part IV of the *AGLC*) and the addition of several new chapters for materials from foreign jurisdictions (in Part V). Important inclusions are:

- clarified rules for subsequent references;
- rules on the use of paragraph numbers in pinpoint references for cases and secondary sources;
- a rule requiring publisher information in citations of books;
- a rule on citing definitions in legislative materials;
- revised and comprehensive rules on material from the United Nations, European supranational institutions and the World Trade Organization;

- new rules for citing international criminal tribunal decisions and decisions in investor–state disputes;
- new chapters for materials from China, Hong Kong, France, Germany, Malaysia, Singapore and South Africa; and
- a chapter providing guidance on how to cite legal materials from jurisdictions not specifically covered by the *AGLC*.

Acknowledgements

Members of the Melbourne University Law Review Association and the Melbourne Journal of International Law have been involved in production of this edition of the *AGLC* over the last four years. Additionally, the third edition of the *AGLC* has been subject to a comprehensive external feedback process, which took place from September to December 2009. Of course, the Review and the Journal had previously received much feedback on the *AGLC*, which was also very helpful in compiling the third edition and for which we are grateful.

We thank first and foremost the past and present members of the '*AGLC3* Committee' for their work in revising and expanding the *AGLC*: Xiu Jing Chang, James Ellis, David Foster, Christopher Hibbard, Errol Lloyd, Luke Pallaras, Miranda Webster and Anna Zhang. The 2008 leaders of the Committee, May-Ling Low and Sunny Leow, deserve our gratitude for laying the groundwork for the third edition of the *AGLC*.

We would like to express our thanks to all those from the Melbourne Law School, from external bodies and organisations and past Members of the Review and Journal who took the time to provide us with feedback on an Exposure Draft of the third edition. This process resulted in a table of over 150 pages of suggestions for improvements to the *AGLC*, all of which we have carefully considered and many of which we have gratefully adopted. Our thanks go to Elizabeth Adeney, Renée Amyot, Alice Anderson, Adrian Bates, Laura Bellamy, Debbie Bennett, Bruce Bott, Sonia Brownhill, Adam Bushby, Howard Choo, Philip Chung, Katherine Cooke, the Hon Justice Clyde Croft, Danielle Davies, Michael Edwards, Stan Emmerson, Caroline Falshaw, Angela Fassoulas, Michele Frankeni, Robin Gardiner, Andrew Godwin, Tatum Hands, Rich Hewett, Carole L Hinchcliff, Rebecca Hughes, Tanya Josev, Chian Kee, Dakshinee Kodituwakku, Karen Kong, Jürgen Kurtz, Sunny Leow, Jeremy Leung, Dylan Lino, May-Ling Low, Bernard Lyons, Ian Malkin, Zach Meyers, Andrew D Mitchell, David Morgan, Lois Nichol, Morgan Nyland, Megan O'Brien, Ann O'Connell, Marianna Parry, Imelda Payne, Claire Riethmuller, Michelle Sanson, Dorothy Shea, Alison Shield, Alissa Sputore, Stacey Steele, Ruth Talbot-Stokes, Dominique Thiriet, Marcia Townsend, Kay Tucker, Tania Voon and Joseph Wenta. We thank especially David Foster and Xiu Jing Chang, who coordinated this external feedback process, and Ian Malkin, whose thorough, detailed and thoughtful feedback from a teaching and learning perspective was invaluable.

We would also like to express our sincere gratitude to Members of the Review and the Journal who, on a voluntary basis, have contributed in myriad ways to the production of the third edition. We are very grateful to Michelle Janczarski and Jordan Wilson-Otto for their tireless work revising the list of law report abbreviations in the Appendix. We acknowledge in this regard the assistance of Branko Ananijevski, Ella Biggs, Evgenia Bourova, Jeannette Chan, Olaf Ciolek, Martin Clark, David Davies, Shane Dawson, Kylie Finnin, Brendan Fitzgerald, Katherine Gardiner, Aditi Gorur, Liam Hickey, Rudi Kruse, Timothy Lau, Julian Law, Loretta Li, Lu Li, Amy Lim, Elliot Luke, Christopher Lum, Yin Lin Ma, Cassandra Marsh, Courtney McLennan, Laura Morfuni, Stephen Muirhead, Kristina Ong, Emma Poole, Mary Quinn, Claire Roberts, Felicity Ryburn, Darryl Slabe, Julia Wang, Ingrid Weinberg and Renshao Xu. We are also grateful to Nicholas Butera, Matthew Jaensch, Duy Nguyen and Darryl Slabe for their assistance with the cover and layout of the *AGLC*. We express our gratitude to Nirmalan Amirthanesan, Blake Ericksen, Greg Roebuck, Jenny Si and Tessa Setiadi for their dedicated administrative work in facilitating publication.

We thank all past and present Members of the Review and the Journal, and others, who participated in proofreading the final drafts of the *AGLC*: Claire Agius, Daniel Allman, Genevieve Bourke, Alex Bowen, Nicholas Butera, Xiu Jing Chang, Martin Clark, Andrew Currie, Shane Dawson, Leah Deery, James Ellis, Tim Farhall, Brendan Fitzgerald, David Foster, Simon G Frauenfelder, Katherine Gardiner, Aditi Gorur, Christopher Hibbard, Martin Ivanovski, Michelle Janczarski, Grace Jennings-Edquist, Duncan Kauffman, James Kearney, Dakshinee Kodituwakku, Rudi Kruse, Julian Law, Sunny Leow, Lu Li, Jessica Liang, Jian Liu, Errol Lloyd, Christopher Lum, Cassandra Marsh, Laura Morfuni, Simin Ngan, Jack O'Connor, Kristina Ong, Mevelyn Ong, Alexandra Phelan, Michelle Phillips, Jordina Rust, Tiong Tjin Saw, Michael Ting, Kathryn Tomasic, Vicki Toong Zi Jun, Alexandra Tran, Christopher Tran, Julia Wang, Katherine Wangmann, Ingrid Weinberg, Tiffany Wong, Zoe Wong, Fei Wu, Renshao Xu, Celine Yim, Albert Yu, Sarah Zeleznikow and Suzanne Zhou. We thank especially Luke Pallaras, Mary Quinn, Miranda Webster and Anna Zhang, whose proofreading and hard work ensured the *AGLC* was completed.

We wish to acknowledge the Melbourne Law School's continuing support of the Review and the Journal and of the *AGLC*. We also wish to acknowledge the generous support of the sponsors of the third edition of the *AGLC*: Arnold Bloch Leibler, Freehills and Mallesons Stephen Jaques.

Our task in compiling the third edition of the *AGLC* was made infinitely easier by the very solid base from which we started. In this regard, we acknowledge the General Editor of the first edition, Andrew D Mitchell, and the General Editors of the second edition, Lucy Kirwan and Jeremy Masters, as well as all those from the Review who contributed to the publication of both previous editions. In addition, we thank David Brennan, Howard Choo, Michael Crommelin AO, Bruce 'Ossie' Oswald, John Tobin and the 2006, 2007 and 2008 Editors of the Review and the Journal for their efforts in bringing about the successful collaboration between the Review and the Journal that has led to this third edition.

Finally, like the General Editors of the second edition, we wish to thank all students, practitioners, academics, judges, court officers and staff, law school administrators, law librarians, law journal editors and others who have supported the *AGLC*. We look forward to the Review and Journal receiving feedback on possible improvements to the *AGLC* for its fourth edition.

Sara Dehm and David Heaton
General Editors, *Australian Guide to Legal Citation* (3rd ed)
Melbourne
March 2010

How to Use This *Guide*

The rules in the *AGLC* have been drafted with maximum usability in mind, and slabs of text have been avoided where possible. However, some complexity in the rules is inevitable due to the variety of sources cited and the precision required in legal citation. Like most things in life, legal citation and the application of the rules in the *AGLC* should be undertaken with a good measure of common sense.

Conventions Adopted in the Rules

To avoid repetition, words in the singular usually include the plural and vice versa, except where different rules for the singular and plural are specified. Thus, 'the author's name' means the names of one or all authors (depending on the source) in most rules. In contrast, 'the last two authors' in rule 1.14.2 refers to specific authors where there are several.

Examples have also been selected to illustrate the various aspects of each rule and are set out in the same order as these aspects are explained where possible.

Except where a rule specifies otherwise, the rule applies to text (that is, discursive text in the body or in the footnotes of a piece) and to citations.

The most specific rule for a source should be used (for example, the *Charter of the United Nations* should be cited according to rule 8.1, although it is a treaty and could be cited applying the rules in chapter 7).

Finally, brief descriptions of cross-referenced rules (usually preceded by 'so' or 'in particular') have been included for convenience and to highlight the reason for the cross-reference. However, these descriptions are only summaries and do not necessarily capture all requirements of the cross-referenced rule. The cross-referenced rule should be consulted and applied in its entirety as appropriate.

Suggested Approach to Using the *AGLC*

First-time users of the *AGLC* are advised to read through the general rules (chapter 1). The first time a source of a particular kind is cited, it is also advisable to read through the chapter containing the relevant rule.

Users of previous editions will notice that some parts of the *AGLC* have moved. The contents and index should be consulted when looking for a particular rule or a means of citing a particular source. Additionally, the Quick Reference Guide at the back of the *AGLC* has been updated to reflect the rules in the third edition. This provides examples of commonly cited sources, which users familiar with the underlying rules can employ as a model for citations.

Subsequent References

Rules regarding subsequent references have been clarified. 'Ibid' can now be used for all sources, including Acts of Parliament and treaties. Rule 1.4 establishes a system for subsequent references whereby:

- if a chapter contains a rule (generally the last rule in a chapter) on subsequent references, that rule should be followed for all materials within that chapter;
- for rules on foreign jurisdictions in Part V, subsequent references should adhere to the rule for the analogous source in Parts II–III; and
- if a chapter in Part III does not contain a rule on subsequent references, 'above n' should be used as described in rules 1.4.2–1.4.3.

Sources Not Included in the *AGLC*

Where there is no rule for a particular source in the *AGLC*, users should attempt to adapt the closest fitting rule. Such citations should be guided by common sense and the following principles (roughly in order of importance):

- clarity and accuracy — sufficient information to unambiguously identify the source and any pinpoint reference should be included;
- consistency with *AGLC* style and other rules — general rules should always be observed, as should common practice in identifying a certain type of source;
- pinpoint references should appear at the end of citations (and anything qualifying a pinpoint should appear immediately after the pinpoint); and
- aesthetic appeal — convoluted citations should be avoided where possible.

Chapter 25 provides source-specific rules to be applied when citing judicial and legislative materials from foreign jurisdictions that do not have their own chapter in Part V.

In addition, when citing a source for which the *AGLC* does not contain a rule it may be instructive to examine the practice of the *Review* and *Journal* in implementing these principles. The variety of legal sources that exist invariably means that the rules in the *AGLC* are constantly developed and applied by the *Review* and the *Journal* to new situations.

Users are encouraged to inform the *Review* and *Journal* of any sources that they think could usefully be included in future editions of the *AGLC* via the Suggestion Form or via email.

Contents

PART I — GENERAL RULES

PART II — DOMESTIC SOURCES

PART IV — INTERNATIONAL MATERIALS

PART VI — APPENDIX

PART I

GENERAL RULES

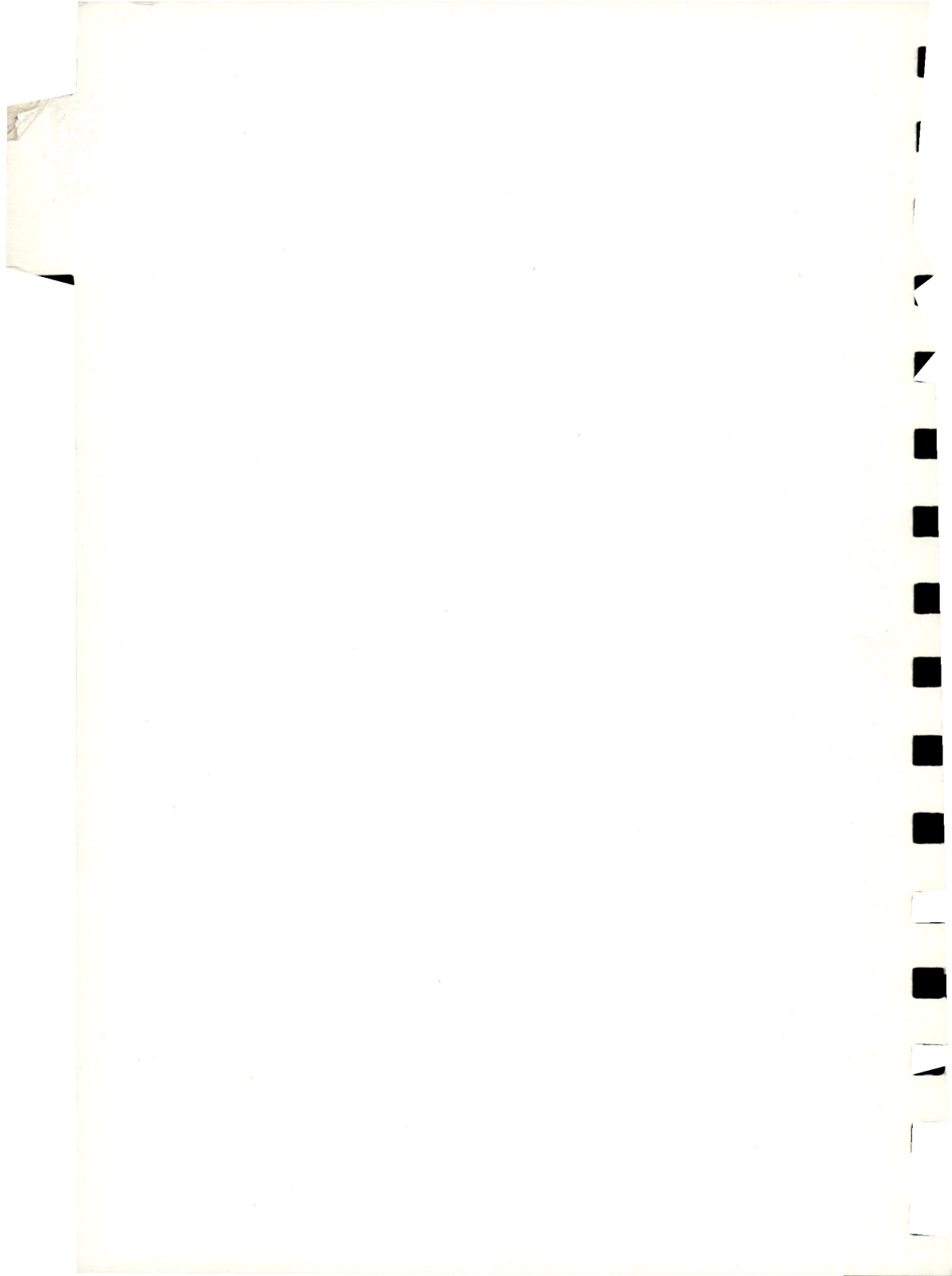

1 General Rules

1.1 General Format of Footnotes

1.1.1 When to Footnote

Rule

Footnotes should be used to:

- provide authority for a proposition;
- acknowledge a source that is relevant to an argument and indicate how it is relevant (for example, to indicate that a source directly supports or directly contradicts an argument);
- provide information that enables the retrieval of relevant sources and quotations that appear in the text; and
- provide other (often tangential or extraneous) information that is not appropriate to include in the text.

Direct quotations should always be followed by a footnote unless their source is provided in full in the text.

The first citation of a source should appear in full.

Examples

Some judges have argued that a presumption of advancement applies wherever there is a 'greater prima facie probability of a beneficial interest being intended'.[1]

This situation is likely to occur only in the rarest of cases, since the court can always make a judgement about the relative credibility of evidence given by living parties.[22]

---

1 *Wirth v Wirth* (1956) 98 CLR 228, 237 (Dixon CJ). See also *Calverley v Green* (1984) 155 CLR 242, 250 (Gibbs CJ).

…

22 In *Gissing v Gissing* [1971] AC 886, 907, Lord Diplock commented that presumptions are easily rebutted if both parties are still alive and capable of giving evidence.

1.1.2 The Position of Footnote Numbers

Rule	A footnote number should immediately follow the portion of text to which it is relevant. It should appear directly after any relevant punctuation (usually a full stop or a comma) other than an em-dash.
Examples	The court describes the best interests of the child as the 'paramount or pre-eminent consideration';[12] it is the 'final determinant' of what orders the court must make.[13] Bainbridge acknowledges that 'the tort creditor has no ability to bargain out of the default rule' of limited liability and that the company is likely to be the cheapest cost avoider (with the ability to organise insurance or take precautions to ensure the accident is prevented).[28] The Gilbert + Tobin Centre of Public Law argued that s 80.2(5) was 'welcome because it would criminalise … incitement to violence against racial, religious, national, or political groups'[34] — consistent with international human rights treaty obligations. The Court of Appeal in *Burger King Corporation v Hungry Jack's Pty Ltd* was also of the opinion that a duty of good faith should be implied in law.[40] Their Honours went on to observe: > The appellant has indeed behaved badly, but no worse than many of his age who have also lived as members of the Australian community all their lives but who happen to be citizens. The difference is the barest of technicalities. It is the chance result of an accident of birth, the inaction of the appellant's parents and some contestable High Court decisions.[55]

1.1.3 Multiple Sources in Footnotes

Rule	If a series of sources is cited within one footnote, a semicolon should be used to separate the sources. The word 'and' should *not* be used to separate the last two sources.
Examples	While a traditional approach insists strictly on offer and acceptance,[89] modern authorities have on occasion relaxed this requirement.[90]

89 See, eg, *Carlill v Carbolic Smoke Ball Co* [1893] 1 QB 256; *Gibson v Manchester City Council* [1978] 2 All ER 583; *MacRobertson Miller Airline Services v Commissioner of State Taxation (WA)* (1975) 133 CLR 125. [**Not:** … [1978] 2 All ER 583 and *MacRobertson Miller* …]

90 See, eg, *Brambles Holdings Ltd v Bathurst City Council* (2001) 53 NSWLR 153, 179–81 (Heydon JA).

1.1.4 Full Stops at the End of Footnotes

Rule

A full stop (or other appropriate closing punctuation) should appear at the end of every footnote.

Examples

46 *R v Gomez* [1993] AC 442.

47 Ibid; *R v Macleod* (2001) 52 NSWLR 389.

50 But what of the second proposition, namely, that Mr Ford was benefited by the receipt of the *means* of obtaining goods and services that he genuinely and subjectively desired?

1.1.5 Pinpoint References

Rule

A 'pinpoint reference' is a reference to a specific page, paragraph, footnote or other section of a source. Pinpoint references should not be preceded by 'at' (except in accordance with rule 1.4.4).

A pinpoint reference to a page should appear as a number. It should not be preceded by 'p' or 'pg'.

A pinpoint reference to a paragraph should appear as a number in square brackets. It should not be preceded by 'para'.

If both a page and a paragraph are referred to, the pinpoint should appear as follows:

Page [Paragraph]

A pinpoint reference to a footnote or endnote within a source should include the page on and/or paragraph in which the footnote or endnote

	appears followed by: n Footnote/Endnote Number Multiple pinpoint references to the same source should be separated by commas.
Examples	[57] H L A Hart, *The Concept of Law* (Clarendon Press, 1970) 15. [79] *Cartwright v Cartwright* [2007] NTSC 32 (9 May 2007) [10]. [**Not:** … (9 May 2007) at [10].] [92] *Futuretronics.com.au Pty Ltd v Graphix Labels Pty Ltd* (2009) 81 IPR 1, 6 [23]. [104] *Davies v Gertig [No 2]* (2002) 83 SASR 521, 528 [57] n 6, 529 [64].
Note	For rules on how pinpoint references involving more than a page, paragraph or footnote number (such as pinpoint references to legislation and treaties) should appear, see subsequent chapters of this *Guide*.

1.1.6 Spans of Pinpoint References

Rule

A span of pinpoint references should be separated by a non-spaced en-dash (–).

Spans of page, paragraph and footnote pinpoint references should appear as follows:

Type of Pinpoint	Rule	Examples
Pages	Page–Page	431–2
Paragraphs	[Para]–[Para]	[57]–[63]
Pages and Paragraphs	Page–Page [Para]–[Para]	312–13 [15]–[18]
Footnotes	Page / [Para] nn Fn–Fn	466 nn 7–8 [88] nn 113–14 23 [40] nn 22–3

In spans of paragraphs, both paragraph numbers should appear separately, enclosed in square brackets (so their numerals should not be shortened according to rule 1.12.1 on number spans).

Examples

57 Karen J Alter, *Establishing the Supremacy of European Law: The Making of an International Rule of Law in Europe* (Oxford University Press, 2001) 182–91.

79 *City of Swan v Lehman Brothers Australia Ltd* [2009] FCAFC 130 (25 September 2009) [50]–[59]. [**Not:** … [50–9].]

92 *Wurridjal v Commonwealth* (2009) 237 CLR 309, 389–90 [196]–[197].

104 Paul L Davies, *Gower's Principles of Modern Company Law* (LBC Information Services, 6th ed, 1997) 348 nn 22–4.

1.2 Introductory Signals for Citations

Rule

An introductory signal may be used before a citation to indicate the relationship between the source and a proposition in the text.

No introductory signal should be used where the source is quoted or directly supports the proposition in the text (for example, if paraphrased).

The following introductory signals may be used:

Introductory Signal	Meaning
See	The source provides qualified support for the proposition in the text.
See, eg,	The source is one of several authorities supporting the proposition.
See also	The source provides additional or general support for the proposition in the text.
See especially	The source is the strongest of several authorities supporting the proposition in the text.

See generally	The source provides background information on the topic discussed in the text.
Cf	The source provides a useful contrast to illustrate the proposition in the text. ('Cf' means 'compare'.)
But see	The source is in partial disagreement with the proposition in the text.
Contra	The source directly contradicts the proposition in the text.

Except for '*contra*', introductory signals should not be italicised.

Examples

1 See, eg, *James v Australia and New Zealand Banking Group Ltd* (1986) 64 ALR 347.

2 Cf *Legislative Instruments Act 2003* (Cth) s 5.

3 *Contra* Giorgio Gaja, 'Expulsion of Aliens: Some Old and New Issues in International Law' (1999) 3 *Cursos Euromediterráneos Bancaja de Derecho Internacional* 283, 293.

1.3 Sources Referring to Other Sources

Rule

The original of any source referred to should be consulted and cited. However, where it is important to show that one source is referred to in another source, the following clauses should be used to join the citations:

Clause	Meaning
quoting	The first-listed source directly quotes the second source.
quoted in	The first-listed source is quoted directly in the second source.
citing	The first-listed source refers to (but does not directly quote) the second source.
cited in	The first-listed source is referred to (but not quoted directly) in the second source.

	These clauses should be preceded by a comma.
Examples	7 *Burger King Corporation v Hungry Jack's Pty Ltd* (2001) 69 NSWLR 558, 570 (Sheller, Beazley and Stein JJA), quoting *Metropolitan Life Insurance Co v RJR Nabisco Inc*, 716 F Supp 1504, 1517 (Walker J) (SD NY, 1989). 8 *Mason v Freedman* [1958] SCR 483, cited in *Shelanu Inc v Print Three Franchising Corporation* (2003) 64 OR (3d) 533, 556.

1.4 Subsequent References

1.4.1 Ibid

Rule	'Ibid' should be used to refer to a source in the *immediately preceding* footnote. However, 'ibid' should not be used where there are multiple sources in the preceding footnote. 'Ibid' can be used regardless of how the source is cited in the preceding footnote (whether in full, using 'ibid' or using 'above n'). If the pinpoint reference is *identical* to that in the preceding footnote, 'ibid' should appear without (repeating) the pinpoint reference. If the pinpoint reference is *different* from that in the preceding footnote, 'ibid' should be followed by the (different) pinpoint reference. There should *not* be a comma (or other punctuation) between 'ibid' and a pinpoint reference. As 'ibid' directs the reader back to the immediately preceding footnote, it should not be used to refer to a source cited earlier in the *same* footnote. (Rather, 'at' should be used in accordance with rule 1.4.4.) 'Ibid' should be capitalised if it appears at the start of a footnote.
Examples	18 Eric Barendt, *Freedom of Speech* (Oxford University Press, 2nd ed, 2005) 163. 19 Ibid. 20 Ibid 174–5.

[21] *Defamation Act 2005* (Vic) s 37.

[22] Ibid s 38.

…

[156] Rosalyn Higgins, *Problems and Process: International Law and How We Use It* (Clarendon Press, 1994). Cf Barendt, above n 18, 67.

[157] Barendt, above n 18, 69. [**Not:** Ibid 69 **or** Barendt, ibid 69.]

…

[204] Higgins, above n 156, 220.

[205] Ibid 222, 239.

1.4.2 Above and Below

Rule

'Above n' should be used where a source has been cited:

- in a previous footnote other than the immediately preceding footnote; or
- in the immediately preceding footnote, if it is not the only source in that footnote.

However, 'above n' should *not* be used for:

- cases, international judicial decisions and other materials in chapters 2, 9, 10, 11 (in accordance with rules 2.14, 9.5, 10.3, 11.4);
- legislation and other materials in chapter 3 (in accordance with rule 3.9);
- certain sources in chapter 6 (in accordance with rule 6.16);
- treaties (in accordance with rule 7.6); and
- UN, WTO, GATT and EU documents (in accordance with rules 8.5, 12.4, 13.3),

and analogous sources in Part V.

Citations using 'above n' should appear as follows:

[Author's Surname], above n [Footnote Number], [Pinpoint].

The 'footnote number' is the footnote in which the source is first cited.

Where the author is a body (such as a government department), the body's name should be included in place of the author's surname.

Where there is no author or editor, the title (or an abbreviated form of the title) should be included in place of the author's surname.

Where works by different authors with the same surname are cited, the authors' full names as they appear on the source should be included in place of the author's surname (to avoid ambiguity).

Where multiple works by the same author are referred to, subsequent references should appear as follows:

[Author's Surname], [Title (Shortened if Necessary)], above n [Footnote Number], [Pinpoint].

'Above' and 'below' may also be used to direct the reader to portions of the text (to particular footnotes, page numbers or numbered parts of the text). To direct the reader to more than one footnote, 'above nn' or 'below nn' should be used.

'*Op cit*', '*loc cit*', '*supra*' and '*infra*' should not be used.

Examples

9 Catharine MacMillan, *Mistakes in Contract Law* (Hart Publishing, 2010) 38.

…

20 MacMillan, above n 9.

…

22 N C Seddon and M P Ellinghaus, *Cheshire and Fifoot's Law of Contract* (LexisNexis, 9th ed, 2008) 867.

…

27 Seddon and Ellinghaus, above n 22, 20.

…

31 'Obama Moves to Bring Russia in from the Cold', *The Age* (Melbourne), 21 September 2009, 10.

…

34 'Obama Moves to Bring Russia in from the Cold', above n 31, 10.

…

39 Sir Anthony Mason, 'Future Directions in Australian Law' (1987) 13 *Monash University Law Review* 149.

40 Keith Mason, *Constancy and Change: Moral and Religious Values in the Australian Legal System* (Federation Press, 1990).

…

43 Keith Mason, above n 40, 28.

…

47 Kim Rubenstein, 'Meanings of Membership: Mary Gaudron's Contributions to Australian Citizenship' (2004) 15 *Public Law Review* 305.

48 Kim Rubenstein, *Australian Citizenship Law in Context* (Lawbook, 2002).

…

61 Rubenstein, *Australian Citizenship Law in Context*, above n 48, 65–74.

62 Rubenstein, 'Meanings of Membership', above n 47, 307–11.

…

74 See above n 21 and accompanying text.

75 See above nn 31–3.

76 See below Part III(A)(1).

1.4.3 Short Titles

Rule

Short titles are an abbreviated form of the title of a source. A short title should appear in italic text and be enclosed in (non-italic) inverted commas and parentheses after the initial citation of a source. It should appear after any pinpoints or parenthetical clauses in the citation. Only one short title should be included in the first citation of a source.

Cases, legislation, certain sources in chapter 6, treaties, international judicial decisions and UN, WTO, GATT and EU documents (and analogous sources in Part V) may be given short titles for subsequent references in accordance with rules 2.14, 3.9, 6.16, 7.6, 8.5, 9.5, 10.3,

11.4, 12.4, 13.3.

For reports and other similar secondary sources (and additionally where indicated throughout the *Guide*), a short title based on the title of the source may be used with an 'above n' reference instead of the author's surname. Subsequent references should then appear as follows:

Short Title, above n Footnote Number, Pinpoint.

Examples

2 Parliamentary Joint Committee on Corporations and Financial Services, Parliament of Australia, *Opportunity Not Opportunism: Improving Conduct in Australian Franchising* (2008) 4 ('*Opportunity Not Opportunism Report*').

…

16 *Opportunity Not Opportunism Report*, above n 2, 7.

1.4.4 At

Rule

Where the same source is cited multiple times within the *same footnote*, the full citation should not be repeated and 'at' should precede subsequent pinpoint references. However, it is not necessary to repeat a pinpoint reference using 'at' if the subsequent pinpoint reference is the same as that immediately beforehand.

Where there are multiple sources in a footnote, 'at' should be used only to refer to the *immediately* preceding source.

'At' can be used regardless of how the source is first cited in a footnote (whether in full, using 'ibid' or using 'above n').

Examples

291 Commonwealth, *Parliamentary Debates*, Senate, 17 June 2008, 2626. The Minister explained that '[t]here may be a number of reasons that prevent a person's immediate removal, … includ[ing] … issues surrounding the acquisition of the person's travel documentation': at 2627. [**Not:** … documentation': ibid 2627.]

292 Ibid 2625. The Minister noted that his Department had 'grouped the data to prevent the identification, or potential identification, of any one person.' [**Not:** … any one person': at 2625.]

…

[378] Cf Andrew Lynch and George Williams, 'Beyond a Federal Structure: Is a Constitutional Commitment to a Federal Relationship Possible?' (2008) 31 *University of New South Wales Law Journal* 395; Tony Blackshield, '*New South Wales v Commonwealth* — Corporations and Connections' (2007) 31 *Melbourne University Law Review* 1135. Blackshield notes a failed 'attempt to confine the scope of s 51(xx)': at 1137. Lynch and Williams argue that the Commonwealth nevertheless has 'inadequate powers to fully regulate industrial relations': Lynch and Williams, above n 378, 397 n 10. [**Not:** … industrial relations': at 397 n 10.]

1.5 Quotations

1.5.1 Short and Long Quotations

Rule

In the body of the text and in the footnotes, short quotations (of three lines or less) should be incorporated within single quotation marks.

Long quotations (of more than three full lines) should appear indented from the left margin, in a smaller font size, and without quotation marks. Legislative and treaty extracts, regardless of length, may also appear this way.

Where a long quotation appears in a footnote, the citation of the source should appear on the line directly preceding or following the quotation.

Examples

Priestley JA stated that 'there is a close association of ideas between the terms unreasonableness, lack of good faith, and unconscionability.'[67]

The Judge stated:

> Thus elaborating, the first question is whether 'a financial benefit is given' within the meaning of s 229 of the *Corporations Act* (in relation to the prohibition on related party benefits without member approval). The second question is whether the exception for arm's length terms in s 210 of the *Corporations Act* is made out …[135]

The *Constitution* provides in s 92 that:

> On the imposition of uniform duties of customs, trade, commerce, and intercourse among the States, whether by means of internal carriage or ocean navigation, shall be absolutely free.

---

[138] The claims are inferred from the rhetorical question:

> Do we respond [to the problems in remote communities] with more of what we have done in the past? Or do we radically change direction with an intervention strategy matched to the magnitude of the problem?

Commonwealth, *Parliamentary Debates*, House of Representatives, 7 August 2007, 10 (Malcolm Brough, Minister for Families, Community Services and Indigenous Affairs and Minister Assisting the Prime Minister for Indigenous Affairs).

1.5.2 Punctuation Introducing Quotations

Rule

A short quotation should be integrated into the sentence. No specific punctuation is required to introduce it. It may be introduced by a colon.

No punctuation should be used where a sentence leads seamlessly into a long quotation. However, a colon is typically the appropriate punctuation to introduce a long quotation.

Examples

This was most obvious in relation to proof of title to land, which 'necessitated tracing title back through an unbroken chain of events and documents, perhaps as far as the Crown grant.'[7]

As the Privy Council commented: 'it does not, in their Lordships' opinion, assist to rationalise the defence … as concerned to protect security of receipts and then to derive from that rationalisation a limitation on the defence.'[8]

However, he ultimately rejected the submission that the detention of these children was indefinite and explained that

> the period of detention had a clear terminus. This (putting it broadly) is the voluntary election of the children (through their parents) to leave Australia or the completion of the legal proceedings brought by the parents on the children's behalf …[9]

In 2005, the matter finally reached the House of Lords, whereupon Baroness Hale declared:

> My Lords, this is, and has always been, a case about children, their rights and the rights of their parents and teachers. Yet there has been no one here or in the courts below to speak on behalf of the children. … The battle has been fought on ground selected by the adults.[10]

1.5.3 Quotations within Quotations

Rule

In short quotations (integrated within the text), double quotation marks should be used for a quotation within the quoted text, single quotation marks for a further quotation inside that, and so forth.

In long quotations, single quotation marks should be used for a quotation within the quoted text, double quotation marks for a further quotation inside that, and so forth.

Quotation marks in quoted text should be changed to adhere to this rule.

Examples

He observed that 'the threshold for determining that an international organisation has "effective control" over an operation ought to be high.'

They summarised Kolb's view as follows:

> Kolb describes good faith as a general principle of international law that has as its aim 'to blunt the excessively sharp consequences sovereignty and its surrogates … may have in the international society, in ever-increasing need of cooperation' …

1.5.4 Punctuation within Quotations

Rule

Punctuation marks at the end of quoted text (full stops, commas, etc) should not be included in a quotation unless the punctuation mark forms part of and is important to the quotation. Other punctuation marks within a quotation should be retained in quoted text.

Hyphens, en-dashes and em-dashes in quotations should be altered to adhere to rule 1.6.3. Full stops in abbreviations in quotations should be omitted to adhere to rule 1.6.1.

Examples

As Walker observed, the 'call for states to grant asylum to those persecuted because of prostitution or homosexuality was made over 20 years ago'. [**Original:** … over 20 years ago, and since then …]

Carmody J goes on to offer the following interpretation of the 'paramount but not sole' formulation appearing in previous cases:

> The best interests of the child(ren) concerned, both in the short and longer term, and not the interests or needs of the parents (let alone the interests of either one of them) are the paramount consideration. However, they are not the sole factor. [**Original:** … sole factor. The …]

The observation that 'there is a sharp student–teacher dichotomy that ought to be observed' was repeated. [**Original:** … a sharp student-teacher dichotomy …]

1.5.5 Capitalisation at the Start of Quotations

Rule

If a quotation begins a sentence, the first letter of the quotation should be capitalised. Otherwise, the first letter of the quotation should not be capitalised. Both may require use of square brackets to indicate amendment to the quotation (see rule 1.6.6).

Where a colon precedes a quotation, the first letter of the quotation should appear as it does in the original (whether capitalised or not).

Examples

According to the *Oxford English Dictionary*, an 'exception' is

> [s]omething that is excepted; a particular case which comes within the terms of a rule, but to which the rule is not applicable; a person or thing that does not conform to the general rule affecting other individuals of the same class.[30]

Subsequently, in *Dextra*, the Privy Council asserted inequitability as the central rationale of the defence:

> The defence should be regarded as founded on a principle of justice designed to protect the defendant from a claim to restitution in respect of a benefit received … in circumstances in which it would be inequitable to pursue that claim, or to pursue it in full.[94]

1.5.6 Ellipses

Rule

Omissions from a quotation should be indicated by an ellipsis (…). A space should precede and follow an ellipsis (however, a space should *not* separate an ellipsis and a footnote number, in accordance with rule 1.1.2).

Where the omitted text immediately follows a complete sentence, a full stop (or other closing punctuation) at the end of that sentence should be included *before* an ellipsis.

A full stop should not be included *after* an ellipsis (whether to show that words before the end of the sentence have been omitted, or to show that an omission falls between complete sentences in the source).

'Leaders' (ellipses at the start of quotations) should not be included.

An ellipsis should be added to or replace any punctuation at the end of a long quotation if the quotation does not end with an appropriate closing punctuation mark.

Examples

In applying *Sullivan*, his Honour considered that the High Court had

> emphasised … that foreseeability of harm to the fathers was not sufficient to ground a duty of care. … *Sullivan v Moody* is not on all fours with the present case because it involved a statutorily imposed duty … Notwithstanding this difference, in my view *Sullivan v Moody* gives guidance … [**Not:** … imposed duty … . Notwithstanding …]

In *Australian Capital Television*, McHugh J noted:

> If the institutions of representative and responsible government are to operate effectively … the business of government must be examinable and the subject of scrutiny, debate and ultimate accountability at the ballot box. The electors must be able to ascertain and examine the performances of their elected representatives …[84]

1.5.7 Editing Quotations

Rule

If a quotation is altered, the alteration should be included within square brackets (in accordance with rule 1.6.6). Omissions from a quotation should be indicated by an ellipsis (in accordance with rule 1.5.6).

Spelling and capitalisation within quotations generally should not be changed (except as required by rule 1.5.5).

All case names, statute titles, treaty titles and titles of sources that should be italicised according to the rules in this *Guide* should also be italicised where they appear in quotations (in accordance with rule 1.8.2).

Examples

The Court observed that 'the [Commonwealth] Act was clearly within power.' [**Original:** … the Act was clearly within power. …]

Additionally, in Tasmania, an as yet insufficiently tested provision in the *Anti-Discrimination Act 1998* (Tas) appears to enlarge the concept and application of anti-vilification laws in relation to conduct which 'offends, humiliates, … insults or ridicules'. [**Original:** … offends, humiliates, intimidates, insults or ridicules …]

As Bunjevac has observed:

> According to the International Organization of Securities Commissions, this perception was significant in structured finance ratings because the rating served as an independent informational input about complex transactions. [**Not:** … Organisation …]

1.5.8 [sic]

Rule

'[sic]' (meaning 'thus') should be inserted after a significant error in material being quoted. Insignificant errors should be left as they appear in the original and should not be followed by '[sic]'.

The term '[sic]' should not be used to mark non-Australian English spelling or non-standard capitalisation.

Although a quotation is obviously the work of another author, '[sic]' may be inserted after discriminatory or offensive expressions in quotations. The preferable solution, where possible, is to paraphrase the passage to avoid any such expression.

Example

He stated brazenly: 'They misunderestimated [sic] me.'

1.5.9 Emphasis and Citations in Quotations

Rule

Any change of emphasis in or omission of citations from a quotation should be indicated in parenthetical clauses after the citation. The parenthetical clauses should follow any pinpoint reference.

Where italics appear in or are added to quoted text for emphasis, the following parenthetical clauses should be used:

Parenthetical Clause	Meaning
(emphasis in original)	The emphasis was in the original text and has not been changed.
(emphasis added)	There was no emphasis in the original text and emphasis has been added.
(emphasis altered)	The emphasis in the original text has been removed or changed.

Any omission of citations from a quotation should be indicated by '(citations omitted)' immediately after the pinpoint (regardless of whether one or several citations have been omitted). However, where possible, a quotation within a quotation should be attributed to its original source in accordance with rule 1.3.

If multiple parenthetical clauses are necessary, they should be enclosed in separate sets of parentheses.

Examples

[16] *Commonwealth v WMC Resources Ltd* (1998) 194 CLR 1, 91–2 (emphasis in original) (citations omitted).

[17] Julie Mertus, 'Considering Nonstate Actors in the New Millennium: Toward Expanded Participation in Norm Generation and Norm Application' (2000) 32 *New York University Journal of International Law and Politics* 537, 552–3 (citations omitted).

1.6 Punctuation

1.6.1 Full Stops

Rule

Full stops should be used only to mark the end of a sentence or

	footnote. Full stops should not be used in abbreviations, after initials or after heading numbers or letters. If a quotation or an element of a citation includes full stops in abbreviations or after initials, the full stops should be omitted. This should *not* be indicated in the quotation or the citation element, with an ellipsis or otherwise.
Examples	Dr Messrs Mr Mrs Ms A-G LLB Cth NSW Qld cf eg et al ie D H Lawrence James Hadley, *Introduction to Roman Law in Twelve Academical Lectures* (D Appleton, 1873). [**Not:** … (D. Appleton, 1873).]

1.6.2 Commas

Rule	Among other uses, commas should be used to separate items in a list of more than two (including the last two items where necessary to avoid ambiguity). Commas should appear on both sides of a subordinate clause within a sentence or not at all. They should *not* be used only before, or only after, a subordinate clause.
Examples	It was agreed that there would be significant implications for solicitors, barristers and the judiciary. Methods of transport included car, horse and cart, and hovercraft. The effect of any equality guarantee would have been so far-reaching that, even if currently out of favour, it cannot be ignored. [**Not:** The effect of any equality guarantee would have been so far-reaching that even if currently out of favour, it cannot be ignored.]

1.6.3 Em-Dashes, En-Dashes, Hyphens and Slashes

Rule	An em-dash (—) may be used to indicate an interruption within a sentence or in place of a colon. Em-dashes may also be used on both sides of a parenthetical remark or apposition.

	An en-dash (–) is half the length of an em-dash and may be used to indicate a span between two numbers (see rules 1.1.6, 1.12.1 and 1.13.2). An en-dash should be used in preference to a forward slash (/) to mark a tension or disjunction between two concepts. However, a forward slash may be used to separate alternatives. A hyphen (-) is half the length of an en-dash and is used to connect the parts of a compound word. Hyphenation should adhere to rule 1.9.
Examples	There was no clear ratio in the decision — indeed, with seven judgments, this was to be expected. [**em-dash**] Once again, those who might have thought otherwise — presumably including Judge McDonald in her dissent in *Tadić* — were in fact conflating two fundamentally different types of liability. [**em-dashes**] There was much discussion on pages 14–22. [**en-dash**] tort–contract dichotomy [**en-dash**] a yes/no question [**slash**] evidence-based policymaking [**hyphen**]

1.6.4 Quotation Marks

Rule	Single (and double) quotation marks should be used for quotations in accordance with rules 1.5.1 and 1.5.3. Single quotation marks may be used to indicate that a word is being used in an unconventional sense.
Example	The State Department 'confirmed' the accuracy of the information by not formally objecting to its publication.

1.6.5 Parentheses

Rule	A full stop or other punctuation ending a sentence should be placed before a closing parenthesis only if the entire sentence appears within the parentheses.

Example	There can be no doubt of the importance of such a law. (That does not mean, of course, that its comparative merits cannot be debated.) [**Not:** (That does not mean, of course, that its comparative merits cannot be debated).]

1.6.6 Square Brackets

Rule	Square brackets should be used to indicate an adjustment to a quotation (for example, where a letter that was upper-case in the original text has been changed to lower-case or vice versa). They may also be used to enclose comments that did not appear in the original text being quoted. Square brackets should also be used to enclose information in citations of translations (see rule 5.6 and chapter 25).
Example	As Kirby J noted, '[t]he Minister did not appoint [Justice Mathews] as reporter until her consent was first signified.'

1.7 Capitalisation

Rule	Capitalisation should be consistent throughout a document. Generally, words should be capitalised only where they: • appear at the beginning of a sentence, title or heading; or • are proper nouns. However, where it is important to expression or meaning, other words may be capitalised. In the titles of all cited materials and in all headings, the first letter of the following should be capitalised: • the first word in a title or heading (and a subtitle or subheading); and

- all other words in the title except articles ('the', 'a', 'an'), conjunctions (for example, 'and', 'but') and prepositions (for example, 'on', 'with', 'before').

However, phrases in foreign languages appearing in titles and headings should be capitalised in accordance with convention in that language.

The following words should generally be capitalised wherever they occur:

Act (or 'Bill') of Parliament	Attorney-General
Bar (that is, the group of practising barristers)	Cabinet
Commonwealth	Crown
Executive Council (but 'the executive')	Governor
	Governor-General
Her Majesty, the Queen	her Honour, his Honour, their Honours
Imperial	
Minister (of the Crown)	Ombudsman
Parliament (but 'parliamentary')	Premier
Prime Minister	

The following words should generally appear in lower case (except at the beginning of a sentence, in a title or in a heading):

common law (and other names of legal classification such as 'administrative law')	federal
	government
	internet
judiciary	legislature
local government	press (that is, the media)
statute	

'Court' should be capitalised when used to refer to a specific court (such as the High Court or the Court of Appeal). However, 'a court' and 'the court' when used in a general sense (absent reference to a specific court) should not be capitalised.

'State' and 'Territory' should be capitalised (whether used as a noun or an adjective) when referring to a specific state or territory. However, when used generally they should not be capitalised.

Examples

In a negligence claim, the court must judge the reasonableness of the defendant's act or omission.

	The High Court had handed down its judgment in *Cole v Whitfield*,[22] but not in *Bath v Alston Holdings Pty Ltd*.[23] The Court's decision in *Cole* nevertheless proved difficult to apply. The State of New South Wales has always taken a different approach from that of other states.

1.8 Italicisation

1.8.1 Italicisation for Emphasis

Rule	Words within the text may be italicised for emphasis. If words in a quotation are italicised for emphasis, a parenthetical clause must be inserted in the footnote to indicate this (in accordance with rule 1.5.9).
Example	Rather, the suggested changes would act as a signalling mechanism to parent companies that their control, and their wrongdoing *through* that control, would result in a statutory piercing of the veil.

1.8.2 Italicisation of Source Titles

Rule	All case names, statute titles, treaty titles and titles of other materials that should be italicised according to the rules in this *Guide* should appear in italics in the text and footnotes (regardless of whether a full citation of the source is included). They should also be italicised in quotations and in citations (for example, within the titles of journal articles) whether or not they are italicised and/or cited in full in the original source. Where source titles are italicised in a quotation, this need *not* be indicated by a parenthetical clause in the footnote or by '[sic]'.
Examples	However, there is one key provision — s 39(1) — of the *Charter* that is unique:

> If, otherwise than because of this *Charter*, a person may seek any relief or remedy in respect of an act or decision of a public authority on the ground that the act or decision was unlawful, that person may seek that relief or remedy on a ground of unlawfulness arising because of this *Charter*. [**Original:** … Charter … Charter …]

Ann Elizabeth Mayer, 'Reflections on the Proposed United States Reservations to *CEDAW*: Should the *Constitution* Be an Obstacle to Human Rights?' (1996) 23 *Hastings Constitutional Law Quarterly* 727.

1.8.3 Italicisation of Foreign Words

Rule

Foreign words and phrases should be italicised unless they appear in the latest edition of the *Macquarie Dictionary*.

Accordingly, the following examples of foreign words and phrases should not be italicised:

ab initio	ad hoc	ad idem
amicus curiae	bona fide	caveat emptor
de facto	de jure	et al
ex gratia	ex parte	ex post facto
habeas corpus	inter alia	laissez-faire
non est factum	obiter dictum	per se
prima facie	quid pro quo	raison d'être
ratio decidendi	sui generis	terra nullius
ultra vires	vice versa	vis-a-vis

The following are examples of foreign words and phrases that should be italicised:

contra proferentem	*ex ante*	*jus ad bellum*
lex fori	*ne bis in idem*	*non-refoulement*
quantum meruit	*res ipsa loquitur*	*stare decisis*

1.9 Spelling and Hyphenation: Official Dictionary

Rule

Spelling should comply with the latest edition of the *Macquarie Dictionary*. Where alternative spellings are given, the first-listed should be used unless there is good reason to do otherwise.

Hyphenation should also comply with the latest edition of the *Macquarie Dictionary*. If a compound expression does not appear in the *Macquarie Dictionary*, it should be hyphenated (not spelt as one word).

Generally, if a hyphenated word should be capitalised according to rule 1.7, the letter following the hyphen should also be capitalised.

Examples

home-buyer	peacekeeping	pre-industrial
re-enact	reinvigorated	decision-maker
multidimensional	policymaker	nonpayment

Peter Birks (ed), *Wrongs and Remedies in the Twenty-First Century* (Clarendon Press, 1996). [**Not:** … *Twenty-first Century*…]

1.10 Grammar: Official Guide

Rule

Grammar should be guided by the latest edition of *Fowler's Modern English Usage*.

1.11 Inclusive Language

Rule

Gender-inclusive language should be used. The words 'he', 'his' and 'him' should not be employed as the supposedly neutral third-person singular. It is acceptable to use 'he or she', 'she or he' or any derivative form ('his', 'her' and 'him'). It is also acceptable to use 'they' (and derivative forms 'their' and 'them') as neutral singular pronouns.

Authors should avoid terms such as 'the reasonable man', 'chairman' and 'spokesman'. Neutral terms such as 'the reasonable person', 'chairperson' and 'spokesperson' should be substituted. However, it may be appropriate to retain gender-specific language where this accurately conveys the intended meaning in the relevant context (for example, in the sentence: 'A plaintiff may be liable in negligence to her own foetus while driving.')

1.12 Numbers and Currency

1.12.1 Numbers

Rule

Numbers under 10 should be written in words. Numerals should be used for:

- numbers over nine;
- numbers of sections, pages, paragraphs, clauses, editions and other elements of citations;
- ratios, mathematical expressions, decimal numbers, etc; and
- series of related quantities, numbers, ages, etc.

However:

- a sentence should never begin with a numeral (even if it is a date) — words should be used instead; and
- a number 10 or above may be written out in full where it forms part of a proper noun.

In numbers of five digits or more, a space (not a comma) should be used to separate each group of three digits.

In numbers expressed in terms of millions or billions, the relevant term should be written out in full (not abbreviated to 'm' or 'bn' etc).

Where a span of numbers is referred to, only the minimum number of digits necessary should be included in the second number (for example, 87–8, 436–62). However, for numbers whose last two digits are 10–19, the last two digits should always be included (for example, 11–14, 215–19).

The above rules also apply to ordinal numbers (for example, second, 40th). The letters in ordinal numbers over nine should appear in superscript.

Examples

one	six	nine
10 per cent	19	673
8700 [**Not:** 8,700 **or** 8 700]	10 695 [**Not:** 10,695]	2 000 000
2.6 million [**Not:** 2.6m **or** 2.6 m]	7 billion	3.9 trillion

The High Court split 4:3.

	The government announced a Ten Point Plan in response to *Wik*. In June 2008, the Minister informed the Senate that as of 7 May 2008 there were 25 people in immigration detention following the cancellation of their visas. Of those 25 persons, only 1 had been in Australia for less than 5 years, with the remaining 24 having been in Australia for between 11 and 45 years prior to visa cancellation. first / third / ninth 10th / 21st / 52nd

1.12.2 Currency

Rule	Currency amounts should appear in figures, immediately preceded by an appropriate symbol (or commonly used code) indicating denomination. The currency denomination need not be specified if it is obvious from the context.
Examples	AUD100 / $1600 / A$16 000 HK$1.3 million / USD200 000 / US$300 000 £150 / ¥250 000 / €47 373.75 The Court awarded $110 000 in damages under the *Trade Practices Act 1974* (Cth). The declared value of the cargo was US$6600.

1.13 Dates

1.13.1 Full Date

Rule	The 'full date' should be written in the form: [Day] [Month] [Year] The day should not be an ordinal number. If the day of the week is included in addition to the full date, the name

	of the day should precede the full date and should not be followed by a comma.
Examples	15 June 1985 [**Not:** 15th June 1985] Thursday 6 March 1987 [**Not:** Thursday, 6 March 1987]

1.13.2 Spans of Dates

Rule	Spans of years should include the first year in full, an en-dash, and the last two digits of the final year. However, if the final year occurs in a different century from the first, the final year should appear in full. Spans of days in the same month should include both dates in full separated by an en-dash. Spans of dates over different months and spans of full dates should be separated by a spaced en-dash.
Examples	1986–87 1999–2009 21–22 September [**Not:** 21–2] 17 July – 19 August 1 January – 29 February 1996 22 March 1946 – 27 August 1947

1.13.3 Decades and Centuries

Rule	When referring to decades, an apostrophe should *not* be placed between the year and the 's'. If only the last two digits of the year are included, an apostrophe should precede them. Centuries should be indicated using ordinal numbers (which should adhere to rule 1.12.1).
Examples	1970s or '70s [**Not:** 1970's **or** '70's] 21st century

1.14 Names

1.14.1 General Rule

Rule	Initials in names should be separated by a space and should not be

followed by full stops (see rule 1.6.1).

Conventional titles such as 'Ms' or 'Mr' may be included in discursive text before a person's name (in both the body and the footnotes), but should not be included in authors' names in citations.

Honorific titles or titles indicating qualification, such as 'the Hon', 'Dr' or 'Professor', may be included in discursive text (in both the body and the footnotes) before a person's name. They should not be used in an author's name in citations, except for 'Sir', 'Dame' and peerage titles (such as 'Lord', 'Baroness', 'Earl' and 'Viscount').

Postnominals, such as 'AM' (Member of the Order of Australia) and 'LLB' (Bachelor of Laws), should not be included after the name of an individual in either the text or the footnotes (unless relevant). They should never be included after the name of an author in a citation.

Examples

Referring to an individual discursively in the text or footnotes:	Referring to an author in a citation:
Associate Professor Tania Voon	Tania Voon
Dame Nellie Melba	Dame Nellie Melba
Lord Nicholls	Lord Nicholls
Professor Ian Malkin	Ian Malkin
Baroness Hale	Baroness Hale
Dr Cockburn	John Cockburn
Ms Sharon Rodrick	Sharon Rodrick
Mr Gageler SC	Stephen Gageler
H L A Hart	H L A Hart

1.14.2 Authors of Secondary Sources

Rule

In citations of secondary sources, authors' names should appear exactly as they do on the source (subject to the other rules in this chapter). This may require the same author's name to appear differently in citations of several of their works.

Where there are two or three authors, the names of all authors should be included and the word 'and' should separate the names of the last two authors. All surnames should be included in 'above n' references.

Where there are more than three authors, the name of the author appearing first on the source should be included, followed by 'et al'. The first listed author's surname and 'et al' should be included in 'above n' references.

Examples

14 P D Finn, 'The Fiduciary Principle' in T G Youdan (ed), *Equity, Fiduciaries and Trusts* (Carswell, 1989) 1, 4. [**Not:** Paul Finn, 'The Fiduciary Principle' …]

15 Kathy Bowrey and Natalie Fowell, 'Digging Up Fragments and Building IP Franchises' (2009) 31 *Sydney Law Review* 185.

16 Robert Cryer et al, *An Introduction to International Criminal Law and Procedure* (Cambridge University Press, 2007). [**Not:** Robert Cryer, Håkan Friman, Darryl Robinson and Elizabeth Wilmshurst, …]

…

19 Bowrey and Fowell, above n 15, 187.

20 Cryer et al, above n 16, 124.

1.14.3 Publications Authored by or Produced on Behalf of a Body

Rule

If a publication is authored by a body (for example, a government department or a non-governmental organisation), the name of that body should appear as the author.

Where a government department is the author and the jurisdiction is not apparent from the department's name, the abbreviated jurisdiction may be included in parentheses after the department's name. The abbreviations in rule 3.1.3 should be used.

If a subdivision of a body or an individual writing on behalf of a body is the author, both the name of the subdivision or individual and the body should be included in the form:

Individual/Subdivision, Body

	Where there are multiple subdivisions, only the most specific subdivision should be included (unless this creates ambiguity).
Examples	Queensland Government, *ClimateSmart 2050 — Queensland Climate Change Strategy 2007: A Low Carbon Future* (2007). Department for Women (NSW), *Heroines of Fortitude: The Experiences of Women in Court as Victims of Sexual Assault* (1996). Criminal Justice Sexual Offences Taskforce, Attorney-General's Department (NSW), *Responding to Sexual Assault: The Way Forward* (2006). Russell Cocks, Law Institute of Victoria, *Ethics Handbook: Questions and Answers* (2004) 133.

1.14.4 Judges

Rule	Judges writing curially (that is, in a judgment) should be referred to by their surname and their judicial title (such as 'Justice') or peerage title (such as 'Lord'), both in the text and in citations. Typically, but not always, the judicial title should be indicated by an abbreviation placed after the judge's name (in accordance with rules 2.9.1, 9.2.8, 23.1.6 and 24.1.8). Honorifics (such as 'the Hon') should not be included when citing a judge writing curially. Where a judge's first name or initials appear on a case and are necessary to unambiguously identify the judge, they should be included. When citing a judge writing extra-curially (both in the text and in citations), the unabbreviated judicial or peerage title (such as 'Justice' or 'Chief Justice') should be included before the judge's name, unless the judge has a title (such as 'Sir', 'Dame' or a peerage title) that makes a judicial title unnecessary. When citing a former judge (writing extra-curially), their former judicial title should not be included. 'Sir', 'Dame' or any peerage title should be included. Honorifics may be included in the text, but not in citations (in accordance with rule 1.14.1). In both curial and extra-curial writing, any territorial designation of a peer (such as 'of Chieveley') should not be included unless necessary to avoid confusion.

Examples

Context	Example(s)
Citing a judge writing curially (in text):	As Dixon J noted in *Essendon Corporation v Criterion Theatres Ltd*, …
Citing a judge writing curially (in a citation):	58 *Essendon Corporation v Criterion Theatres Ltd* (1947) 74 CLR 1, 18 (Dixon J).
Citing a judge writing extra-curially (in text):	Opening the Law Librarians' Symposium, Sir Daryl Dawson stated: 'The modern law library is something which I could not have envisioned in my student days.' … Justice Virginia Bell … Lord Hoffmann …
Citing a judge writing extra-curially (in a citation):	99 Sir Anthony Mason, 'Future Directions in Australian Law' (1987) 13 *Monash Law Review* 149; Lord Cooke, 'Foreword' in Janet McLean (ed), *Property and the Constitution* (Hart Publishing, 1999) v; Justice Michael Kirby, 'Transnational Judicial Dialogue, Internationalisation of Law and Australian Judges' (2008) 9 *Melbourne Journal of International Law* 171.
Citing a former judge (in text):	As pointed out by the Hon Mary Gaudron in a recent speech, …
Citing a former judge (in a citation):	104 Michael Kirby, 'The Dreyfus Affair — Lessons for Today' (Speech delivered at the Melbourne Law School, Melbourne, 1 September 2009).
Including the territorial designation of a peer	This was a different approach from that of Lord Nicholls. [**Not:** … Lord Nicholls of Birkenhead] **But:** Lord Keith of Avonholm had a very different view of negligence from that held by Lord Keith of Kinkel.

1.15 Headings and Titles

1.15.1 Title and Author

Rule

Titles should be capitalised, centred and in bold type. The name(s) of the author(s) should be in large and small capitals and centred.

Example

REFLECTIONS ON THE WORLD TRADE ORGANIZATION AND THE PROSPECTS FOR ITS FUTURE

BRYAN MERCURIO*

1.15.2 Heading Levels

Rule

Headings should appear as follows:

Heading Level	Attributes
I HEADING LEVEL ONE	Upper-case Roman numeral not italicised; heading in large and small capitals and centred
A *Heading Level Two*	Upper-case letter not italicised; heading italicised and centred
1 *Heading Level Three*	Arabic numeral not italicised; heading italicised and left-aligned
(a) Heading Level Four	Lower-case letter and heading italicised and left-aligned
(i) Heading Level Five	Lower-case Roman numeral and heading italicised and left-aligned

Capitalisation in headings should adhere to rule 1.7.

1.16 Bibliographies

Rule

Where a bibliography is required, it should list all sources that were relied upon (not only those referred to in the text and footnotes).

The bibliography may be divided into the sections below. However, a section may be omitted and other categories or subdivisions may be included as needed (with appropriate renumbering).

A *Articles/Books/Reports*

B *Cases*

C *Legislation*

D *Treaties*

E *Other*

All sources listed in the bibliography should be cited as set out in these rules (cases should be set out as if referred to in the text). However:

- an author's first name and surname should be inverted and separated by a comma — for works by two or more authors, only the *first* author's name and surname should be inverted; and
- full stops should *not* follow the citations.

Sources should be listed in alphabetical order according to:

- the surname of the first-listed author;
- where the author is an institution, the first word of the name of the institution (excluding 'the'); or
- where there is no author, the first word of the title.

Where two authors have the same surname, the authors should be sorted alphabetically according to their first names. Where more than one work by an author is listed, the works should be listed in chronological order.

Example

BIBLIOGRAPHY

A *Articles/Books/Reports*

Eastwood, Christine, Sally Kift and Rachel Grace, 'Attrition in Child Sexual Assault Cases: Why Lord Chief Justice Hale Got It Wrong' (2006) 16 *Journal of Judicial Administration* 81

Foster, Michelle, *International Refugee Law and Socio-Economic Rights: Refuge from Deprivation* (Cambridge University Press, 2007)

McLachlin, Beverley, 'Academe and the Courts: Professor Mullan's Contribution' in Grant Huscroft and Michael Taggart (eds), *Inside and Outside Canadian Administrative Law: Essays in Honour of David Mullan* (University of Toronto Press, 2006) 9

B *Cases*

Lane v Morrison [2009] HCA 29 (26 August 2009)

Northern Cameroons (Cameroon v United Kingdom) (Preliminary Objections) [1963] ICJ Rep 15

C *Legislation*

Aerodrome Landing Fees Act 2003 (Vic)

Australian Constitution

D *Treaties*

Convention against Torture and Other Cruel, Inhuman or Degrading Treatment or Punishment, opened for signature 10 December 1984, 1465 UNTS 85 (entered into force 26 June 1987)

E *Other*

New South Wales, *Parliamentary Debates*, Legislative Assembly, 15 December 1909

PART II

DOMESTIC SOURCES

2 Cases

Examples	*R v Tang*	(2008)	237	CLR	1	, 7
	Bakker v Stewart	[1980]		VR	17	, 22
Element	Case Name	Year	Volume	Law Report Series	Starting Page	Pinpoint
Rule	2.1	2.2	2.2	2.3	2.4	2.5

2.1 Case Name

2.1.1 Parties' Names: General Rule

Rule

A citation of an Australian case should include the parties' names in italics as they appear on the first page of the report, except that:

- punctuation should adhere to rule 1.6.1 (so full stops should not be used in abbreviations);
- capitalisation should adhere to rule 1.7;
- where the parties are individuals, given names and initials should be omitted;
- only the first-named plaintiff and first-named defendant should be cited ('*& Anor*' or '*& Ors*' should not be used to indicate other parties); and
- where the case involves more than one action, only the first action should be cited.

Examples

Alati v Kruger (1955) 94 CLR 216.

Momentum Productions Pty Ltd v Lewarne (2009) 254 ALR 223. [**Not:** *Momentum Productions Pty Ltd v Richard John Lewarne* …]

Hot Holdings Pty Ltd v Creasy (1996) 185 CLR 149. [**Not:** *Hot Holdings Pty Ltd v Creasy and Ors* …]

Tame v New South Wales (2002) 211 CLR 317. [**Not:** *Tame v New South Wales; Annetts v Australian Stations Pty Ltd* …]

2.1.2 Business Corporations and Firms

Rule

Where a party is a business corporation or firm, the following abbreviations should be used:

Word	Abbreviation
and	&
Company	Co
Limited	Ltd
Proprietary	Pty
Incorporated	Inc
(in liquidation)	(in liq)
(in provisional liquidation)	(in prov liq)
(administrator appointed)	(admin apptd)
(manager appointed)	(mgr apptd)
(receiver appointed)	(rec apptd)

Other (including foreign) words and phrases designating corporate status (for example, GmbH, AG, plc, SA, Sarl, etc) or a special status under incorporation legislation (for example, rec and mgr apptd) should be abbreviated according to convention.

'*Trading as*' or '*t/as*', trading names and former company names should not be included.

Where 'the' forms part of a company or firm name, it should be included.

Examples

Andrew Shelton & Co Pty Ltd v Alpha Healthcare Ltd (2002) 5 VR 577.

Australian Competition and Consumer Commission v C G Berbatis Holdings Pty Ltd (2003) 214 CLR 51.

Lumbers v W Cook Builders Pty Ltd (in liq) (2008) 232 CLR 635. [**Not:** … *Pty Ltd (in liquidation)* …]

Olivaylle Pty Ltd v Flottweg GmbH & Co KGaA [No 3] (2008) 76 IPR 152.

The Mond Staffordshire Refining Co Ltd v Harem (1929) 41 CLR 475. [**Not:** *Mond Staffordshire Refining Co Ltd v Harem trading as 'Mulsol' Laboratories* …]

2.1.3 The Commonwealth and the States and Territories

Rule	Where the Commonwealth of Australia is a party, '*Commonwealth*' should be used. Where a party is an Australian state or territory, only the name of that State or Territory should be used (for example, '*Queensland*', not '*State of Queensland*'). 'The' should be omitted from such names.
Examples	*Wong v Commonwealth* (2009) 236 CLR 573. [**Not:** … *The Commonwealth* …] *New South Wales v Amery* (2006) 230 CLR 174. [**Not:** *State of New South Wales* …]

2.1.4 The Crown

Rule	*Rex* ('the King') and *Regina* ('the Queen') should be abbreviated to '*R*' where the Crown is the first-named party. Where the Crown is the respondent, '*The King*' or '*The Queen*' (as appropriate) should be written out in full.
Examples	*R v Reid* [2007] 1 Qd R 64. *Nydam v The Queen* [1977] VR 430. *Kemp v The King* (1951) 83 CLR 341.

2.1.5 Governmental Entities, Foreign Governments and International Organisations

Rule	Where a governmental entity or instrumentality, a foreign government or an international organisation is a party, its name should appear in the conventional shortened form (if any exists), rather than the full elaborate form. However, the full form should be used where this is necessary to avoid ambiguity. 'The' should be omitted from such names.

Examples

BP Refinery (Westernport) Pty Ltd v Shire of Hastings (1977) 180 CLR 266. [**Not:** … *President, Councillors and Ratepayers of the Shire of Hastings* …]

Papua New Guinea v Daera Guba (1973) 130 CLR 353. [**Not:** *Administration of the Territory of Papua New Guinea* …]

O'Donoghue v Ireland (2008) 234 CLR 599. [**Not:** … *Republic of Ireland* …]

European Community v Commissioner of Patents (2006) 68 IPR 539.

But: *Zoeller v Federal Republic of Germany* (1989) 23 FCR 282.

2.1.6 Ministers and Officers of the Commonwealth, States and Territories, and Government Departments

Rule

Where a Minister of the Crown or government officer is a party, their title should appear in the conventional shortened form (if any exists), rather than the full elaborate form.

Where both the title and name of a Minister or officer are included in the report, only the title should be included (and the name omitted). However, where only their name is included in the report, this should be included.

Where the jurisdiction of the Minister or officer is included in their title (but not evident in the conventional shortened form), it should not appear in full, but should appear in parentheses in an abbreviated form after their title (using the abbreviations in rule 3.1.3).

Where a secretary, under secretary or officer of a government department is a party and the name of the department appears in the case name, their position and the name of the department (separated by a comma) should be included. If the jurisdiction of the department is included in its title, it should appear in parentheses in an abbreviated form after the department name (using the abbreviations in rule 3.1.3).

'The' should be omitted from such titles.

Examples

MacCormick v Federal Commissioner of Taxation (1984) 158 CLR 622. [**Not:** *MacCormick v Commissioner of Taxation of the Commonwealth of Australia* …]

M238 of 2002 v Minister for Immigration and Multicultural and Indigenous Affairs [2003] FCAFC 260 (21 November 2003). [**Not:** … *Ruddock, The Minister for Immigration* …]

Hicks v Ruddock (2007) 156 FCR 574.

Zhu v Treasurer (NSW) (2004) 218 CLR 530. [**Not:** *Zhu v Treasurer of New South Wales* …]

Houssein v Under Secretary, Department of Industrial Relations and Technology [1980] 2 NSWLR 398.

2.1.7 Attorneys-General and Directors of Public Prosecutions

Rule

Where an Attorney-General is a party, '*Attorney-General*' should be used in the text and '*A-G*' in a footnote citation.

Where a party is a Director of Public Prosecutions, '*Director of Public Prosecutions*' should be used in the text and '*DPP*' in a footnote citation.

Both should be followed by the abbreviated form of the relevant jurisdiction within parentheses (see rule 3.1.3), even if it is not included in the report.

'The' should not precede '*A-G*' or '*DPP*' in a citation.

Examples

In *Director of Public Prosecutions (NSW) v RHB*,[2] the Court of Criminal Appeal of New South Wales reconsidered a sentence imposed for murder.

16 *DPP (Vic) v Finn* (2008) 186 A Crim R 235.

17 *Bradshaw v A-G (Qld)* [2000] 2 Qd R 7, 13.

2.1.8 *Re*

Rule	Procedural phrases such as '*In re*' and '*In the matter of*' should be shortened to '*Re*'.
Examples	*Re Judiciary and Navigation Acts* (1921) 29 CLR 257. [**Not:** *In re Judiciary and Navigation Acts* …] *Re Palmer; George v McIntyre* (1902) 2 SR (NSW) 200.
Note	'*Re*' means 'in the matter of' and is commonly used when a court acts in an advisory or guardianship capacity, as it does in cases involving the interpretation of wills or trusts. For example, if *Re Smith* were a trusts case, Smith would be the testator or settlor. Extended case names such as *Roberts v Jones; Re Williams* can occur where, for example, Williams left property to Jones to hold on trust for Roberts and Roberts sues Jones to enforce the will. In speech, '*Re*' should be rendered 'in the matter of'.

2.1.9 *Ex parte*

Rule	'*Ex parte*' should not be abbreviated and '*Ex*' should be capitalised.
Examples	*Re McBain; Ex parte Australian Catholic Bishops Conference* (2002) 209 CLR 372. *J Boag & Son Brewing Ltd v Cascade Brewery Co Pty Ltd; Ex parte Banks Paton Australia Pty Ltd* (1997) 7 Tas R 119. *R v Kirby; Ex parte Boilermakers' Society of Australia* (1956) 94 CLR 254.
Notes	'*Ex parte*' indicates that the party to an action is acting in the absence of the other party. For example, *Ex parte Wilson* indicates that Wilson brought the action. Extended case names such as *Ex parte Wilson; Re Ho* can occur where, for example, Wilson brings an action concerning the rights of Zhang (a third party) under Ho's will.

	Case names such as *R v Chan; Ex parte Owen* can refer to applications for prerogative writs (administrative law remedies) and contempt proceedings. In the case of a prerogative writ, the above citation would mean that Owen has made an application for a prerogative writ against Chan.

2.1.10 *ex rel*

Rule	When citing a relator action, the first-named relator should always be included and should be introduced by the abbreviation '*ex rel*'.
Example	[227] *A-G (Vic) ex rel Dale v Commonwealth* (1945) 71 CLR 237. [**Not:** *A-G (Vic) (at the relation of Dale and Others)* …]
Note	The abbreviation '*ex rel*' stands for '*ex relatione*', which means 'upon the relation or information of'. Where a legal action is brought by the Attorney-General at the request of a private individual who lacks the necessary standing to sue in their own name, the private individual is termed the 'relator' and the case 'the relator action'. In pre-20th century law reports, '*ex rel*' ordinarily denoted that the reporter did not personally witness the proceedings but obtained an account second-hand.

2.1.11 *v*

Rule	A '*v*' should generally separate the parties' names. It should not be followed by a full stop and should be italicised.
Example	*K-Generation Pty Ltd v Liquor Licensing Court* (2007) 99 SASR 58.
Note	In speech, the '*v*' between the parties' names is rendered 'and' in a civil action and 'against' in a criminal action both in Australia and the United Kingdom. It is not pronounced 'versus' as it is in the United States of America.

2.1.12 Admiralty Cases

Rule	For admiralty cases in rem, only the name of the vessel in question should appear as the case name. For admiralty cases in personam, the parties' names (separated by '*v*') followed by a semicolon and the name of the vessel at issue should appear as the case name. 'The' should be included in names of vessels.
Examples	*The Maria Luisa [No 2]* (2003) 130 FCR 12. [**Not:** *Kent v Vessel 'Maria Luisa' [No 2]* …] *Great Peace Shipping Ltd v Tsavliris Salvage (International) Ltd; The Great Peace* [2003] QB 679.
Note	Admiralty cases in rem are proprietary actions brought against the ship itself, and the ship (not a person) is named as the respondent. Admiralty cases in personam are actions between private parties that relate to a ship.

2.1.13 Multiple Proceedings between the Same Parties

Rule	For multiple proceedings under the same name, the number of the decision should be indicated in square brackets if the number appears *in the case name itself*. Where there are multiple proceedings under the same name, but the case names do not (all) include numbers, it may be appropriate to give the cases descriptive short titles to differentiate them (see rule 2.1.14).
Examples	*Bahr v Nicolay [No 2]* (1988) 164 CLR 604. *Wentworth v Rogers [No 5]* (1986) 6 NSWLR 534. *Kuwait Airlines Corporation v Iraqi Airways Co [Nos 4 and 5]* [2002] 2 AC 883.

The litigation commenced by Mrs Cubillo went through many stages.[6]

---

6 See *Cubillo v Commonwealth* (1999) 89 FCR 528 ('*Cubillo Strike-Out Application*'); *Cubillo v Commonwealth [No 2]* (2000) 103 FCR 1 ('*Cubillo Trial*'); *Cubillo v Commonwealth* (2001) 112 FCR 455 ('*Cubillo Appeal*').

2.1.14 Abbreviated and Popular Case Names

Rule

Where a case is commonly referred to by a popular name or is referred to more than once, the popular name or an abbreviated version of the case name may be included as a short title and used in subsequent references to the case. A popular case name may also be included as a short title to identify a case (even where the case is not referred to subsequently).

The short title should adhere to rule 1.4.3 (so should be italicised and placed within single inverted commas and parentheses following the initial citation). It may be placed in the text or in the footnotes.

In subsequent references, the short title should replace the parties' names. Otherwise, the citation should appear as normal.

Examples

Several Justices on the Court have shown an extreme aversion to '[t]op-down reasoning'.[1] This aversion has emerged in several different contexts. … Those arguing for judicial acknowledgment of restitution for unjust enrichment have not been immune to this criticism.[4]

The external affairs power has been interpreted widely in many recent decisions, such as *Commonwealth v Tasmania* (1983) 158 CLR 1 ('*Tasmanian Dam Case*').[9]

---

1 See, eg, *McGinty v Western Australia* (1996) 186 CLR 140, 232 (McHugh J) ('*McGinty*'). See also *Roxborough v Rothmans of Pall Mall Australia Ltd* (2001) 208 CLR 516, 544–5 (Gummow J) ('*Roxborough*').

…

4 See *Roxborough* (2001) 208 CLR 516, 544–5 (Gummow J), 579 (Kirby J). Gummow J relied upon the comments of McHugh J in *McGinty* (1996) 186 CLR 140, 232.

…

9 See also *Victoria v Commonwealth* (1996) 187 CLR 416 (‘*Industrial Relations Act Case*’).

2.1.15 Omitting the Case Name

Rule

The case name should be omitted in a footnote citation if the case name appears in full (or as a defined short title in accordance with rule 2.1.14) in the sentence accompanying the footnote.

Examples

In *Thomas v Mowbray*,[12] the control order regime established under the schedule to the *Criminal Code Act 1995* (Cth) survived a constitutional challenge.

Toohey J, in *Mabo v Queensland [No 2]*, also discussed fiduciary obligations.[14]

But: In *Al-Kateb*, several High Court Justices discussed the role of international law in Australian constitutional interpretation.[20]

---

12 (2007) 233 CLR 307.

…

14 (1992) 175 CLR 1, 204.

…

20 *Al-Kateb v Godwin* (2004) 219 CLR 562.

2.2 Year and Volume

Rule	Volumes of law report series are organised either by year or by volume number. Where the volumes of a law report series are organised by volume number, the year in which the decision was handed down (often, but not necessarily, the year in which the case was reported) should appear in parentheses '( )'. Where the volumes of a law report series are organised by year, the year of the volume in which the case is reported should appear in square brackets '[ ]'. If more than one volume is produced in a single year, the volume number should be included between the year and the report series abbreviation.
Examples	*R v Lester* (2008) 190 A Crim R 468. *Sent v Andrews* (2002) 6 VR 317. [**Not:** … (2002–03) 6 VR 317] *King v King* [1974] Qd R 253. *Rowe v McCartney* [1976] 2 NSWLR 72.
Notes	On occasion, a law report series may change from being organised by year to volume number or vice versa. The system used for the volume in which the relevant case appears should be used. Where a law report series organised by year contains decisions that were handed down before the year of the volume, the year of the volume (not that of the decision) should nevertheless be included. The discrepancy between the year of the volume and the year of decision may be explained discursively if it is important.

2.3 Law Report Series

2.3.1 Authorised/Unauthorised and Generalist/Specific Report Series

Rule

A reported version of a case should be cited in preference to an unreported version.

Where a case appears in an 'authorised' report series, this series should be cited in preference to any other reported version. Where a case has not been reported in an authorised report series, an unauthorised report series should be cited.

Generalist (unauthorised) report series should be cited in preference to subject-specific (unauthorised) report series, which sometimes include extracts rather than the full decision.

If the only report of a case is a partial report and the relevant part is not extracted, the case should be cited as unreported (in accordance with rule 2.8).

Examples

Balchin v Anthony (2008) 22 NTLR 52. [**Not:** … [2008] NTSC 2 (4 January 2008).]

Rural Press Pty Ltd v Australian Competition and Consumer Commission (2003) 216 CLR 53. [**Not:** … (2003) 203 ALR 217.]

Mar Mina (SA) Pty Ltd v City of Marion (2008) 163 LGERA 24.

Scott v CAL No 14 Pty Ltd [No 2] (2009) 256 ALR 512. [**Not:** … (2009) 52 MVR 45.]

But: *Tobacco Control Coalition Inc v Philip Morris (Australia) Ltd* [2000] FCA 1004 (27 July 2000) [69], [74]. [**Not:** … [2000] ATPR (Digest) ¶46-205.]

Note

Authorised reports usually indicate that they are the 'authorised reports' of the court in the opening pages of each volume. Judgments reproduced therein have been approved by a judge or their associate.

2.3.2 Abbreviations for Report Series

Rule

The name of the report series should be abbreviated using the abbreviations contained in the Appendix to this *Guide*. The name of the report series should not appear in italics.

The following are the most commonly cited Australian authorised (or preferred) report series:

Court/Jurisdiction	Report Series	Years
High Court of Australia	CLR	1903–
Federal Court of Australia	FCR	1984–
Australian Capital Territory	ACTR (in ALR)	1973–2008
	ACTLR	2007–
New South Wales	SR (NSW)	1901–59
	NSWR	1960–70
	NSWLR	1971–
Northern Territory	NTR (in ALR)	1979–91
	NTLR	1990–
Queensland	QSR	1902–57
	Qd R	1958–
South Australia	SALR	1899–1920
	SASR	1921–
Tasmania	Tas LR	1904–40
	Tas SR	1941–78
	Tas R	1979–
Victoria	VLR	1875–1956
	VR	1957–
Western Australia	WALR	1898–1958
	WAR	1958–

Commonly used unauthorised Australian report series are: ALR, ALJR, FLR, Fam LR, NTR.

Names of report series that do not appear in the Appendix should be written out in full and not italicised.

Example

Arnold v Regent Press Pty Ltd [1957] QSR 211.

2.4 Starting Page

Rule

The first page of the case should appear after the abbreviated form of the report series. If the case is identified by a unique reference rather than a starting page, that reference (including accompanying symbols) should be used instead of a starting page number.

Examples

Theophanous v Herald & Weekly Times Ltd (1994) 182 CLR 104.

Borg v Commissioner, Department of Corrective Services [2002] EOC ¶93-198.

Overlook Management BV v Foxtel Management Pty Ltd [2002] Aust Contract Reports ¶90-143, 91 970.

Note

CCH report series often use a unique reference instead of a starting page.

2.5 Pinpoint Reference

Rule

Pinpoint references should adhere to rules 1.1.5–1.1.6 and be preceded by a comma and a space. Where the pinpoint reference is to the first page of the report, the page number should be repeated. In accordance with rule 1.1.5, a series of pinpoint references should be separated by commas rather than 'and'.

Where cases are paginated, pinpoint references should be to pages. Page numbers should adhere to rule 1.12.1.

Where a report has both page numbers and paragraph numbers, page numbers should *always* be included in a pinpoint reference. In accordance with rules 1.1.5–1.1.6, paragraph numbers *may* be included *in addition*.

Where pages and paragraph numbers are included in pinpoint references, both a page number and a paragraph number should be included after 'ibid' unless exactly the same page(s) *and* paragraph(s) are referred to in the 'ibid' citation.

Examples

Re Mackenzie Grant & Co (1899) 1 WALR 116, 116.

De L v Director-General, Department of Community Services (NSW) [No 2] (1997) 190 CLR 207, 211, 221–2.

Garry Rogers Motors (Aust) Pty Ltd v Subaru (Aust) Pty Ltd [1999] ATPR ¶41-703, 43 014.

Total Ice Pty Ltd v Maroochy Shire Council [2009] 1 Qd R 82, 89–92 [18]–[19], 93 [24].

At trial, it was held that 'the appellants had not proved that they had suffered any loss or damage.'[49] On appeal, it was pointed out that the appellants may have suffered loss 'if the outgoings for which they were liable included sums of a kind which had not been taken into account in forming the estimate they were given.'[50] This was so even though the appellants may have received value for their payments.[51] Yet the case had been dismissed at first instance.[52]

---

49 *Murphy v Overton Investments Pty Ltd* (2004) 216 CLR 388, 402 [29].

50 Ibid 404 [32].

51 Ibid.

52 Ibid 404 [33].

2.6 Court

Rule

Generally, the name of the court should not be included in a citation of a reported case. However, where it is important to identify the court and the court is not otherwise apparent (for instance, from the report series or the text), the name of the court may be included in parentheses, following any pinpoint references and parenthetical clauses.

The jurisdiction of the court should not be indicated where it is otherwise apparent (as is the case for authorised state law reports).

Examples	[22] *Aldrick v EM Investments (Qld) Pty Ltd* [2000] 2 Qd R 346 (Court of Appeal). [23] *Chief Executive Officer of Customs v Labrador Liquor Wholesale Pty Ltd* (2001) 188 ALR 493, 498 (emphasis added) (Queensland Court of Appeal).

2.7 Parallel Citations

Rule	Parallel citations should not be used in citations of Australian cases. In accordance with rule 2.3.1, the most authoritative available version of a case should be cited.
Example	*Perre v Apand Pty Ltd* (1999) 198 CLR 180. [**Not:** *Perre v Apand Pty Ltd* (1999) 198 CLR 180; 164 ALR 606; [1999] HCA 36.]
Note	Parallel citations are used in citations of the United Kingdom Nominate Reports (see rule 23.1.3) and early United States Supreme Court decisions (see rule 24.1.3).

2.8 Unreported Decisions

2.8.1 Decisions with a Medium Neutral Citation

Example	*Quarmby v Keating*	[2009]	TASSC	80	(9 September 2009)	[11]
Element	Case Name	Year	Unique Court Identifier	Judgment Number	Full Date	Pin-point

Rule	Unreported decisions with a medium neutral citation (a citation system that does not depend on publisher or medium) should be cited as shown above. However, a medium neutral citation should only be used where the medium neutral citation was allocated *by the court itself*. Where this is not the case, unreported judgments should be cited in accordance with rule 2.8.2.

Case names should adhere to rule 2.1. Pinpoint references should appear as paragraph numbers, and should adhere to rules 1.1.5–1.1.6. There should be no punctuation between the full date and any pinpoint.

The following are the current preferred unique court identifiers for Australian Supreme and superior Commonwealth courts, and the years for which the courts allocated judgment numbers themselves:

Court	Unique Court Identifier	Years
High Court of Australia	HCA	1998–
High Court of Australia — Special Leave Dispositions	HCASL	2008–
Federal Court of Australia	FCA	1999–
Federal Court of Australia — Full Court	FCA	1999–2001
	FCAFC	2002–
Family Court of Australia	FamCA	1998–
Family Court of Australia — Full Court	FamCA	1998–2007
	FamCAFC	2008–
Supreme Court of the Australian Capital Territory (including Full Court)	ACTSC	1998–
Australian Capital Territory Court of Appeal	ACTCA	2002–
Supreme Court of New South Wales	NSWSC	1999–
New South Wales Court of Appeal	NSWCA	1999–
New South Wales Court of Criminal Appeal	NSWCCA	1999–
Supreme Court of the Northern Territory (including Full Court)	NTSC	1999–
Northern Territory Court of Appeal	NTCA	2000–
Northern Territory Court of Criminal Appeal	NTCCA	2000–
Supreme Court of Queensland	QSC	1998–
Queensland Court of Appeal	QCA	1998–
Supreme Court of South Australia (including Full Court until end of 2009)	SASC	1999–
Supreme Court of South Australia — Full Court	SASCFC	2010–
Supreme Court of Tasmania (including Full Court until end of 2009)	TASSC	1999–

Tasmanian Court of Criminal Appeal	TASCCA	2010–
Supreme Court of Tasmania — Full Court	TASFC	2010–
Supreme Court of Victoria	VSC	1998–
Victorian Court of Appeal	VSCA	1998–
Supreme Court of Western Australia	WASC	1999–
Western Australian Court of Appeal (including Full Court until end 2004)	WASCA	1999–

A list of current, commonly used Australian unique court identifiers is set out in Table A.

Examples

Maguire v Leather [2009] HCASL 48 (12 March 1999).

Minister for Immigration and Citizenship v SZIAI [2009] HCA 39 (23 September 2009) [27].

R v De Gruchy [2006] VSCA 10 (9 February 2006) [4]–[5] (Vincent JA).

Notes

In accordance with rule 2.3.1, a case should generally not be cited as unreported if it has been reported.

Although some online databases are allocating medium neutral designations retrospectively, such designations have not been used in past citations of unreported cases. To avoid confusion and to unambiguously identify decisions, medium neutral citations should not be used to cite decisions prior to the years listed above.

2.8.2 Decisions without a Medium Neutral Citation

Example	*Barton v Chibber*	(Unreported,	Supreme Court of Victoria,	Hampel J,	29 June 1989)	3
Element	Case Name	Unreported Description	Court	Judge(s)	Full Date	Pin-point

Rule

Unreported decisions without a medium neutral citation allocated by the court should be cited as shown above.

	Case names should adhere to rule 2.1. Judges' names should adhere to rule 2.9.1. Pinpoint references are generally to page numbers and refer to the copy of the judgment itself (as delivered by the court). If paragraph numbers are used instead of or in addition to page numbers, they should appear in square brackets (in accordance with rules 1.1.5–1.1.6). There should be no punctuation between the closing parenthesis after the full date and any pinpoint.
Example	*Ross v Chambers* (Unreported, Supreme Court of the Northern Territory, Kriewaldt J, 5 April 1956) 77–8.
Notes	In accordance with rule 2.3.1, a case should generally not be cited as unreported if it has been reported. Older unreported judgments are sometimes compiled by courts into bound volumes, but even if citing an unreported case from such a volume, there is no need to refer to the volume or include a starting page.

2.9 Identifying Judges and Counsel

2.9.1 Identifying Judicial Officers

Rule	Where appropriate, the judicial officer(s) whose judgment is being cited may be identified in parentheses after a pinpoint reference. However, a judicial officer should not be included in a footnote citation if their identity is otherwise apparent. 'Per' should not be used. Judicial officers' names should appear in accordance with rule 1.14.4. The following abbreviations of judicial offices in Australia should appear after judicial officers' names in the text and in citations (including where the name appears at the start of a sentence). However, those titles marked with an asterisk (*) should always appear in full before judicial officers' names.

Judicial Office	Abbreviation/Title
Acting Chief Justice	ACJ
Acting Justice of Appeal	AJA
Acting Justices of Appeal	AJJA
Acting Justice	AJ
Acting Justices	AJJ
Acting President	AP
Associate Justice	AsJ
Auxiliary Judge	AUJ
Chief Judge Administrator	CJA
Chief Judge at Common Law	CJ at CL
Chief Judge in Equity	CJ in Eq
Chief Judge of the Commercial Division	CJ Comm D
Chief Justice	CJ
Commissioner	Commissioner*
Deputy Chief Justice/District Court Judge	DCJ
Federal Magistrate	FM
Judge	Judge*
Judicial Registrar	JR
Justice of Appeal	JA
Justices of Appeal	JJA
Justice	J
Justices	JJ
Magistrate	Magistrate*
Master	Master*
President	P
Senior Judge Administrator	SJA
Senior Judge	SJ
Senior Judges	SJJ
Senior Puisne Judge	SPJ
Vice-President	V-P

Examples

Kartinyeri v Commonwealth (1998) 195 CLR 337, 383 (Gummow and Hayne JJ).

Ruddock v Vadarlis (2001) 110 FCR 491, 495 [4]–[7] (Black CJ).

	Vigolo v Bostin (2002) 27 WAR 121, 130 (Sheppard AUJ). *R v Merritt* (2004) 59 NSWLR 557, 567 [35]–[38] (Wood CJ at CL). *Ottobrino v Espinoza* (1995) 14 WAR 373, 377 (Commissioner Buss). *Re Zoudi* (2006) 14 VR 580, 587–9 [24]–[28] (Maxwell P, Buchanan, Nettle, Neave and Redlich JJA). *R v Hoxha* (Unreported, Victorian Court of Appeal, Charles, Callaway JJA and Vincent AJA, 1 November 1995).

2.9.2 Subsequent Elevation

Rule	When identifying a judge, their judicial office at the time of the decision should be used. The phrase 'as he/she then was' should not be included.

2.9.3 Statements Made during Argument

Rule	When citing a statement made during argument, the words 'during argument' should be included in separate parentheses after the judge's or counsel's name. '*Arguendo*' should not be used. When referring to statements by counsel during argument, their initials (if included in the report) and any designation as Queen's Counsel ('QC'), King's Counsel ('KC') or Senior Counsel ('SC') should be included.
Examples	*Stephens v Abrahams [No 2]* (1903) 29 VLR 229, 239 (Williams J) (during argument), 242–3 (Isaacs KC) (during argument). *Combet v Commonwealth* (2005) 224 CLR 494, 497 (S J Gageler SC) (during argument).

2.10 Case History

Rule

The subsequent history of a case may be indicated after a citation of the case by including the abbreviations 'affd' for 'affirmed' or 'revd' for 'reversed', preceded by a comma and followed by the citation of the subsequent decision.

If the case name remains the same or the parties' names are merely reversed, the name of the subsequent decision should be omitted.

Examples

Perpetual Trustees Victoria Ltd v Ford (2008) 70 NSWLR 611, 640–2 (Harrison J), revd [2009] NSWCA 186 (8 July 2009).

Harkins v Butcher (2002) 55 NSWLR 558, affd *Butcher v Lachlan Elder Realty Pty Ltd* (2004) 218 CLR 592.

2.11 Quasi-Judicial Decisions

2.11.1 Administrative Decisions

Rule

Administrative decisions and determinations (including those of tribunals) should generally be cited in the same way as reported and unreported cases, except that:

- often '*and*' is used to separate party names, rather than '*v*' — this should appear as it does in the decision itself;
- the title of the decision may be a number or code, rather than party names;
- tribunal members may be referred to by a title other than 'Mr' or 'Ms' (such as 'Dr', 'Prof', etc);
- the titles 'Member', 'Deputy Member' and 'Senior Member' (in addition to those in rule 2.9.1, which should be used for judicial officers sitting in tribunals) are often used for administrative decision-makers and should appear before the name of the decision-maker (if they have no other title); and

- the initials or first names of tribunal members should be omitted, unless they are necessary to avoid ambiguity (in accordance with rule 1.14.4).

Examples

Re Pochi and Minister for Immigration and Ethnic Affairs (1979) 26 ALR 247.

McMahon v Boroondara City Council [2002] VCAT 626 (5 July 2002) [26]–[28] (Member Avery).

Application by AAPT Ltd [No 2] [2009] ACompT 6 (9 September 2009) [6.1]–[6.5] (Finkelstein J, Member Davey and Prof Round).

Dr Gerber stated:

> when dealing with rugby footballers, it seems to me to be a fruitless exercise to parse and analyse their every utterance in an attempt to comprehend their meaning. In the hands of rugby league footballers, the spoken word — like the game itself — is rough at the best of times …[21]

[21] *AAT Case 7422* (1991) 22 ATR 3450, 3456 [28]. He later commented (at 3458 [45]) that:

> Whatever the capital gains tax provisions sought to achieve is still firmly locked in the mind of the parliamentary draftsman who, for purposes of comprehension and enlightenment, might as well have enacted Pt IIIA in Swahili.

Note

Administrative decisions are often reported in the ALD, ATR and state administrative decision series. Many administrative tribunals have medium neutral unique 'court' identifiers, some of which are listed in Table A.

2.11.2 Arbitrations

Rule

Arbitral decisions should be cited as follows:

[*Case Name*] ([Award Description], [Forum], [Case/Award] No [Number], [Full Date]) [Pinpoint].

Only information appearing on the arbitral decision should be included. If the parties' names are omitted from an arbitral decision, the other elements should be included but should not appear in parentheses. 'Case/Award' should be replaced by the appropriate designation used by the relevant forum. If there is no forum, the arbitrator's name may be included instead.

Where the parties' names are included, there should be no punctuation between the closing parenthesis after the full date and any pinpoint. If the parties' names are not included, a comma should separate the full date and any pinpoint. Pinpoint references should be to pages, paragraphs or both (and should adhere to rules 1.1.5–1.1.6).

Where an arbitral decision is reproduced in a report series, book or periodical, a citation of the reproduction should be included after the above information, preceded by 'reported in'. A starting page should be included. Pinpoints should be to the page numbers of the reproduction, and may also include paragraph numbers in addition.

Examples

Sandline International Inc v Papua New Guinea (Award, Sir Edward Somers, Sir Michael Kerr and Sir Daryl Dawson, 9 October 1998) [10.2].

Beckman Instruments Inc v Overseas Private Investment Corporation (Award and Opinion, American Arbitration Association Commercial Arbitration Tribunal, Case No 16 199 00209 87G, 20 February 1988) reported in (1988) 27 ILM 1260, 1263.

Meiki Co Ltd v Bucher-Guyer SA (Preliminary Award, International Chamber of Commerce, Case No 2114 of 1972, 10 October 1972) reported in Sigvard Jarvin and Yves Derains (eds), *Collection of ICC Arbitral Awards: 1974–1985* (Kluwer, 1990) 49, 51.

Final Award, Netherlands Arbitration Institute, Case No 1930, 12 October 1999 reported in (2001) 26 *Yearbook — Commercial Arbitration* 181, 184 [5]–[6].

2.12 Transcripts of Proceedings

2.12.1 General Rule

Rule

Transcripts of proceedings should be cited as follows:

Transcript of Proceedings, [*Case Name*] ([Court], [Proceeding Number], [Judge(s)], [Full Date of Proceedings]) [Pinpoint].

A proceeding number (the number assigned by the court to the matter) should be included only if it appears on the transcript. The names of all judges hearing the matter should be included after the proceeding number.

Pinpoint references should be to page numbers or line numbers (where line numbering is continuous across a transcript). If a pinpoint is included, a speaker's name may be included after it (in accordance with rule 2.9) but '(in argument)' should not be included.

Examples

Transcript of Proceedings, *Celano v Swan* (County Court of Victoria, 09/0867, Judge Lacava, 27 August 2009) 11 (S M Petrovich).

Transcript of Proceedings, *R v MSK* (Supreme Court of New South Wales, Hidden J, 18 May 2005) 112, 143, 151, 156.

2.12.2 High Court of Australia from July 2003

Rule

Transcripts of proceedings in the High Court of Australia with 'HCATrans' numbers appearing on the transcript itself should be cited as follows:

Transcript of Proceedings, [*Case Name*] [[Year]] HCATrans [Number] ([Full Date of Proceedings]) [Pinpoint].

Pinpoint references should be to line numbers. If a pinpoint is included, a speaker's name may be included after it (in accordance with rules 2.9.1–2.9.2), but '(in argument)' should not be included.

Transcripts of other High Court proceedings should be cited according to rule 2.12.1.

Examples	Transcript of Proceedings, *Ruhani v Director of Police* [2005] HCATrans 205 (19 April 2005). Transcript of Proceedings, *Mulholland v Australian Electoral Commission* [2004] HCATrans 8 (12 February 2004) 2499–517 (Callinan J and J B R Beach QC), 2589–93 (McHugh J).
Note	High Court transcripts contain 'HCATrans' numbers from July 2003.

2.13 Submissions in Cases

Rule	Submissions in cases should be cited as follows: [Party Name], '[Title of Submission]', Submission in [*Case Name*], [Proceeding Number], [Full Date], [Pinpoint]. A title of submission and a proceeding number (the number assigned by the court to the matter) should be included only if they appear in the submission. Pinpoints may be to page numbers, paragraph numbers or both (see rules 1.1.5–1.1.6).
Example	Attorney-General (Cth), 'Outline of Submissions of the Attorney-General of the Commonwealth as Amicus Curiae', Submission in *Humane Society International Inc v Kyodo Senpaku Kaisha Ltd*, NSD 1519/2004, 25 January 2005, [10], [20]–[22], [28].

2.14 Subsequent References

Rule	'Ibid' should be used for all materials in this chapter (in accordance with rule 1.4.1). In other subsequent references, citations should appear in full each time a source is referred to. However, for citations of cases and quasi-judicial decisions, a short title may be used in place of the parties' names (in accordance with rule 2.1.14).

'Above n' should not be used for any materials in this chapter.

Examples

14 *Moore v Haynes* (2008) 23 NTLR 112, 116–17 [19]–[20] ('*Moore*').

15 Ibid 118 [24].

…

19 *Moore* (2008) 23 NTLR 112, 121 [34]. [**Not:** *Moore*, above n 14, 121 [34].]

20 Transcript of Proceedings, *NV Philips Gloeilampenfabrieken v Mirabella International Pty Ltd* (High Court of Australia, No S73 of 1994, Mason CJ, 23 November 1994) 3 (R J Ellicott QC).

21 Ibid (Mason CJ). His Honour commented that it would 'be a sacrifice' not to hear counsel's arguments.

3 Legislative Materials

3.1 Statutes (Acts of Parliament)

Example	*Crimes Act*	*1958*	(Vic)	s 3
Element	Title	Year	Jurisdiction	Pinpoint
Rule	3.1.1	3.1.2	3.1.3	3.1.4–3.1.6

3.1.1 Title

Rule

A citation of an Australian Act of Parliament should begin with the short title of the Act in italics. The long title of the Act should be used only if the Act does not contain a short title.

Titles should appear as they do in the statute book, subject to chapter 1. In particular:

- punctuation should adhere to rule 1.6.1 (so full stops should not be used in abbreviations); and
- capitalisation should adhere to rule 1.7.

Where multiple Acts have the same title but contain different numbers in their short titles (for example, '*(No 1)*' and '*(No 2)*'), the number should be included and should appear in parentheses.

Examples

Evidence Act 1995 (NSW).

Social Welfare Ordinance 1964 (NT).

Law and Justice Legislation Amendment Act (No 2) 1992 (Cth).

Law and Justice Legislation Amendment Act (No 4) 1992 (Cth).

Note

Statutes of the Australian Capital Territory and the Northern Territory were previously referred to as ordinances. However, these ordinances became known as Acts after the ACT (in 1988) and the NT (in 1978) attained self-government.

3.1.2 Year

Rule

The year in which the Act was originally passed should appear in italics following the title. The year should be included whether or not the Act includes it in the short title.

Example

Meteorites Act 1973 (Tas). [**Not:** *Meteorites Act* 1973 (Tas).]

Notes

Citations of an Act refer to that Act as amended (and consolidated). Regardless of when a particular provision was introduced, the year included should be that of original enactment. Generally, a principal Act rather than an amending Act should be cited (but see rule 3.8).

For the ACT and the NT, the year is that in which the original ordinance (which may subsequently have become an Act) was promulgated.

3.1.3 Jurisdiction

Rule

An abbreviated form of the jurisdiction in which the Act was passed should appear in parentheses following the year. The jurisdiction should not be italicised.

The following abbreviations should be used for Australian jurisdictions:

Jurisdiction	Abbreviation
Commonwealth	Cth
Australian Capital Territory	ACT
New South Wales	NSW
Northern Territory	NT
Queensland	Qld
South Australia	SA
Tasmania	Tas
Victoria	Vic
Western Australia	WA

Examples

Misrepresentation Act 1972 (SA).

Charter of Human Rights and Responsibilities Act 2006 (Vic).

3.1.4 Pinpoint Reference

Rule

Pinpoint references to Acts usually comprise an abbreviation and a number, separated by a space.

Pinpoint references should use the following abbreviations (in the text and in citations), except where the pinpoint begins a sentence:

Designation	Abbreviation	Plural	Abbreviation
Appendix	app	Appendices	apps
Article	art	Articles	arts
Chapter	ch	Chapters	chs
Clause	cl	Clauses	cls
Division	div	Divisions	divs
Paragraph	para	Paragraphs	paras
Part	pt	Parts	pts
Schedule	sch	Schedules	schs
Section	s	Sections	ss
Sub-clause	sub-cl	Sub-clauses	sub-cls
Subdivision	sub-div	Subdivisions	sub-divs
Sub-paragraph	sub-para	Sub-paragraphs	sub-paras
Subsection	sub-s	Subsections	sub-ss

The words ‘item’ and ‘items’ may be used to refer to items in a table or schedule, or numbered paragraphs in an amending Act. They should not be abbreviated.

Numbered or lettered subsections should appear in parentheses immediately following the section number. The section number and subsection number should *not* be separated by a space (for example, ‘s 3(a)’, not ‘s 3 (a)’).

In references to a section and a subsection, a paragraph and a sub-paragraph, etc, the abbreviation that corresponds to the highest ‘level’ of the section or paragraph etc in the pinpoint should be used (for example, ‘s 31(1)’, not ‘sub-s 31(1)’).

Where multiple combinations of an abbreviation and a number are needed to form one pinpoint reference, there should be no comma between each abbreviation–number combination (for example, ‘pt III div 2’, not ‘pt III, div 2’).

Where an Act uses a decimal numbering system (often in the form Chapter . Part . Section), pinpoints should contain the whole of the decimal number preceded by the abbreviation for the lowest 'level' of section, part, chapter, etc, cited (for example, 's 2.3.5', not 'ch 2.3.5').

Examples

s 2	s 108	sub-s (3)
pt V	s 5(1) [**Not:** s5(1)]	s 2(3) [**Not:** s 2 (3)]
ch III	s 14(1)(a)	s 28(1)(a)(i)
pt 7 div 3 sub-div 8	s 13 [**Not:** pt 2 s 13]	cl 14(3)(a)

Despite there being no requirement to show fault, actions under *Trade Practices Act 1974* (Cth) pt VA have been rare.

She drew attention to sub-s (1). Subsection (1) provides that 'a registered trade mark is personal property'.

The judge referred to s 8(3) in argument. [**Not:** … sub-s 8(3) …]

Social Security (Administration) Act 1999 (Cth) s 123TE.

Aboriginal and Torres Strait Islander Act 2005 (Cth) pt 3A div 2.

Civil Liability Act 2003 (Qld) ch 2 pt 1 div 4.

Crimes at Sea Act 1999 (Vic) sch 1 cl 2.

Aboriginal Land Rights (Northern Territory) Amendment Act 2006 (Cth) sch 1 item 46.

A New Tax System (Goods and Services Tax) Act 1999 (Cth) s 38-10(1) items 1–2.

Gambling Regulation Act 2003 (Vic) s 3.2.1.

Legal Profession Act 2004 (Vic) pt 2.3.

Income Tax Assessment Act 1997 (Cth) s 20-110(1)(a).

Notes

The most specific pinpoint that is appropriate should be included. Thus 'pt 3 div 7' is appropriate where speaking generally of that division, but 's 58' is appropriate where dealing with an individual section. Because section numbering is usually continuous throughout an Act, it is unnecessary to indicate chapters, parts, divisions, etc, when citing a section.

Some recent taxation statutes contain sections in the form of a division number immediately followed by a hyphen and a section number (for example, 's 26-52'). A hyphen (not an en-dash) should be used between the division and section numbers in such pinpoints.

3.1.5 Multiple Pinpoint References

Rule

The plural abbreviation of the highest 'level' of sections, subsections, etc, cited should precede multiple pinpoints (see rule 3.1.4).

Consecutive pinpoints should be separated by an en-dash (–) (for example, 'sub-ss (2)–(3)'). Hyphens (-) should *not* be used (in accordance with rule 1.1.6).

Non-consecutive pinpoints should each be separated by a comma and a space (for example, 'paras (3), (5)'). The word 'and' should *not* be used to separate the final two pinpoints (in accordance with rule 1.1.5).

Spans of section numbers should adhere to rule 1.12.1. In spans of alphanumeric sections, divisions, parts, etc, of an Act, the whole section number etc should be repeated (for example, 'ss 22A–22D', not 'ss 22A–D').

Where an Act uses a decimal numbering system, each section number, part number, etc, in spans and in non-consecutive pinpoints should be written out in full (for example, 'ss 3.2.5–3.2.7', not 'ss 3.2.5–7').

Examples

ss 2–3

ss 42–9

ss 5, 7, 9 [**Not:** … 7 and 9]

ss 6(7)(b)–(d) [**Not:** s 6(7)(b)–(d)]

sub-ss (2)–(7)

ss 29(2)–(5) [**Not:** sub-ss 29(2)–(5)]

sub-paras (4)–(8)

ss 3(a)–(c) [**Not:** ss 3(a), (b), (c)]

cls (1)–(3)

ss 92(1), (4), (7)

divs 3–4

ss 8(2), (5)(a)–(b) [**Not:** ss 8(2), 8(5)(a)–(b)]

ss 5, 7, 9, 28

HSI, as an 'interested person', sought a declaration and injunction against Kyodo for contravening ss 229–30 of the *Environment Protection and Biodiversity Conservation Act 1999* (Cth).

Unpublished works are dealt with in sub-ss (2)–(3).

Liquor Act 2007 (NSW) ss 5(1)(a)–(b).

Fair Trading (Reinstatement of Regulations) Act 2008 (Tas) ss 4(2)(a)–(b), (4), 5(b).

Gas Supply Act 2003 (Qld) ch 2 pt 1 div 3 sub-div 2, ch 3 pt 1.

Unlawful Assemblies and Processions Act 1958 (Vic) ss 5–6, 10–12, 26–9. [**Not:** … 26–29.]

Wrongs Act 1958 (Vic) ss 28F–28G, 28J. [**Not:** … ss 28F–G, J.]

See *Gambling Regulation Act 2003* (Vic) s 3.2.1. Sections 3.2.1–3.2.2 allow the Commission to authorise gambling. [**Not:** … Sections 3.2.1–2 …]

3.1.6 Definitions

Rule

Unnumbered definitions should be cited as follows:

s [Section Number] (definition of '[Defined Term]')

's [Section Number]' should be replaced with the schedule number (or other portion of an Act) containing the definition as appropriate.

If there are multiple paragraphs in the definition and a particular paragraph is referred to, a reference to that paragraph should be included, preceded by 'para'. No comma should separate the defined term and 'para'.

If definitions are contained in numbered sections of an Act, each definition should be cited as a normal section (in accordance with rules 3.1.4–3.1.5).

Examples

Property Law Act 1958 (Vic) s 3 (definition of 'legal practitioner').

Evidence Act 2008 (Vic) Dictionary pt 1 (definition of 'civil proceeding').

Greenhouse Gas Storage Act 2009 (Qld) sch 2 (definition of 'GHG well' para (1)). [**Not:** … (definition of 'GHG well', para (1)).]

Corporations Act 2001 (Cth) s 9 (definition of 'administrator' para (a)(i)). [**Not:** … (Cth) s 9(a)(i).]

Human Rights Act 2004 (ACT) s 5. [**Not:** … s 5 (definition of 'human rights').]

Note

Definitions are usually contained in a single section or a schedule of an Act, but are usually not individually numbered. When Acts are amended, new terms are often inserted in alphabetical order between existing terms.

3.2 Australian Constitutions

Rule

The *Constitution of the Commonwealth of Australia* may be cited as the *Australian Constitution*, the *Commonwealth Constitution*, or simply the *Constitution* if there is no ambiguity as to which constitution is being cited.

Where necessary, the *Australian Constitution* may also be referred to within its enacting legislation as:

Commonwealth of Australia Constitution Act 1900 (Imp) 63 & 64 Vict, c 12, s 9.

Constitutions of the Australian states should be cited as normal statutes.

Examples

Australian Constitution s 51(ii).

Australian Capital Territory (Self-Government) Act 1988 (Cth) s 22(1); *Northern Territory (Self-Government) Act 1978* (Cth) s 6; *Constitution Act 1902* (NSW) s 5; *Constitution Act 1867* (Qld) s 2; *Constitution Act 1934* (SA) s 5; *Constitution Act 1934* (Tas) s 9(1); *Constitution Act 1975* (Vic) s 16; *Constitution Act 1889* (WA) s 2(1).

3.3 Delegated Legislation

Example	*Police Regulations*	*2003*	(Vic)	reg 6
Element	Title	Year	Jurisdiction	Pinpoint

3.3.1 General Rule

Rule

Delegated legislation (for example, regulations, rules and orders) should be cited in the same manner as primary legislation (in accordance with rule 3.1).

Examples

Heritage Regulation 2006 (ACT) reg 5(1).

County Court (Court Fees) Order 2001 (Vic) O 3.

3.3.2 Pinpoint Reference

Rule

The abbreviations in rule 3.1.4 as well as the following additional abbreviations should be used to refer to pinpoints in delegated legislation:

Designation	Abbreviation	Plural	Abbreviation
Order	O	Orders	OO
Regulation	reg	Regulations	regs
Rule	r	Rules	rr
Sub-regulation	sub-reg	Sub-regulations	sub-regs
Sub-rule	sub-r	Sub-rules	sub-rr

Examples

Migration Regulations 1994 (Cth) regs 2.01–2.02.

Uniform Civil Procedure Rules 2005 (NSW) rr 3.4(1)(b), (2A)(a)–(b).

Federal Court Rules 1979 (Cth) OO 3, 5, 7 r 4A.

Supreme Court (General Civil Procedure) Rules 2005 (Vic) r 3.01.

High Court Rules 2004 (Cth) r 42.02.2.

Notes

In some court rules, for example the *Supreme Court (General Civil Procedure) Rules 2005* (Vic) and the *High Court Rules 2004* (Cth), the numbering of the rules is continuous, and the decimal rule number includes the number of the order. In such cases, *only* a rule number need be included as a pinpoint (for example, 'r 8.01'). An order number is not needed, but may be used when referring generally to the order as a whole (for example, 'O 8').

In other court rules, for example the *Federal Court Rules 1979* (Cth), both the order number and the specific rule within the order (if the latter is cited) must be included (for example, 'O 9 r 4'). In lists of pinpoints to such court rules, it may be necessary to repeat the order number to unambiguously identify the pinpoints cited.

3.4 Quasi-Legislative Materials

3.4.1 Gazettes

Rule

Gazettes should be cited as follows:

[Jurisdiction], [*Gazette Title*], No [Gazette Number], [Full Date], [Pinpoint].

Where multiple notices appear in the same gazette or on the same page, the author and title of the notice (if available) should also be included as follows:

[Author], '[Title of Notice]' in [Jurisdiction], [*Gazette Title*], No [Gazette Number], [Full Date], [Starting Page], [Pinpoint].

Examples

Commonwealth, *Gazette: Special*, No S 489, 1 December 2004.

'Australian Capital Territory Teaching Service' in Australian Capital Territory, *Australian Capital Territory Gazette*, No 1, 24 May 1989, 3.

Minister for Lands (WA), '*Land Acquisition and Public Works Act 1902* — *Native Title Act 1993* (Commonwealth) — Notice of Intention to Take Land for a Public Work' in Western Australia, *Western Australian Government Gazette*, No 27, 18 February 1997, 1142, 1143.

3.4.2 Orders and Rulings of Government Instrumentalities and Officers (ASIC Class Orders, Taxation Rulings, etc)

Rule

Orders and rulings of government instrumentalities and officers that are not appropriate to cite as delegated legislation (see rule 3.3) and are not published in a gazette (see rule 3.4.1) should be cited as follows:

Instrumentality/Officer, *Instrument Title*, Document Number, Full Date, Pinpoint.

Only the official title of an officer (not their name) should be included. Where a government department or an officer promulgates the instrument, the jurisdiction should be included in parentheses after the name of the department or officer if it is not obvious or otherwise apparent (using the abbreviations in rule 3.1.3).

A document number should be included only if it appears on the instrument. The document number should be reproduced using any abbreviations as they appear on the instrument (adhering to rule 1.6.1, so full stops should not be used in abbreviations).

Examples

Australian Taxation Office, *Income Tax: Carrying on a Business as a Professional Artist*, TR 2005/1, 12 January 2005.

Australian Securities and Investments Commission, *ASIC Class Order — Credit Rating Agencies*, CO 05/1230, 15 December 2005, para 4.

Minister for Immigration and Citizenship (Cth), *Direction [No 41] — Visa Refusal and Cancellation under Section 501*, 3 June 2009.

3.4.3 Legislation Delegated to Non-Government Entities (ASX Listing Rules, Professional Conduct Rules, etc)

Rule

Delegated legislation and quasi-legislative instruments issued by non-government entities should be cited in the same way as orders and rulings of government instrumentalities and officers (in accordance with rule 3.4.2) as far as possible.

Terms designating the issuing body as a company (for example, 'Pty', 'Ltd', 'Co', 'Inc') should be omitted from its name, as should 'the' at the start of the name.

Where such delegated legislation does not include a document number or is frequently updated, the full date may be replaced with the date of the version cited (or the effective date of the provision cited) as follows:

[Issuing Body], [*Title*] (at [Full Date]) [Pinpoint].

Examples

Australian Securities Exchange, *Listing Rules* (at 11 January 2010) r 1.3.3.

Law Society of New South Wales, *Professional Conduct and Practice Rules* (at 11 December 1995) r 2.1.

Victorian Bar, *Practice Rules — Rules of Conduct and Compulsory Continuing Legal Education Rules* (at 1 August 2005) rr 24–5. [**Not:** The Victorian Bar Inc, …]

Note

If a source has provisions with different effective dates, the effective date of the provision cited should be included.

3.4.4 Court Practice Directions and Practice Notes

Rule

If a court practice direction or practice note is reproduced in a report series, it should be cited as follows:

[Court], *Practice Direction/Note No* [*Number*] — [*Title of Practice Direction/Note*] [Citation of Report Series], [Pinpoint].

The citation of the report series should adhere to rule 2.3. Pinpoint references should be to pages or pages and paragraphs (in accordance with rule 2.5).

Court practice directions and practice notes not published in a report series should be cited as follows:

[Court], *Practice Direction/Note No* [*Number*] — [*Title of Practice Direction/Note*], [Full Date], [Pinpoint].

Examples	Supreme Court of Victoria, *Practice Note No 5 of 2006 — Criminal Division: Case Management by Section 5 Hearings* (2006) 16 VR 702, 703. High Court of Australia, *Practice Direction No 3 of 2006 — Amendment of Practice Direction No 1 of 2000*, 5 September 2006. Federal Court of Australia, *Practice Note No 1 — Appeals to a Full Court*, 3 January 2008, pt B.
Note	Practice directions and practice notes are often reproduced in the issuing court's authorised report series and should be cited from there where available.

3.5 Bills

Rule	Bills should be cited in the same manner as Acts, except the title and year should not be italicised. 'Clause' and 'sub-clause' are usually the appropriate pinpoint designations.
Examples	Corporations Amendment Bill (No 1) 2005 (Cth). Carbon Pollution Reduction Scheme Bill 2009 (Cth) cl 83. Migration Amendment (Immigration Detention Reform) Bill 2009 (Cth) sch 1 item 9.

3.6 Explanatory Memoranda, Statements and Notes

Rule	Explanatory Memoranda (also known in some jurisdictions as Explanatory Statements or Explanatory Notes) should be cited as follows: Explanatory Memorandum, [Citation of Bill] [Pinpoint].

	'Explanatory Memorandum' should be replaced with 'Explanatory Statement' or 'Explanatory Note(s)' where appropriate. The citation of the Bill should appear in accordance with rule 3.5. Pinpoints should be to pages or pages and paragraphs of the memorandum, statement or note (and should adhere to rules 1.1.5–1.1.6).
Example	Explanatory Memorandum, Charter of Human Rights and Responsibilities Bill 2006 (Vic). Explanatory Notes, Adoption Bill 2009 (Qld) 5–6, 29.
Note	Chapter 6 contains rules on citing other parliamentary documents. Second reading speeches are sections of parliamentary debates and should be cited in accordance with rule 6.1.1. Bills digests and alert digests should be cited in accordance with rule 6.1.5.

3.7 Order of Parallel Australian Statutes and Bills

Rule	When citing equivalent Acts or Bills across multiple Australian jurisdictions, Commonwealth Acts or Bills should appear first, followed by state and territory Acts or Bills in alphabetical order *of jurisdiction.* Parallel Acts and Bills should be ordered in this way even if legislation from all Australian jurisdictions is not cited, unless there is good reason to do otherwise (for example, where the order is important to meaning).
Examples	*Trade Practices Act 1974* (Cth) s 52(1); *Fair Trading Act 1992* (ACT) s 12(1); *Fair Trading Act 1987* (NSW) s 42(1); *Consumer Affairs and Fair Trading Act 1990* (NT) s 42(1); *Fair Trading Act 1989* (Qld) s 38(1); *Fair Trading Act 1987* (SA) s 56(1); *Fair Trading Act 1990* (Tas) s 14(1); *Fair Trading Act 1999* (Vic) s 9(1); *Fair Trading Act 1987* (WA) s 10(1). *Oaths and Affirmations Act 1984* (ACT) s 14(1); *Oaths Act 1939* (NT) s 8; *Oaths Act 1867* (Qld) s 5; *Oaths Act 1936* (SA) s 13; *Oaths, Affidavits and Statutory Declarations Act 2005* (WA) s 5(1).

3.8 Legislative History: Amendments, Repeals and Insertions

Rule	Where it is appropriate or important, the legislative history of an Act or provision may be indicated by referring to both the original and the amending legislation. The following expressions should be used, preceded by a comma, to link the two Acts (thereby indicating the legislative history): • 'as amended by'/'later amended by'/'amending'; • 'as repealed by'/'repealing'; and • 'as inserted by'/'inserting'. The term used will depend upon which Act amended, inserted or repealed the other Act or provision. They are not interchangeable. 'Amending/repealing/inserting' and 'as amended by/as repealed by' should also be used for Bills.
Examples	*Anti-Discrimination Act 1977* (NSW) s 4(1), as amended by *Anti-Discrimination (Amendment) Act 1994* (NSW) sch 1 item 1. *Anti-Discrimination (Amendment) Act 1994* (NSW) sch 1 item 1, amending *Anti-Discrimination Act 1977* (NSW) s 4(1). *Copyright Act 1968* (Cth) s 40(3), later amended by *Copyright Amendment Act 2006* (Cth) sch 6 item 11. *Crimes Act 1914* (Cth) s 24A(g), as repealed by *Anti-Terrorism Act (No 2) 2005* (Cth) sch 7 item 2. *Anti-Terrorism Act (No 2)* 2005 (Cth) sch 7 item 2, repealing *Crimes Act 1914* (Cth) s 24A(g). *Crimes Act 1958* (Vic) s 3B, as inserted by *Crimes (Homicide) Act 2005* (Vic) s 3. *Crimes (Homicide) Act 2005* (Vic) s 3, inserting *Crimes Act 1958* (Vic) s 3B.

Family Assistance and Other Legislation Amendment (2008 Budget and Other Measures) Bill 2009 (Cth) sch 2 item 1, repealing *Social Security (Administration) Act 1999* (Cth) s 144(ka).

Social Security (Administration) Act 1999 (Cth) s 144(ka), repealed by Family Assistance and Other Legislation Amendment (2008 Budget and Other Measures) Bill 2009 (Cth) sch 2 item 1.

3.9 Subsequent References

3.9.1 Legislative Materials in Their Entirety

Rule

'Ibid' should be used for all materials in this chapter (in accordance with rule 1.4.1).

In other subsequent references, citations should appear in full each time a source is referred to. However:

- Acts (see rule 3.1);
- delegated legislation (see rule 3.3);
- quasi-legislative materials *except for* gazettes (see rules 3.4.2–3.4.4); and
- Bills (see rule 3.5)

may be given a short title the first time they are cited. The short title should adhere to rule 1.4.3 (so should be italicised and placed within single inverted commas and parentheses following the initial citation). The short title may be placed in the text or in the footnotes. Subsequent references to these sources should appear as follows:

[*Short Title*] [Pinpoint].

'Above n' should not be used for any materials in this chapter.

Examples

9 *Historic Shipwrecks Act 1976* (Cth).

10 Ibid s 7.

11 Ibid s 9. [**Not:** Ibid 9.]

[12] *Northern Territory National Emergency Response Act 2007* (Cth) s 3 ('*NTNER Act*').

...

[16] *NTNER Act* s 5. [**Not:** *NTNER Act*, above n 12, s 5.]

[17] Australian Securities and Investments Commission, *Covered Short Sales*, CO 08/751, 22 September 2008 ('*Covered Short Sales Class Order*').

...

[19] *Covered Short Sales Class Order* paras 3–4.

3.9.2 Individual Parts of Legislative Materials

Rule

A short title may be given to a portion of an Act, a piece of delegated legislation or a Bill (in accordance with rule 1.4.3). The short title should be placed after the pinpoint to the relevant portion.

In subsequent references, pinpoints following the short title refer to sections, items, etc, within that portion of an Act. (For example, if the citation '*Trade Practices Act 1974* (Cth) sch pt 1 ('*Competition Code*')' is included, a subsequent reference to '*Competition Code* s 45' is a reference to the s 45 *within* the Competition Code — that is, within sch pt 1 of the Act.)

In accordance with rule 1.4.3, only one short title should be introduced in a single citation.

Example

[16] *Criminal Code Act 1995* (Cth) sch 1 ('*Criminal Code*').

...

[22] *Criminal Code* s 80.2(5).

Note

Short titles for a portion of an Act will often be appropriate for schedules of Acts, where the rest of the Act operates as 'machinery' to apply the schedule.

PART III

SECONDARY SOURCES

4 Journal Articles

Examples	Andrew Kenyon,	'Problems with Defamation Damages?'	(1998)	24	*Monash University Law Review*	70	, 74
	Martin Dockray,	'Why Do We Need Adverse Possession?'	[1985]		*Conveyancer and Property Lawyer*	272	, 275
Element	Author	Title	Year	Volume and Issue	Journal	Page	Pin-point
Rule	4.1	4.2	4.3	4.4	4.5	4.6	4.7

4.1 Author

4.1.1 Signed Articles

Rule

The name of the author of a journal article should appear in accordance with chapter 1. In particular:

- names should adhere to rules 1.14.1–1.14.2 (so should appear exactly as they do on the source, subject to other general rules, and initials should be separated by a space);
- authors' titles should adhere to rule 1.14.1 (so all titles should be omitted except for 'Sir', 'Dame' and peerage titles);
- punctuation should adhere to rule 1.6.1 (so full stops should not be used after initials or in abbreviations);
- names of bodies should adhere to rule 1.14.3;
- names of judges should adhere to rule 1.14.4; and
- names of multiple authors should adhere to rule 1.14.2.

Examples

Justice Michael Kirby, 'Is Legal History Now Ancient History?' (2009) 83 *Australian Law Journal* 31.

Gary Edmond et al, 'Law's Looking Glass: Expert Identification Evidence Derived from Photographic and Video Images' (2009) 20 *Current Issues in Criminal Justice* 337. [**Not**: Gary Edmond, Katherine Biber, Richard Kemp and Glenn Porter, …]

4.1.2 Unsigned Articles

Rule

For unsigned journal articles, the type of article (such as 'Comment' or 'Note') should appear in place of the author's name.

Example

Note, 'Unfixing *Lawrence*' (2005) 118 *Harvard Law Review* 2858.

Note

'Comments' and 'Notes' are common in American law journals. They are usually short, anonymous pieces written by students.

4.2 Title

Rule

The title of a journal article should appear (unitalicised) within single quotation marks as it does on the first page of the article. It should appear in accordance with chapter 1. In particular:

- punctuation should adhere to rule 1.6.1 (so full stops should not be used after initials or in abbreviations);
- capitalisation should adhere to rule 1.7; and
- italicisation should adhere to rule 1.8.2 (so titles of cases, Acts, treaties, etc, in the article title should be italicised).

Where there is no punctuation in the source separating the title from a subtitle, a colon or an em-dash should be inserted.

Examples

Helen Rhoades, 'The Dangers of Shared Care Legislation: Why Australia Needs (Yet More) Family Law Reform' (2008) 36 *Federal Law Review* 279.

Antonio Cassese, 'The *Nicaragua* and *Tadić* Tests Revisited in the Light of the ICJ Judgment on Genocide in Bosnia' (2007) 18 *European Journal of International Law* 649, 651. [**Not:** … 'The Nicaragua and Tadić Tests Revisited …]

4.3 Year

Rule	For journals organised by volume number, the year of publication should appear in parentheses. For journals organised by year, the relevant year should appear in square brackets.
Examples	Ted Schneyer, 'Some Sympathy for the Hired Gun' (1991) 41 *Journal of Legal Education* 11. Jessica Palmer, 'Chasing a Will-o'-the-Wisp? Making Sense of Bad Faith and Wrongdoers in Change of Position' [2005] *Restitution Law Review* 53.
Note	For journals organised by volume number, where a volume spans multiple years (for example, the volume is for 1992–93), the year included should be that in which the article cited was published. For journals organised by year, where a volume spans multiple years, the span of years should be included in square brackets (and should appear in accordance with rule 1.13.2).

4.4 Volume and Issue

Rule	For journals organised by volume number, the volume number should appear after the year, preceded by a space. (Journals organised by year have no volume number.) If all issues within a volume of a journal are consecutively paginated, the issue number should be omitted. If the issues within a volume are not consecutively paginated: • for journals organised by volume number, the issue number should appear in parentheses immediately after the volume number (for example, '33(2)'); and • for journals organised by year, the issue number should appear in parentheses, preceded by a space, after the year (for example, '[1999] (4)').

If one bound edition of a journal is designated as containing multiple issues (and under this rule the issue numbers must be included), the issues should be separated by an en-dash and enclosed inside parentheses after the volume number or year (as appropriate) (for example, '21(2–3)' and '[1957] (5–6)').

Where an issue identifier other than a number is used (for example, a season or a month) and the issue identifier must be included (that is, pagination is non-consecutive), this should appear preceded by a space and enclosed in parentheses after the volume number or year (for example, '31 (Winter)' and '[1982] (Summer)').

Examples

Heather Douglas, 'Assimilation and Authenticity: The "Ordinary Aboriginal Person" and the Provocation Defence' (2006) 27 *Adelaide Law Review* 199, 199, 201–2.

W M C Gummow, 'Carrying on Passing Off' (1974) 7 *Sydney Law Review* 224, 224. [**Not:** … (1974) 7(2) *Sydney Law Review* 224 …]

Jeremy Masters, 'Easing the Parting' (2008) 82(11) *Law Institute Journal* 68, 69–71.

John Kleinig, 'Paternalism and Personal Integrity' [1983] (3) *Bulletin of the Australian Society of Legal Philosophy* 27.

James Boyle, 'The Second Enclosure Movement and the Construction of the Public Domain' (2003) 66(1–2) *Law and Contemporary Problems* 33, 37. [**Not:** … (2003) 66(1)–(2) …]

Notes

The issues within a volume are 'consecutively paginated' where issues subsequent to the first continue the pagination (that is, the numbering of subsequent issues does *not* begin again at page 1).

Where issues are published very frequently and/or are commonly indexed by full date, it may be more appropriate to use a newspaper-style citation (see rule 6.5).

4.5 Journal

Rule	The full title of the journal (as it appears on the title page) should appear in italics, following the year and any volume or issue number. The journal title should *not* be abbreviated. 'The' should not be included at the start of a journal title.
Examples	*University of New South Wales Law Journal* [**Not:** *UNSWLJ* **nor** *The University of New South Wales L J*] *Columbia Law Review* [**Not:** *Colum L Rev* **nor** *The Columbia Law Review*]

4.6 Starting Page

Rule	The number of the first page of an article should follow the title of the journal or periodical. No punctuation should separate the starting page from the title. For forthcoming articles, the starting page should be replaced with '(forthcoming)'.
Examples	Janet Halley, 'Rape in Berlin: Reconsidering the Criminalisation of Rape in the International Law of Armed Conflict' (2008) 9 *Melbourne Journal of International Law* 78. Michelle Foster, '*Non-Refoulement* on the Basis of Socio-Economic Deprivation: The Scope of Complementary Protection in International Human Rights Law' [2009] *New Zealand Law Review* (forthcoming).

4.7 Pinpoint Reference

Rule	Pinpoint references should appear after the starting page, preceded by a comma and a space. They should adhere to rules 1.1.5–1.1.6. Generally, pinpoint references should be to page numbers. (Paragraph numbers *may* be included *in addition* to page numbers, but this is rarely necessary.) Where the pinpoint reference is to the first page of an article, the page number should be repeated.
Examples	Marjorie Florestal, 'Is a Burrito a Sandwich? Exploring Race, Class, and Culture in Contracts' (2008) 14 *Michigan Journal of Race and Law* 1, 3 n 6, 13–15, 47–51, 58. Gordon Goldberg, 'Certain Contemporary Confusions Concerning Consideration, a Common Count and Conversion' [2000] *Restitution Law Review* 189, 189.

4.8 Articles Published in Parts

Rule	If an article has been published in multiple parts, a full citation should be given for each part cited. '(Pt Number)' should be inserted between the title and the year (regardless of whether the other parts are cited). Any reference to the part within the title of the article should be omitted.
Examples	R N Gooderson, 'Claim of Right and Dispute of Title' (Pt 1) [1966] *Cambridge Law Journal* 90; R N Gooderson, 'Claim of Right and Dispute of Title' (Pt 2) [1966] *Cambridge Law Journal* 216. Jacobus tenBroek, 'California's Dual System of Family Law: Its Origin, Development, and Present Status' (Pt 1) (1964) 16 *Stanford Law Review* 257. [**Not:** … 'California's Dual System of Family Law: Its Origin, Development, and Present Status — Part I' …]

4.9 Articles Published in Electronic Journals

Rule

Articles from electronic journals should only be cited where a printed edition (of the journal or the article cited) does not exist.

Articles appearing in journals that are only available online should, as far as possible, be cited in the same manner as articles in printed journals. However, it will often not be possible to include a volume number, issue number or starting page. Pinpoint references should be to page numbers or paragraph numbers if available (in accordance with rules 1.1.5–1.1.6), but otherwise may be to numbered parts of the article.

A URL should always follow the citation to electronic articles. The URL should adhere to rule 6.15.6 (so the date of retrieval should *not* be included).

Examples

Kate Lewins, 'What's the *Trade Practices Act* Got to Do with It? Section 74 and Towage Contracts in Australia' (2006) 13(1) *eLaw Journal: Murdoch University Electronic Journal of Law* 58, 59 <https://elaw.murdoch.edu.au/archives/issues/2006/1/eLaw_Lewins_13_2006_05.pdf>.

William van Caenegem, 'Copyright Liability for the Playing of "Music on Hold" — *Telstra Corporation Ltd v Australasian Performing Right Association Ltd*' (1996) 2 *High Court Review* [9]–[12] <http://www.austlii.edu.au/au/journals/HCRev/1996/9.html>.

Note

If an article appears in a printed journal, even where a similar version is available online, the printed journal should be cited instead, in accordance with the other rules in this chapter.

4.10 Symposia

Rule	Where a symposium is referred to as a whole, it should be cited in the same manner as an article in a journal, except that: • 'Symposium' should appear instead of an author's name; • the title of the symposium should appear in inverted commas; and • the starting page should be that on which the first article in the symposium (or any symposium title page or introductory section) begins. Individual articles within a symposium should be cited as regular journal articles (in accordance with the other rules in this chapter).
Example	Symposium, 'Contemporary Human Rights in Australia' (2002) 26 *Melbourne University Law Review* 251.

5 Books

Example	Malcolm N Shaw,	*International Law*	(Cambridge University Press, 6th ed, 2008)	578
Element	Author	Title	Publication Details	Pinpoint
Rule	5.1	5.2	5.3	5.4

5.1 Author

5.1.1 General Rule

Rule

The name of the author of a book should appear in accordance with chapter 1. In particular:

- names should adhere to rules 1.14.1–1.14.2 (so should appear exactly as they do on the source, subject to other general rules, and initials should be separated by a space);
- authors' titles should adhere to rule 1.14.1 (so all titles should be omitted except for 'Sir', 'Dame' and peerage titles);
- punctuation should adhere to rule 1.6.1 (so full stops should not be used after initials or in abbreviations);
- names of bodies should adhere to rule 1.14.3;
- names of judges should adhere to rule 1.14.4; and
- names of multiple authors should adhere to rule 1.14.2.

Examples

Ronald Dworkin, *Law's Empire* (Harvard University Press, 1968).

Lorelle Frazer, Scott Weaven and Owen Wright, Asia-Pacific Centre for Franchising Excellence, *Franchising Australia 2008 — Survey* (2008).

Sarah Joseph, Jenny Schultz and Melissa Castan, *The International Covenant on Civil and Political Rights: Cases, Materials, and Commentary* (Oxford University Press, 2nd ed, 2004).

Paul Rishworth et al, *The New Zealand Bill of Rights* (Oxford University Press, 2003).

5.1.2 Editors

Rule	The name of the editor of a book should appear in the same manner as an author's name and should be followed by '(ed)' for one editor or '(eds)' for multiple editors.
Examples	R G Frey (ed), *Utility and Rights* (Basil Blackwell, 1985). Jason W Neyers, Erika Chamberlain and Stephen G A Pitel (eds), *Emerging Issues in Tort Law* (Hart Publishing, 2007). John Bowers et al (eds), *Blackstone's Employment Law Practice 2009* (Oxford University Press, 2009).

5.2 Title

Rule	The title of a book should appear in italics as it appears on the title page of the book. It should appear in accordance with chapter 1. In particular: • punctuation should adhere to rule 1.6.1 (so full stops should not be used after initials or in abbreviations); and • capitalisation should adhere to rule 1.7. Where there is no punctuation on the title page separating the title from a subtitle, a colon or an em-dash should be inserted.
Examples	Alistair Pound and Kylie Evans, *An Annotated Guide to the Victorian Charter of Human Rights and Responsibilities* (Lawbook, 2008). Prue Vines, *Law and Justice in Australia — Foundations of the Legal System* (Oxford University Press, 2nd ed, 2009).

5.3 Publication Details

5.3.1 Publisher

Rule	A brief version of the publisher's name should be included in parentheses after the title. It should be followed by a comma. Sufficient information to identify the publisher (and no more) should be included. The publisher's name should appear as on the title page (or in the publication information), except that: • 'the' at the start of the name should be omitted; • abbreviations related to the publisher's corporate status ('Pty', 'Ltd', 'Co', etc) should be omitted; • geographical designations ('Australia', 'A/Asia', etc) in company names should be omitted, unless they are an important part of the name; and • subdivisions within companies should be omitted. A publisher's name should only be included if it appears in the book. A publisher's name should *not* be included where the publisher's and the author's names are the same.
Examples	Ngaire Naffine, *Law's Meaning of Life: Philosophy, Religion, Darwin and the Legal Person* (Hart Publishing, 2009). David Brown and Meredith Wilkie (eds), *Prisoners as Citizens: Human Rights in Australian Prisons* (Federation Press, 2002). [**Not:** … The Federation Press …] Clive Turner, *Australian Commercial Law* (Lawbook, 29th ed, 2009). [**Not:** … Lawbook Co … **nor** … Lawbook Company …] Martin Davies and Ian Malkin, *Torts* (LexisNexis Butterworths, 5th ed, 2008). [**Not:** … LexisNexis Butterworths Australia …] McGill Law Journal, *Canadian Guide to Uniform Legal Citation* (Carswell Thomson, 4th ed, 1998). [**Not:** … Carswell Thomson Professional Publishing …]

	Elizabeth Ellis, *Principles and Practice of Australian Law* (Thomson Reuters, 2nd ed, 2009). [**Not:** … Thomson Reuters (Professional) Australia Ltd …] Martin Vranken, *Death of Labour Law? Comparative Perspectives* (Melbourne University Press, 2009). Law Institute of Victoria, *Legal Directory 2006* (2005). [**Not:** … *Legal Directory 2006* (Law Institute of Victoria, 2005).]
Notes	Usually, it is sufficient to include only the first two or three words of a publisher's name, especially where the publisher is readily identifiable. The name of a printer of a book (that is not also its publisher) should not be included, even if no publisher appears on the book. A publisher's name is often unnecessary for documents where a government or government department is the author, as these are usually self-published.

5.3.2 Edition Number and Date of First Publication

Rule	Where there are multiple editions of a book and an edition number (for example, '2nd edition') appears in the book being cited, the edition number should be included after the publisher's name. It should appear as follows: [Ordinal Edition Number] ed, The ordinal number of the edition should adhere to rule 1.12.1 (so the letters in the ordinal number should appear in superscript). For older books, the year of first publication and the year of the publication being cited may be included instead of an edition number. This should appear as follows: first published [Year of First Publication], [Year of Edition Cited] ed) Information concerning reprints should not be included. Where no edition number is indicated in the book, no edition number should be included.

Examples	Patricia Birnie, Alan Boyle and Catherine Redgwell, *International Law & the Environment* (Oxford University Press, 3rd ed, 2009). Thomas Hobbes, *Leviathan* (Clarendon Press, first published 1651, 1909 ed). Sir Matthew Hale, *Historia Placitorum Coronae* (London Professional Books, first published 1736, 1971 ed) vol 1, 635. George Orwell, *Animal Farm: A Fairy Story* (Secker and Warburg, first published 1945, 1998 ed) 23.
Note	Where the book does not contain an edition number but has been republished in multiple years, the year of first publication and year of the publication being cited should generally replace an edition number. This is typically the case for books published prior to the 20th century or popular books republished by several publishers.

5.3.3 Revised Editions

Rule	Where a book is a 'revised', 'expanded' or 'updated' edition but the revision does not have a new edition number, this should be indicated by including 'revised ed': • for a revision of a numbered edition, after the edition number and preceded by a space (for example, '2nd revised ed'); or • for an unnumbered revised edition (generally a revision of the first edition), after the publisher's name and preceded by a comma.
Examples	E J Cohn and W Zdzieblo, *Manual of German Law* (Oceana Publications, 2nd revised ed, 1968) vol 1. Peter Birks, *An Introduction to the Law of Restitution* (Clarendon Press, revised ed, 1989) 18.
Note	An unnumbered revised edition is generally a revision of the first edition of a work and should be designated 'revised ed'. '1st revised ed' should be used only where the edition number appears in the book.

5.3.4 Publication Year

Rule	The year of publication should appear following the name of the publisher and any edition number. A completed multi-volume work that was published over a range of years should include the first and final years of publication as a span (in accordance with rule 1.13.1). If publication is still in progress, the first year and an en-dash should appear.
Examples	Andrew D Mitchell and Jennifer L Beard, *International Law: In Principle* (Thomson Reuters, 2009). B Edgeworth, C J Rossiter and M A Stone, *Property Law: Cases and Materials* (LexisNexis Butterworths, 7th ed, 2004). Jonathan I Charney, Lewis M Alexander and Robert W Smith (eds), *International Maritime Boundaries* (Martinus Nijhoff, 1993–2002). Jeremy Bentham, *Rationale of Judicial Evidence* (Garland Publishing, first published 1802–12, 1978 ed) vol 1. Pamela Andre (ed), *Documents on Australian Foreign Policy 1937–49* (Department of Foreign Affairs and Trade, 1975–) vol XVI, 159.

5.4 Pinpoint Reference

5.4.1 General Rule

Rule	A pinpoint reference should be preceded by a space. There should be no punctuation between the closing parenthesis (containing the publication details) and the pinpoint reference. Pinpoint references should adhere to rules 1.1.5–1.1.6. If a book has page numbers, pinpoint references should be to page numbers. If a book has page numbers and paragraphs, pinpoint references *may* be to page numbers *and* paragraph numbers. If the book has only numbered paragraphs, a pinpoint reference should be to a paragraph. When referring to a numbered chapter of a book, 'chapter' should be abbreviated 'ch' in footnote citations.

Examples	Margaret C Jasper, *Home Mortgage Law Primer* (Oceana Publications, 3rd ed, 2009) 70–7. [**Not:** … (Oceana Publications, 3rd ed, 2009), 70–7.] Charles Mitchell and Stephen Watterson, *Subrogation: Law and Practice* (Oxford University Press, 2007) 9 [2.02]. James Edelman and Elise Bant, *Unjust Enrichment in Australia* (Oxford University Press, 2006) ch 4.

5.4.2 Multi-Volume Books

Rule	If the book contains more than one volume, the number of the volume cited should appear after the publication details, preceded by 'vol'. A comma should separate the volume number from any further page or paragraph pinpoint references (for example, 'vol 4, 466' refers to page 466 in volume 4).
Examples	Sir Gerald Fitzmaurice, *The Law and Procedure of the International Court of Justice* (Grotius Publications, 1986) vol 2, 430. J Guéron et al (eds), *The Economics of Nuclear Power Including Administration and Law* (Pergamon Press, 1956–59) vol 1, 396.
Note	Where the volumes of a book were published in different years, the span of years over which *all* volumes were published should be included in the publication information, in accordance with rule 5.3.4.

5.5 Chapters in Edited Books

Example	Peter Millett,	'Proprietary Restitution'	in	Simone Degeling and James Edelman (eds),	*Equity in Commercial Law*	(Lawbook, 2005)	123	, 138
Element	Author	Chapter Title	in	Editor	Book Title	Publication Details	Starting Page	Pinpoint

Rule

Chapters in edited books should be cited as shown above.

The chapter title should be enclosed in single inverted commas. There should be no other punctuation between the chapter title and 'in'. The starting page is that on which the chapter cited begins.

Where multiple chapters from an edited collection are cited, the details of the edited collection should be included in full in the first reference to *each* chapter.

Subsequent ('above n') references to a chapter from an edited collection should use the names of the authors of the particular chapter and refer to the footnote in which the *chapter* is first cited.

Examples

22 Meg Russell, 'Reform of the House of Lords: Lessons for Bicameralism' in Nicholas Aroney, Scott Prasser and J R Nethercote (eds), *Restraining Elective Dictatorship: The Upper House Solution?* (University of Western Australia Press, 2008) 119.

…

43 Janet Ransley, 'Illusions of Reform: Queensland's Legislative Assembly since Fitzgerald' in Nicholas Aroney, Scott Prasser and J R Nethercote (eds), *Restraining Elective Dictatorship: The Upper House Solution?* (University of Western Australia Press, 2008) 248, 252. [**Not:** … in Aroney, Prasser and Nethercote (eds), above n 22, 248, 252.]

...

45 Russell, above n 22, 122.

46 Ransley, above n 43, 255. [**Not:** Ransley, above n 22, 255.]

5.6 Translations

Example	Jean-Paul Sartre,	*Being and Nothingness: An Essay on Phenomenological Ontology*	(Hazel E Barnes trans,	Methuen, 1958)	151	[trans of: *L'Etre et le Néant* (first published 1943)]
Element	Original Author	Translation Title	Translator	Translation Publication Information	Pinpoint	Original Title and Year

Rule

Translations should be cited as shown above.

The original title may be included in square brackets after any pinpoint. However, if the translation title appears in the original language, it is not necessary to include the original title.

The year in which the original work (used by the translator) was first published, or its edition number and year of publication, may also be included in square brackets after any pinpoint. If the original title is included, the year (or year and edition number) should appear in parentheses after the original title. If the original title is not included, the year (or year and edition number) should appear in square brackets (without parentheses).

In accordance with rule 1.7, titles in a foreign language should be capitalised in accordance with convention in that language.

Examples

The Qur'an (Tarif Khalisi trans, Harvard University Press, 1972).

Friedrich Nietzsche, *Thus Spoke Zarathustra: A Book for Everyone and No One* (R J Hollingdale trans, Penguin Books, 1961) 210–13 [trans of: *Also sprach Zarathustra: Ein Buch für Alle und Keinen* (first published 1883–85)].

Hans-Georg Gadamer, *Truth and Method* (Garrett Barden and John Cumming trans, Crossroad, 1975) [trans of: *Wahrheit und Methode: Grundzüge einer philosophischen Hermeneutik* (2nd ed, 1965)].

Emmanuel Levinas, *Entre nous* (Michael B Smith and Barbara Harshav trans, Athlone Press, 1998) 27 [first published 1991].

6 Other Sources

6.1 Government Documents

6.1.1 Parliamentary Debates

Rule

Parliamentary debates (or 'Hansard') should be cited as follows:

[Jurisdiction], *Parliamentary Debates*, [Chamber], [Full Date of Debate], [Pinpoint] ([Name of Speaker]).

Names of speakers should adhere to rule 1.14. If a speaker's name is included, their first and last names should appear. 'MP', 'MLC', 'MLA', 'Senator' and other designations indicating membership of Parliament should not be included in the speaker's name. If it is relevant, the position of the speaker within a ministry or shadow ministry (or any part of their position which is relevant) may be included after their name, preceded by a comma.

Examples

Commonwealth, *Parliamentary Debates*, Senate, 18 June 2008, 2642–4 (Bob Brown).

Victoria, *Parliamentary Debates*, Legislative Assembly, 4 May 2006, 1289–95 (Rob Hulls, Attorney-General).

The second reading speech for the Migration Amendment Bill 1983 (Cth) was incorporated by reference in the Senate.[23]

[23] Commonwealth, *Parliamentary Debates*, Senate, 7 September 1983, 373–4 (John Button). [**Not:** … 373–4 (John Button, Minister for Industry and Commerce).]

6.1.2 Parliamentary Papers

Rule

Parliamentary papers should be cited as follows:

[Jurisdiction], [*Title*], Parl Paper No [Number] ([Year]) [Pinpoint].

Example	Commonwealth, *Australia's Aid Program in the Pacific: Joint Standing Committee on Foreign Affairs, Defence and Trade*, Parl Paper No 211 (2007) 24.

6.1.3 Parliamentary Research Papers, Notes and Briefs

Rule

Parliamentary research papers, notes and briefs should be cited as follows:

[Author], '[Title]' (Research Paper No [Number], Parliamentary Library, [Legislature], [Year]) [Pinpoint].

Where the document is a research note or brief, 'Research Paper' should be modified accordingly. Where the document is prepared by a body other than a parliamentary library, that body's name should replace 'Parliamentary Library'.

Examples

Scott Bennett, 'The Rise of the Australian Greens' (Research Paper No 8, Parliamentary Library, Parliament of Australia, 2008) 15.

Jeffrey Robertson, 'North Korean Nuclear Issues and the Role of Parliamentary Diplomacy' (Research Note No 23, Parliamentary Library, Parliament of Australia, 2007).

6.1.4 Parliamentary Committee Reports

Rule

Parliamentary committee reports should be cited as follows:

[Committee], [Legislature], [*Title*] ([Year]) [Pinpoint].

Where a committee is from one chamber of Parliament and this is not apparent from the committee's name, the name of the chamber should be added to the start of the committee's name.

Pinpoint references should adhere to rules 1.1.5–1.1.6. Pinpoints should be to page numbers (if available). Where a committee report has page and paragraph numbers, paragraph numbers *may* be included *in addition* to page numbers. Where a report has only page numbers or paragraph numbers, pinpoints should be to page numbers or paragraph numbers as appropriate.

Examples

Law Reform Committee, Parliament of Victoria, *Inquiry into Alternative Dispute Resolution and Restorative Justice* (2009) 26.

Senate Legal and Constitutional References Committee, Parliament of Australia, *Administration and Operation of the Migration Act 1958* (2006) 280–1 [9.30]–[9.38]. [**Not:** Legal and Constitutional References Committee, Senate, Parliament of Australia …]

6.1.5 Bills Digests and Alert Digests

Rule

Bills digests, alert digests and similar documents should be cited as follows:

[Author], [*Title*], No [Digest/Alert Number] of [Year], [Full Date], [Pinpoint].

Where a parliamentary committee is the author, the committee's name should adhere to rule 6.1.4. Where a government department is the author and its jurisdiction is not apparent from its name, the abbreviated jurisdiction may be included in parentheses after the department name (in accordance with rule 1.14.3).

Pinpoint references should adhere to rule 6.1.4 (so should include page numbers and *may* include paragraph numbers in addition).

Examples

Senate Standing Committee for the Scrutiny of Bills, Parliament of Australia, *Alert Digest*, No 9 of 2007, 13 August 2007, 11.

Legislation Review Committee, Parliament of New South Wales, *Legislation Review Digest*, No 13 of 2008, 10 November 2008, 6.

Department of Parliamentary Services (Cth), *Bills Digest*, No 75 of 2008–09, 27 January 2009, 8.

6.1.6 Evidence to Parliamentary Committees

Rule

Evidence to a parliamentary committee given during a hearing can generally be found in a 'Committee Hansard' publication. It should be cited as follows:

Evidence to [Committee], [Legislature], [Location], [Full Date], [Pinpoint] ([Name of Speaker]).

The committee's name should adhere to rule 6.1.4. Pinpoint references should adhere to rules 1.1.5–1.1.6 and should generally be to page numbers.

The position of the person giving evidence may be included after their name where it is relevant.

Example

Evidence to Senate Standing Committee on Foreign Affairs, Defence and Trade, Parliament of Australia, Canberra, 26 February 2007, 12 (Angus Houston, Air Chief Marshal).

Note

The page numbers in a Committee Hansard are often preceded by an abbreviation of the Committee name (for example, 'SL&C'). Such abbreviations should be omitted from pinpoint references.

6.1.7 Royal Commission Reports

Rule

Royal commission reports should be cited as follows:

[Jurisdiction], [Name of Royal Commission], [*Title*] ([Year]) [Pinpoint].

The jurisdiction is that of the enactment creating the Royal Commission. Where a Royal Commission is commissioned by multiple jurisdictions, all should be included in alphabetical order.

In accordance with rule 5.4.2, where a report contains multiple volumes the volume number should be included in pinpoint references (even where the volumes are consecutively paginated). Pinpoint references should adhere to rule 6.1.4 (so should include page numbers and *may* include paragraph numbers in addition).

Examples	Commonwealth, Royal Commission into Aboriginal Deaths in Custody, *National Report* (1991) vol 5, 31 [36.3.12]. Commonwealth and New South Wales, Royal Commission of Inquiry into the Activities of the Nugan Hand Group, *Final Report* (1985). New South Wales, Royal Commission into Drug Trafficking, *Report* (1979) vol 2, 555.

6.1.8 Law Reform Commission Reports

Rule	Law reform commission reports should be cited as follows: [Name of Law Reform Commission], [*Title*], [Report/Discussion Paper] No [Number] ([Year]) [Pinpoint]. The type of publication ('Report', 'Discussion Paper', 'Issues Paper', etc) should be included as appropriate. In accordance with rule 5.4.2, where a report, discussion paper, etc, contains multiple volumes, the volume number should be included in pinpoint references (even where the volumes are consecutively paginated). Pinpoint references should adhere to rule 6.1.4 (so should include page numbers and *may* include paragraph numbers in addition).
Examples	Victorian Law Reform Commission, *Civil Justice Review*, Report No 14 (2008). Law Reform Commission, *Reform of Evidence Law*, Discussion Paper No 16 (1980) 4. Australian Law Reform Commission, *For Your Information: Australian Privacy Law and Practice*, Report No 108 (2008) vol 1, 339 [7.7].
Note	The Australian Law Reform Commission ('ALRC') was, prior to 1996, called the 'Law Reform Commission'. Citations of ALRC reports should use the name of the body at the time of the report.

6.1.9 Australian Constitutional Convention Debates

Rule

Debates of the Australasian federal conventions should be cited as follows:

Title, Location, Full Date, Pinpoint (Name of Speaker).

Pinpoint references should adhere to rule 1.1.5–1.1.6 and be to page numbers.

Names of speakers should adhere to rules 1.14 and 6.1.1. In particular:

- first and last names should be included; and
- all titles (such as 'the Hon', 'Mr' and 'Dr') except 'Sir', 'Dame' and peerage titles should be omitted.

Examples

Official Record of the Debates of the Australasian Federal Convention, Sydney, 2 September 1897, 19 (Edmund Barton).

Official Report of the National Australasian Convention Debates, Adelaide, 29 March 1897, 206–7 (Sir John Downer).

Note

The title of the relevant volume of debates should be included as it appears on the source. The titles vary slightly.

6.2 Submissions to Government Inquiries, Committees and Agencies

Rule

Submissions to government inquiries, committees, agencies, etc, should be cited as follows:

Author, Submission No Number to Government Body, *Name of Inquiry*, Full Date, Pinpoint.

For submissions to parliamentary committees or inquiries, 'Government Body' should be replaced with the committee's name and legislature, which should adhere to rule 6.1.4. Where the government body does not allocate a number to submissions, 'No Number' should be omitted. Where the name of the inquiry is not included on the submission, it should be omitted.

	Where a full date is not available, as much of the full date as appears should be included. Pinpoint references should adhere to rule 6.1.4 (so should include page numbers and *may* include paragraph numbers in addition).
Examples	Mobil Oil Australia, Submission No 25 to Australian Competition and Consumer Commission, *Inquiry into the Price of Unleaded Petrol*, 27 July 2007, 6–7. Human Rights Law Resource Centre, Submission No 21 to Senate Standing Committee on Legal and Constitutional Affairs, Parliament of Australia, *Inquiry into the Anti-Terrorism Laws Reform Bill 2009*, 11 September 2009, 3 [6]. Victorian Automobile Chamber of Commerce, Submission to Road Safety Committee, Parliament of Victoria, *Inquiry into Driver Distraction*, October 2005, 6–7. Australian Indigenous Doctors' Association, Submission No 187 to Northern Territory Emergency Response Review, 22 August 2008, [17].
Note	Submissions of parties in cases should be cited in accordance with rule 2.13.

6.3 Legal Encyclopedias

Rule	Legal encyclopedias should be cited as follows: Publisher, *Title of Encyclopedia*, vol Volume Number (at Full Date) Title Number Name of Title, 'Chapter Number Name of Chapter' [Paragraph]. The publisher's name should adhere to rule 5.3.1. Where a legal encyclopedia indicates the date of last update of a chapter, this date should be included. Otherwise, the date of retrieval should be included.

	Pinpoint references should adhere to rules 1.1.5–1.1.6 and should be to paragraphs. Where a legal encyclopedia is viewed online, the volume number should be omitted.
Examples	LexisNexis, *Halsbury's Laws of Australia*, vol 15 (at 25 May 2009) 235 Insurance, '2 General Principles' [235-270]. Lawbook, *The Laws of Australia* (at 31 August 2000) 24 International Trade, '2 Foreign Investment' [24.2.87].

6.4 Looseleaf Services

Rule	Looseleaf services should be cited as follows: Publisher, *Title*, vol Volume Number (at Most Recent Service Number for Pinpoint) Pinpoint. The publisher's name should adhere to rule 5.3.1. Where an author of a looseleaf service is clearly identified, the author's name should be included before the publisher, followed by a comma. Pinpoints should adhere to rules 1.1.5–1.1.6 and should be to paragraphs. However, where a looseleaf service uses a paragraph symbol (¶), this should immediately precede paragraph numbers (which should then not appear in square brackets). Where a looseleaf service is viewed online, the volume number and the comma after the title should be omitted.
Examples	LexisNexis Butterworths, *Civil Procedure: Victoria*, vol 1 (at Service 231) [21.01.1]. Marcus S Jacobs, Thomson Reuters, *International Commercial Arbitration in Australia: Law and Practice*, vol 1 (at Release 5) [3.230]. CCH International, *Japan Business Law Guide*, vol 1 (at 68-1-08) ¶7-200. [**Not**: … ¶[7200].] J W Carter, LexisNexis, *Carter on Contract* (at 10 January 2009) [19-001].

Notes

Printed looseleaf services are updated periodically by replacing old pages with updated pages. The service number is usually a numerical identifier (indicating the sequential number of the update) or a date, and generally appears in a corner of the page.

Electronic 'looseleaf' services may include the most recent service number or a date of last update. If not, the date on which the electronic looseleaf service was accessed should be used as the most recent service number.

6.5 Newspaper Articles

6.5.1 Printed Newspapers

Rule

Newspaper articles from printed newspapers should be cited as follows:

> Author, 'Title', *Newspaper* (Place of Publication), Full Date, Pinpoint.

The author's name should adhere to rule 1.14.

The title of an article should appear (unitalicised) within single quotation marks as it does on the first page of the article. It should appear in accordance with chapter 1. In particular:

- punctuation should adhere to rule 1.6.1 (so full stops should not be used after initials or in abbreviations);
- capitalisation should adhere to rule 1.7; and
- italicisation should adhere to rule 1.8.2 (so titles of Acts etc in the article title should be italicised).

Where there is no punctuation in the source separating the title from a subtitle, a colon or an em-dash should be inserted.

	The full name of the newspaper should be used, including '*The*' where it appears in the masthead. If an article appears in a named section of a newspaper (for example, '*Sport*') and the newspaper is not consecutively paginated, the name of the section should be included before that of the newspaper in the form: *Section*, *Newspaper* If an article appears in a section of a newspaper without a name and the newspaper is not consecutively paginated, this should be indicated in the pinpoint reference (for example, 'C14'). The place of publication should appear as it does on the masthead or publication information of the newspaper. A state or country may also be included to clarify the place of publication (for example, 'Paris, Texas') or where the place of publication may not be known to readers (for example, 'Ouagadougou, Burkina Faso').
Examples	Stephen Howard and Billy Briggs, 'Law Lords Back School's Ban on Islamic Dress', *The Herald* (Glasgow), 23 March 2006, 7. Fabiano Maisonnave, 'Test of Endurance: Coup Leaders Try to Drive Zelaya from Embassy — Honduran Regime Restricts Food and Supplies and Deploys Pop as a Weapon', *The Guardian Weekly* (London), 30 October 2009, 3. Abigail Hunter, 'He Stole My Son, Now I'm Alone in Hell', *Times2*, *The Times* (London), 3 December 2009, 3. Eleanor Laise, 'TCW Slams Gundlach in Lawsuit over His Exit', *The Wall Street Journal* (New York), 8 January 2010, C1.

6.5.2 Unsigned and Untitled Articles

Rule	For unsigned articles, the author's name should be omitted. However, for editorials, 'Editorial' should replace the author's name. Subsequent references to unsigned articles and editorials should include an abbreviated form of the title (in accordance with rule 1.4.2).

For untitled articles, a description of the piece (for example, 'Letter to the Editor') should replace the title. The description should *not* be enclosed in quotation marks.

Examples

'Fury at WA Council Plan', *The Australian Financial Review* (Sydney), 1 May 2006, 5.

Editorial, 'Medicare by Name, No Longer by Nature', *News*, *The Age* (Melbourne), 12 March 2004, 12.

Rose Healy, Letter to the Editor, *The Herald Sun* (Melbourne), 10 June 2002, 16.

6.5.3 Electronic Newspapers

Rule

Electronic newspapers should only be cited where an identical printed edition (of the newspaper or the article cited) does not exist.

Citations of electronic newspaper articles should appear in the same manner as citations of printed newspapers (in accordance with rules 6.5.1–6.5.2). However:

- the place of publication should be replaced with '(online)';
- a pinpoint reference should only be included where the article has pages or paragraphs; and
- a URL should be included after the full date (or any pinpoint reference) and should adhere to rule 6.15.6.

Example

Farrah Tomazin, 'Kinder Wages Breakthrough', *The Age* (online), 19 May 2009 <http://www.theage.com.au/national/education/kinder-wages-breakthrough-20090519-bcwh.html>.

6.6 Television and Radio Transcripts

Rule

Television and radio transcripts should be cited as follows:

Broadcaster, ‘Title of Segment’, *Name of Program*, Full Date (Name of Speaker).

The name of the speaker should be included unless it is otherwise apparent. It should adhere to rule 1.14.

A pinpoint reference may be included after the full date, preceded by a comma, if it appears in the transcript. A URL may be included after the speaker's name (or any pinpoint) in the first reference to a transcript where the transcript is only available online or the URL would aid its retrieval. The URL should appear in accordance with rule 6.15.6.

Example

ABC Radio National, ‘Inventions: Who Owns Them?’, *The Law Report*, 8 September 2009 (Andrew Stewart) <http://www.abc.net.au/rn/lawreport/stories/2009/2678819.htm#transcript>.

6.7 Films and Audiovisual Recordings

Rule

Films and other audiovisual recordings should be cited as follows:

Title (Directed by Name of Director, Studio/Production Company, Year) Pinpoint.

The name of the studio or production company should adhere to rule 5.3.1. Where there are multiple studios or companies, only the first-named studio or company should be included.

Pinpoint references should be to a point in time in the recording, and should appear (depending on the accuracy desired) in the format:

Hours : Minutes : Seconds

Examples

Calling the Ghosts: A Story about Rape, War and Women (Directed by Mandy Jacobson and Karmen Jelincic, Bowery Productions, 1996).

To Kill a Mockingbird (Directed by Robert Mulligan, Brentwood Productions, 1962) 1:43:00.

6.8 Press and Media Releases

Rule

Press and media releases should be cited as follows:

[Author], '[Title]' ([Release Type], [Document Number], [Full Date]) [Pinpoint].

The name of the author should adhere to rule 1.14. The release type should appear as it does on the source (for example, 'Press Release', 'Media Release', 'Press Statement'). A document number should be included only if it appears on the release. The document number should be reproduced using any abbreviations as they appear on the release (adhering to rule 1.6.1, so full stops should not be used in abbreviations).

A URL may be included after the first reference to a release where this would aid its retrieval. It should appear in accordance with rule 6.15.6.

Examples

Department of Defence (Cth), 'Highest East Timorese Honour for Army Officers' (Media Release, MSPA 172/09, 22 May 2009).

Australian Stock Exchange, 'ASX Group Monthly Activity Report — April 2009' (Media Release, 5 May 2009) 1 <http://www.asx.com.au/about/pdf/ma050509_monthly_activity_report_april09.pdf>.

6.9 Working Papers and Similar Documents of Various Bodies

Rule

Working papers and other similar documents of various bodies should be cited as follows:

Author, ' Title ' (Document Type No Number , Institution Name , Full Date) Pinpoint .

The document type should be reproduced as it appears on the source (for example, 'Working Paper', 'Discussion Paper', 'Research Report', etc). Where the document is not part of a numbered series, 'No Number ' should be omitted. The institution name should adhere to rule 1.14.3 (so generally only the most specific subdivision and the umbrella body's name should be included). Where there is not a full date on the source, as much of the full date as appears should be included (for example, 'September 1997' or '1998').

Pinpoint references should adhere to rule 6.1.4 (so should include page numbers and *may* include paragraph numbers in addition).

A URL may be included after the first reference to a working paper or similar document where this would aid its retrieval. It should appear in accordance with rule 6.15.6.

Examples

Jens Tapking and Jing Yang, 'Horizontal and Vertical Integration in Securities Trading and Settlement' (Working Paper No 245, Bank of England, 2004) 11–12.

Paul Memmott and Peter Blackwood, 'Holding Title and Managing Land in Cape York — Two Case Studies' (Research Discussion Paper No 21, Australian Institute of Aboriginal and Torres Strait Islander Studies, 2008) 37.

Caroline O N Moser, Annika Tornqvist and Bernice van Bronkhorst, 'Mainstreaming Gender and Development in the World Bank: Progress and Recommendations' (Report, World Bank, 1998).

	John Howe and Ingrid Landau, '"Light Touch" Labour Regulation by State Governments in Australia: A Preliminary Assessment' (Working Paper No 40, Centre for Employment and Labour Relations Law, The University of Melbourne, December 2006) 6 <http://papers.ssrn.com/sol3/papers.cfm?abstract_id=961528>.
Note	Where a document of a body is published as a book, it should be cited in accordance with chapter 5.

6.10 Theses

Rule	Theses should be cited as follows: [Author], [*Title*] ([Type of Thesis], [Institution], [Year]) [Pinpoint]. A URL may be included after the first reference to a thesis where this would aid its retrieval. It should appear in accordance with rule 6.15.6.
Examples	Denis Joseph Andrew Muller, *Media Accountability in a Liberal Democracy — An Examination of the Harlot's Prerogative* (PhD Thesis, The University of Melbourne, 2005). Amélie Champsaur, *The Regulation of Credit Rating Agencies in the US and the EU: Recent Initiatives and Proposals* (LLM Thesis, Harvard University, 2005) 19–20 <http://www.law.harvard.edu/programs/about/pifs/education/sp19.pdf>.

6.11 Conference Papers

Rule	Conference papers should be cited as follows: [Author], '[Title]' (Paper presented at [Name of Conference], [Location], [Full Date]) [Pinpoint]. A URL may be included after the first reference to a conference paper where this would aid its retrieval. It should appear in accordance with rule 6.15.6.

Example

Anne Orford, 'Roman Law and the Godly Imperium in England's New Worlds' (Paper presented at the Workshop on the Theo-Political Renaissance, Department of English, Cornell University, 25 April 2008).

6.12 Speeches

Rule

Speeches should be cited as follows:

Speaker, 'Title' (Speech delivered at the Name of Forum, Location, Full Date).

A URL may be included after the first reference to a speech where this would aid its retrieval. It should appear in accordance with rule 6.15.6.

Example

Chief Justice Robert French, 'Native Title — A Constitutional Shift?' (Speech delivered at the JD Lecture Series, The University of Melbourne, 24 March 2009) <http://www.hcourt.gov.au/publications_05.html>.

Note

Where a speech has been published in a journal or book, it should be cited in accordance with chapters 4 or 5 respectively.

6.13 Interviews

6.13.1 Interviews Conducted by the Author

Rule

Interviews conducted by the author should be cited as follows:

Interview with Name of Interviewee (Location or Form of Interview, Full Date).

The position of the interviewee may also be included after their name, preceded by a comma.

Examples	Interview with Philip Dunn (Melbourne, 19 October 2005). Interview with Ian Brownlee, Chief Policy Director, Office of the Director of Public Prosecutions (York, 3 August 2007). Interview with Nicola Roxon, Shadow Attorney-General (Doorstop Interview, 2 November 2005).

6.13.2 Interviews Not Conducted by the Author

Rule	Interviews not conducted by the author should be cited as follows: [Name of Interviewer], Interview with [Name of Interviewee] ([Location or Form of Interview], [Full Date]). The position of the interviewee may also be included after their name, preceded by a comma. A URL may be included after the first reference to an interview where this would aid retrieval of the interview. The URL should appear in accordance with rule 6.15.6.
Example	Laurie Oakes, Interview with John Howard, Prime Minister of Australia (Television Interview, 30 October 2005).
Note	Where an interview has been published in a journal or book, it should be cited in accordance with chapters 4 or 5 respectively.

6.14 Written Correspondence

Rule	Written correspondence should be cited as follows: [Type of Correspondence] from [Author] to [Recipient], [Full Date], [Pinpoint]. Types of correspondence include letters, faxes and emails. The position of the correspondents may be included after their names.

Where correspondence is reproduced within another hard copy source, that source may be cited (in accordance with the appropriate rules of this *Guide*). It should appear after the full date (or any pinpoint) and be preceded by ‘in’. Alternatively, a URL may be included where this would aid retrieval of the correspondence (in accordance with rule 6.15.6). A URL should not be preceded by ‘in’.

Examples

Email from Jonathon Barrington to Deborah Horowitz, 17 May 2001.

Letter from Ellen Keen to George Rusden, 28 April 1867 in *Rusden Papers* (Leeper Library, Trinity College, The University of Melbourne) vol 11.

Letter from Deloitte Touche Tohmatsu, Melbourne, to Opes Prime Clients, 1 April 2008, 3 <http://www.deloitte.com.au/media/docs/OpesPrime_groupcircular.pdf>.

Note

Attachments sent via email may be cited in this manner, unless the attachment is covered by another rule in this *Guide*.

6.15 Internet Materials

Example	Board of Examiners,	*Admission Requirements*	(18 February 2010)	Council of Legal Education	<http://www.lawadmissions.vic.gov.au>
Element	Author	Document Title	Full Date	Website Name	Uniform Resource Locator
Rule	6.15.1	6.15.2	6.15.3	6.15.4	6.15.6

Note

A source should be cited using this rule only if it does not exist in a published form and no other rule within this *Guide* applies to it.

Citations of articles in electronic journals should adhere to rule 4.9. Citations of electronic newspapers should adhere to rule 6.5.3. Citations of blogs should adhere to rule 6.15.7.

6.15.1 Author

Rule	The author's name should be included if it is apparent from the web page or document. It should adhere to rule 1.14.
Example	Department of Corrective Services, Government of Western Australia, *Victim–Offender Mediation* <http://www.correctiveservices.wa.gov.au/victim-services/victim-offender-mediation/>.

6.15.2 Document Title

Rule	The title of the particular web page or web document cited should be included in italics after the author's name.
Example	World Health Organization, *Violence against Women: A Priority Health Issue* (1997) <http://www.who.int/gender/violence/prioreng/en/>.

6.15.3 Full Date

Rule	Where available, the full date of last update of the web page should be included after the document name. If this is not shown, the full date of creation should be included. Where there is not a full date on the web page or document, as much of the full date as appears should be included. Where there is no date, the full date should be omitted.
Examples	International Whaling Commission, *IWC Information* (29 September 2009) <http://www.iwcoffice.org/commission/iwcmain.htm>. Law Council of Australia, *Our History* <http://www.lawcouncil.asn.au/about/history.cfm>.

6.15.4 Website Name

Rule	The name of the general website on which the web page or document resides should be included if available. The website name should not appear in italics.

	If the website name is preceded by a document title but no full date, the document title and website name should be separated by a comma. Where the author and website name are identical, the website name should not be included.
Examples	ARM National Committee, *The Australian Republican Movement Policy* (February 2009) Australian Republican Movement <http://www.republic.org.au/page/australian-republican-movement-policy>. Internet Patent News Service, *Patent Database*, Patenting Art and Entertainment <http://www.patenting-art.com/database/dbase1-e.htm>. Innocence Project, *Eyewitness Misidentification* <http://www.innocenceproject.org/understand/Eyewitness-Misidentification.php>. [**Not:** Innocence Project, *Eyewitness Misidentification*, Innocence Project …]

6.15.5 Pinpoint Reference

Rule	Any pinpoint reference should appear before the URL and be preceded by a comma. Pinpoint references should adhere to rule 6.1.4.
Example	Australasian Legal Information Institute, *News* (22 December 2009) AustLII, 2 <http://www.austlii.edu.au/austlii/news/20091222.pdf>.
Note	Web pages do not usually include pinpoints. Where they appear on a web page, pinpoints are usually paragraph numbers, which should be included in citations in square brackets (in accordance with rules 1.1.5–1.1.6).

6.15.6 Uniform Resource Locator ('URL')

Rule	The URL should be enclosed within '< >' symbols. Where the full URL of a document appears cumbersome and the document can be located easily from a general website, the URL of the general website may be included instead. The date of retrieval should *not* be included after the URL.

Examples

Oxfam International, *Flooding in the Philippines Highlights Urgency of Climate Leadership* (28 September 2009) <http://www.oxfam.org/en/pressroom/pressrelease/2009-09-28/flooding-philippines-urgency-climate-leadership>.

National Human Rights Consultation Committee, *Terms of Reference* (2008) National Human Rights Consultation <http://www.humanrightsconsultation.gov.au>. [**Not:** … <http://www.humanrightsconsultation.gov.au/www/nhrcc/nhrcc.nsf/Page/Terms_of_Reference>.]

6.15.7 Blogs and Online Forums

Rule

Posts on blogs and online forums should be cited as follows:

Author of Post, 'Title of Post' on Author of Blog/Forum, *Blog/Forum Name* (Full Date of Post) <URL of Post>.

Only elements that appear on the blog or forum should be included. The URL should adhere to rule 6.15.6 (so where a post is easily accessible from a general website, the URL of the general website may replace the URL of the post).

Examples

Jeremy Gans, 'The *Charter* vs Eviction' on Jeremy Gans, *Charterblog: Analysis of Victoria's Charter of Human Rights* (12 July 2008) <http://charterblog.wordpress.com/2008/07/12/the-charter-vs-eviction>.

Khalid al Nur, 'Politics of Rage, Politics of Change' on *Making Sense of Sudan* (25 September 2009) <http://blogs.ssrc.org/sudan/2009/09/25/politics-of-rage-politics-of-change>.

6.16 Subsequent References

Rule

'Ibid' should be used for all materials in this chapter (in accordance with rule 1.4.1).

'Above n' should be used for all materials in this chapter (in accordance with rule 1.4.2), except for:

- parliamentary debates (rule 6.1.1);
- evidence to parliamentary committees (rule 6.1.6);
- Australian constitutional convention debates (rule 6.1.9);
- interviews (rule 6.13); and
- written correspondence (rule 6.14).

Subsequent references to these listed sources (other than those using 'ibid') should appear in full.

Examples

[5] Commonwealth, *Parliamentary Debates*, House of Representatives, 26 October 2009, 10 858 (Kevin Rudd, Prime Minister).

[6] Ibid.

…

[17] Commonwealth, *Parliamentary Debates*, House of Representatives, 26 October 2009, 10 858 (Kevin Rudd, Prime Minister). [**Not:** Commonwealth, above n 5, 10 858.]

[18] Jyoti Rahman, David Stephan and Gene Tunny, 'Estimating Trends in Australia's Productivity' (Working Paper No 2009-01, Treasury, Australian Government, 2 February 2009) 12 <http://archive.treasury.gov.au/documents/1466/PDF/Trends%20in%20Australia%27s%20Productivity.pdf>.

[19] Ibid 15.

…

[58] Rahman, Stephan and Tunny, above n 18, 14.

[59] *Mad Max 2* (Directed by George Miller, Kennedy Miller Productions, 1981) 1:20.

…

[70] *Mad Max 2*, above n 59, 0:55.

Note

In accordance with rule 1.4.3, short titles may be included in the initial citations of, and replace author names in 'above n' references to, reports and similar documents.

PART IV

INTERNATIONAL MATERIALS

7 Treaties

Examples	*Treaty on the Non-Proliferation of Nuclear Weapons*,		opened for signature 1 July 1968,	729 UNTS 161	(entered into force 5 March 1970)	art 3
	Agreement regarding the Transfer of the Administration of Justice in the Territories of Northern Slesvig,	Denmark–Germany,	signed 12 July 1921,	8 LNTS 397	(entered into force 17 January 1922)	art 2
	Statute of the International Renewable Energy Agency,		opened for signature 26 January 2009,	[2009] ATNIF 23	(not yet in force)	art V
Element	Treaty Title	Parties' Names	Date Opened for Signature or Signed	Treaty Series	Date of Entry into Force	Pin-point
Rule	7.1	7.2	7.3	7.4	7.3	7.5

7.1 Treaty Title

Rule

A citation of a treaty should include the treaty title in italics as it appears on the first page of the treaty. However:

- purely procedural components of the title (which are not part of the substantive name, such as the date and place of signature) should be omitted;

	• punctuation should adhere to rule 1.6.1 (so full stops should not be used in abbreviations); and • capitalisation should adhere to rule 1.7.
Example	*International Covenant on Economic, Social and Cultural Rights*, opened for signature 16 December 1966, 993 UNTS 3 (entered into force 3 January 1976). [**Not**: *International Covenant on Economic, Social and Cultural Rights. Adopted by the General Assembly of the United Nations on 16 December 1966*, opened for signature …]
Note	If parties' names are included in the treaty title, they should be reproduced in citations exactly as they appear in that title, even if they appear in an elaborate form.

7.2 Parties' Names

Rule	For multilateral treaties with more than three signatories, the names of states parties should not be included after the treaty title. If the names of states parties to a bilateral or trilateral treaty appear in the treaty title, they should not be repeated after the title. If they do not appear in the title, they should be included (unitalicised) after the treaty title, preceded and followed by a comma and joined by en-dashes. The conventional shortened forms of states parties' names should be used (if any exist), rather than their full elaborate forms (for example, 'Venezuela', not 'Bolivarian Republic of Venezuela'). However, the full form should be used if necessary to avoid ambiguity (for example, to differentiate the 'Democratic Republic of the Congo' from the 'Republic of the Congo').
Examples	*Convention Relating to the Non-Fortification and Neutralisation of the Aaland Islands*, opened for signature 20 October 1921, 9 LNTS 211 (entered into force 6 April 1922). [**Not:** … *Aaland Islands*, Germany–Denmark–Estonia–Finland–France etc …]

Agreement on Cultural and Educative Integration between the Republic of Venezuela and the Republic of Peru, signed 12 January 1996, 2408 UNTS 125 (entered into force 13 March 1997) art 4. [**Not:** … *between the Republic of Venezuela and the Republic of Peru*, Venezuela–Peru, signed …]

International Agreement on the Scheldt, Belgium–France–Netherlands, signed 3 December 2002, 2351 UNTS 13 (entered into force 1 December 2005) art 3(1)(a).

7.3 Date Opened for Signature or Signed and Date of Entry into Force

7.3.1 Opened for Signature (Open Multilateral Treaties)

Rule

Multilateral treaties that are opened for signature to states generally should be cited as follows:

[*Treaty Title*], opened for signature [Date of Conclusion], [Treaty Series] (entered into force [Date of Entry into Force]).

The date of entry into force is the date on which the treaty first commences for any state party.

Example

Convention Relating to the Status of Refugees, opened for signature 28 July 1951, 189 UNTS 137 (entered into force 22 April 1954).

Note

Where a treaty is adopted by the United Nations General Assembly, the date of adoption is generally the date of conclusion.

7.3.2 Signed by All Parties (Closed Multilateral or Bilateral Treaties)

Rule	Treaties that are signed by all parties and are not opened for signature to others (often bilateral and trilateral treaties) should be cited as follows: *Treaty Title*, signed Date of Conclusion, Treaty Series (entered into force Date of Entry into Force). Where the date of conclusion and entry into force are the same, such treaties should be cited as follows: *Treaty Title*, Treaty Series (signed and entered into force Date of Conclusion and Entry into Force).
Examples	*Agreement between the Government of Australia and the Government of the United Kingdom of Great Britain and Northern Ireland Providing for the Reciprocal Recognition and Enforcement of Judgments in Civil and Commercial Matters*, signed 23 August 1990, [1994] ATS 27 (entered into force 1 September 1994). *Agreement Relating to Co-operation on Antitrust Matters*, Australia–United States of America, 1369 UNTS 43 (signed and entered into force 29 June 1982).

7.3.3 Treaties Not Yet in Force

Rule	For treaties that are not yet in force, '(not yet in force)' should replace the date of entry into force.
Example	*Convention on Cluster Munitions*, opened for signature 3 December 2008, [2008] ATNIF 24 (not yet in force).
Note	Drafts of treaties should be cited in accordance with the appropriate rules of this *Guide* for the source type. They are commonly contained in UN documents (see chapter 8). Where it is not otherwise apparent that a reference is to a draft treaty, this should be clarified discursively.

7.4 Treaty Series

Rule

A citation of a treaty series should be included and the series name should be abbreviated.

Where the treaty series is organised by volume, the citation should appear as follows:

[Volume Number] [Treaty Series Abbreviation] [Starting Page]
(for example, '23 UNTS 35').

Where the treaty series is organised by year, the citation should appear as follows:

[[Year of Volume]] [Treaty Series Abbreviation]
[Starting Page or Treaty Number]
(for example, '[2010] ATS 5').

Where the treaty series is organised by sequential order of deposit independent of year (that is, the treaty is the nth treaty ever deposited in the series), the citation should appear as follows:

[Treaty Series Abbreviation] No [Sequential Number]
(for example, 'CETS No 207').

Parallel citations should not be used.

For treaties to which Australia is a party, the following treaty series and abbreviations should be used:

Treaty Series	Abbreviation
United Nations Treaty Series	UNTS
League of Nations Treaty Series	LNTS
Australian Treaty Series	ATS
Australian Treaties Not Yet in Force	ATNIF

ATS or ATNIF should only be used where the treaty is not reported in the UNTS or LNTS. Where the treaty is not reported in these treaty series, the other treaty series listed below should be used.

For treaties to which Australia is not party, the following treaty series should be used in order of preference:

- UNTS or LNTS;
- an official treaty series of a state party; or
- another international or regional treaty series.

The latter two categories include:

Treaty Series	Abbreviation
Canada Treaty Series	CTS
Consolidated Treaty Series	ConTS
Council of Europe Treaty Series	CETS
European Treaty Series	ETS
Pacific Islands Treaty Series	PITS
United States Treaties and Other International Agreements	UST

For treaties between members of the European Union that do not appear in the UNTS or an official treaty series of a member (as well as in accordance with rule 13.1.2), the *Official Journal of the European Union* should be cited.

If a treaty is not published in a treaty series, other sources containing the treaty, such as *International Legal Materials* (abbreviated 'ILM'), should be cited.

Examples

Vienna Convention on the Law of Treaties, opened for signature 23 May 1969, 1155 UNTS 331 (entered into force 27 January 1980).

Agreement between the Government of Australia and the Government of Samoa Relating to Air Services, signed 11 August 2000, [2001] ATS 18 (entered into force 29 October 2001).

Convention on Cybercrime, opened for signature 23 November 2001, ETS No 185 (entered into force 1 July 2004) art 4(1).

Military Convention between Bulgaria and Greece, signed 22 September 1912, 217 ConTS 134 (entered into force 5 October 1912).

Convention on the International Recovery of Child Support and Other Forms of Family Maintenance, opened for signature 23 November 2007, 47 ILM 257 (not yet in force).

Notes

The very first page of a treaty (as it appears in a treaty series) should be included as the starting page, even though this page does not usually indicate a page number and contains only the title, party names and other formal details.

Although *International Legal Materials* is not technically a treaty series or report series, it may be abbreviated 'ILM' and treated for citation purposes as if it were both.

7.5 Pinpoint Reference

Rule

A pinpoint reference should follow the date of entry into force, preceded by a space. A pinpoint reference should *not* be preceded by any punctuation.

Pinpoint references should be to the articles, paragraphs, sections, etc, of a treaty. They should *not* be to the pages of the treaty series. Pinpoint references should adhere to rules 1.1.5–1.1.6. They should use the abbreviations in rule 3.1.4 (for example, 'art', 'para', 's') as appropriate. In accordance with rule 3.1.4, the highest 'level' of article, paragraph, etc, in the pinpoint should be used (for example, 'art 31.1', not 'para 31.1'). The designator 'annex' should always be written out in full.

Examples

International Convention on the Elimination of All Forms of Racial Discrimination, opened for signature 21 December 1965, 660 UNTS 195 (entered into force 4 January 1969) art 3.

Convention on the Privileges and Immunities of the United Nations, opened for signature 13 February 1946, 1 UNTS 15 (entered into force 17 September 1946) s 9. [**Not:** … (entered into force 17 September 1946), s 9.]

Agreement Establishing the Advisory Centre on WTO Law, opened for signature 30 November 1999, 2299 UNTS 249 (entered into force 15 July 2001) annex II.

Note

Articles are commonly separated from paragraphs by parentheses (for example, 'art 33(1)') or decimal points (for example, 'art 33.1'). Both Roman numbering (for example, 'art XX') and Arabic numbering (for example, 'art 12') are common in treaties. The form of pinpoint reference in the treaty cited should be used in citations.

7.6 Subsequent References

Rule

'Ibid' should be used for all materials in this chapter (in accordance with rule 1.4.1).

In other subsequent references, citations should appear in full each time a treaty is referred to. However, treaties referred to frequently may be given a short title the first time they are cited. The short title should adhere to rule 1.4.3 (so should be italicised and placed within single inverted commas and parentheses following the initial citation). The short title may be placed in the text or in the footnotes. Subsequent references should take the form:

[*Short Title*] [Pinpoint].

A short title may be given to a portion of a treaty (for example, an annex, an appendix or a schedule) in accordance with rule 1.4.3. The short title should be placed after the pinpoint to the relevant portion. Pinpoints following the short title in subsequent references refer to sections, paragraphs, etc, within that portion of a treaty.

'Above n' should not be used for treaties.

Examples

[15] *Treaty on the Zone of Cooperation in an Area between the Indonesian Province of East Timor and Northern Australia*, signed 11 December 1989, 1654 UNTS 105 (entered into force 9 February 1991) art 4(2)(a) ('*Timor Gap Treaty*').

...

[69] *Timor Gap Treaty* art 6(1).

70 *Convention on the Prohibition of the Development, Production, Stockpiling and Use of Chemical Weapons and on Their Destruction*, opened for signature 13 January 1993, 1974 UNTS 45 (entered into force 29 April 1997) annex ('*Annex on Chemicals*').

…

73 *Annex on Chemicals* pt B sch 2 para 2.

8 United Nations Materials

8.1 Constitutive Document

Rule	The *Charter of the United Nations* should be cited as follows: *Charter of the United Nations* Pinpoint .
Example	*Charter of the United Nations* art 51.
Note	The *Statute of the International Court of Justice* should be cited in accordance with rule 9.1.

8.2 Official Documents of the United Nations

Rule

A citation of a United Nations ('UN') document should include the elements listed in the table below that appear in the document. The elements should be included in the order shown below. (The examples in the table are not taken from a single document.)

Element	Example	Rule
Author	H S Amerasinghe,	8.2.1
Title	*Informal Single Negotiating Text Part IV Presented by the President of the Conference,*	8.2.2
Resolution or Decision Number	GA Res 3314,	8.2.3
Official Records	UN GAOR,	8.2.4
Committee Number	4th Comm,	8.2.5
Session (and Part) Number	34th sess, 28th sess, 1st pt,	8.2.6
Meeting Number	75th mtg,	8.2.7

Agenda Item	Agenda Item 2,	8.2.8
Supplement	Supp No 3,	8.2.9
UN Document Number	UN Doc A/RES/150	8.2.10
Full Date	(20 August 2008)	8.2.11
Annex	annex I	8.2.12
Pinpoint Reference	[2]	8.2.13

Elements before the UN document number should be separated by (non-italic) commas. Elements after the UN document number should generally not be separated by any punctuation, but the full date should appear in parentheses.

In accordance with rule 1.12.1, all ordinal numbers in citations should appear in figures and their letters should be superscript.

In accordance with rule 1.6.1, full stops should not be used in abbreviations. However, full stops should be included *within* a UN document number (in accordance with rule 8.2.10).

Example *Millennium Summit of the United Nations*, GA Res 54/254, UN GAOR, 54th sess, 93rd plen mtg, Agenda Item 49(b), Supp No 49, UN Doc A/RES/54/254 (23 March 2000, adopted 15 March 2000) para 3.

Note For examples of commonly cited types of UN documents, see rule 8.6.

8.2.1 Author

Rule Where an individual or body (other than a principal organ of the UN) is identified as the author of a document, the individual's or body's name should be included.

The author's official position may be included if it is not evident from the document title. It should be included after their name, preceded by a comma.

Examples	Fatma Zohra Ksentini, *Report of the Special Rapporteur on Human Rights and the Environment*, UN Doc E/CN.4/Sub.2/1994/9 (6 July 1994). Giorgio Gaja, Special Rapporteur, *Second Report on the Responsibility of International Organizations*, UN Doc A/CN.4/541 (2 April 2004).

8.2.2 Title

Rule	The title of a document should appear in italics.
Example	Human Rights Committee, *General Comment No 33: The Obligations of States Parties under the Optional Protocol to the International Covenant on Civil and Political Rights*, 94th sess, UN Doc CCPR/C/GC/33 (25 June 2009).
Note	Not every UN document has a title (for example, Security Council resolutions generally do not have titles).

8.2.3 Resolution or Decision Number

Rule

When citing a resolution or decision, the organ and the resolution or decision number should be included. They should appear using the abbreviations below:

Organ and Type	Abbreviation
Economic and Social Council Decision	ESC Dec
Economic and Social Council Resolution	ESC Res
General Assembly Decision	GA Dec
General Assembly Resolution	GA Res
Security Council Decision	SC Dec
Security Council Resolution	SC Res

Examples

United Nations Declaration on the Rights of Indigenous Peoples, GA Res 61/295, UN GAOR, 61st sess, 107th plen mtg, Supp No 49, UN Doc A/RES/61/295 (13 September 2007). [**Not:** … General Assembly Resolution 61/295 …]

SC Res 1441, UN SCOR, 57th sess, 4644th mtg, UN Doc S/RES/1441 (8 November 2002).

8.2.4 Official Records

Rule

Where a document is contained in the *Official Records* of a UN organ, this should be indicated using the following abbreviations:

Organ and Official Records	Abbreviation
General Assembly Official Records	UN GAOR
Security Council Official Records	UN SCOR
Economic and Social Council Official Records	UN ESCOR
Trusteeship Council Official Records	UN TCOR

Examples

Universal Declaration of Human Rights, GA Res 217A (III), UN GAOR, 3rd sess, 183rd plen mtg, UN Doc A/810 (10 December 1948).

SC Res 1734, UN SCOR, 61st sess, 5608th mtg, UN Doc S/RES/1734 (22 December 2006).

Sub-Commission on the Promotion and Protection of Human Rights, *Norms on the Responsibilities of Transnational Corporations and Other Business Enterprises with Regard to Human Rights*, UN ESCOR, 55th sess, 22nd mtg, Agenda Item 4, UN Doc E/CN.4/Sub.2/2003/12/Rev.2 (13 August 2003).

Amendment of the Rules of Procedure of the Trusteeship Council, UN TCOR, 61st sess, 1705th mtg, Agenda Item 10, UN Doc T/RES/2200 (LXI) (25 May 1994) annex para 3.

8.2.5 Committee Number

Rule	Where a UN document originates from a committee of the General Assembly, this should be indicated by including the committee number as follows: [Ordinal Number of Committee] Comm (for example, '2nd Comm').
Example	*Summary Record of the 35th Meeting*, UN GAOR, 3rd Comm, 47th sess, 35th mtg, Agenda Items 94 and 96, UN Doc A/C.3/47/SR.35 (4 December 1992) 11 [57].
Note	The United Nations General Assembly has six main committees, numbered from the First to the Sixth Committee.

8.2.6 Session (and Part) Number

Rule	Where a document originates from a session of a UN organ, committee or other body, the session number should be included. It should appear as follows: [Ordinal Number of Session] sess (for example, '4th sess'). If the session is organised into parts, the part number should also be included in the same form, preceded by a comma. 'Part' should be abbreviated 'pt' (for example, '4th sess, 3rd pt').
Examples	UN SCOR, 62nd sess, 5663rd mtg, UN Doc S/PV.5663 (17 April 2007). UN GAOR, 6th Comm, 3rd sess, 1st pt, 77th mtg, UN Doc A/C.6/SR.77 (18 October 1948).

8.2.7 Meeting Number

Rule	A meeting number should be included as follows: [Ordinal Number of Meeting] mtg (for example, '37th mtg').

	Where the meeting is a 'plenary meeting', 'mtg' should be replaced with 'plen mtg'.
Examples	SC Res 1546, UN SCOR, 59th sess, 4987th mtg, UN Doc S/RES/1546 (8 June 2004). *Measures to Eliminate International Terrorism*, GA Res 49/60, UN GAOR, 49th sess, 84th plen mtg, Supp No 49, UN Doc A/RES/49/60 (9 December 1994).

8.2.8 Agenda Item

Rule	An agenda item should be included as follows: Agenda Item [Agenda Item Number] (for example, 'Agenda Item 137'). Where more than one agenda item appears on a UN document, 'Agenda Items' should precede the agenda item numbers. The last two agenda item numbers should be separated by 'and'.
Examples	*The Ethiopian Millennium*, GA Res 61/270, UN GAOR, 61st sess, 103rd plen mtg, Agenda Item 44, Supp No 49, UN Doc A/RES/61/270 (27 June 2007, adopted 15 June 2007). *International Migration and Development: Report of the Secretary-General*, UN GAOR, 60th sess, Agenda Item 54(c), UN Doc A/60/871 (18 May 2006). *Gratis Personnel Provided by Governments*, GA Res 53/218, UN GAOR, 53rd sess, 97th plen mtg, Agenda Items 112 and 119, Supp No 49, UN Doc A/RES/53/218 (21 April 1999).
Note	Documents marked with an 'agenda item' are created or distributed in pursuance of an item on a UN body's official agenda.

8.2.9 Supplement

Rule	Where a UN document appears in a supplement to the *Official Records*, the supplement should be included as follows: Supp No [Supplement Number] (for example, 'Supp No 98').
Example	*2005 World Summit Outcome*, GA Res 60/1, UN GAOR, 60th sess, 8th plen mtg, Agenda Items 46 and 120, Supp No 49, UN Doc A/RES/60/1 (24 October 2005).
Note	UN reports, resolutions and decisions are published as supplements to the *Official Records* (which are independently paginated sections within or volumes of the *Official Records*). From the 31st session (1976), General Assembly resolutions were published in Supp No 49.

8.2.10 UN Document Number

Rule	Almost all UN documents are assigned a unique document number, which should be included as follows: UN Doc [Document Number] (for example, 'UN Doc A/RES/54/275'). A document number should appear *exactly* as it does on the document cited (including slashes and full stops). Abbreviations in document numbers should appear in upper case. Where multiple document numbers are necessary (for example, due to an addendum or corrigendum), 'Doc' should be replaced by 'Docs' and only as much of the second document number as is different should be included. The document numbers should be separated by 'and' (for example, 'UN Docs A/63/804 and Corr.1').
Examples	*International Day of Peace*, GA Res 55/282, UN GAOR, 55th sess, 111th plen mtg, Agenda Item 33, Supp No 49, UN Doc A/RES/55/282 (28 September 2001, adopted 7 September 2001) para 3.

SC Res 1905, UN SCOR, 64th sess, 6249th mtg, UN Doc S/RES/1905 (21 December 2009).

The Situation in the Occupied Territories of Azerbaijan: Report of the Secretary General, UN GAOR, 63rd sess, Agenda Item 18, UN Docs A/63/804 and Corr.1 (30 March 2009). [**Not:** … UN Docs A/63/804 and A/63/804/Corr.1 …]

Notes

The following abbreviations, which indicate the body under whose auspices the document was produced, often form the first component of a UN document number:

Abbreviation	Meaning	Abbreviation	Meaning
A	General Assembly	CAT/C	Committee against Torture
CCPR/C	Human Rights Committee	CEDAW/C	Committee on the Elimination of Discrimination against Women
CERD/C	Committee on the Elimination of Racial Discrimination	CRC/C	Committee on the Rights of the Child
DP	UN Development Programme	E	Economic and Social Council
S	Security Council	ST	Secretariat
TD	UN Conference on Trade and Development	UNEP	United Nations Environment Programme

The following abbreviations, which indicate the specific body that authored or received the document, often form the second component of a UN document number:

Abbreviation	Meaning	Abbreviation	Meaning
AC	Ad hoc committee	C	Standing, permanent or main committee
CONF	Conference	CN	Commission
GC	Governing council	PC	Preparatory committee

SC	Sub-Committee	Sub	Sub-Commission
WG	Working group		

The following abbreviations, which indicate a description of the document type or its characteristics, often form the third (sometimes final) component of a UN document number:

Abbreviation	Meaning	Abbreviation	Meaning
CRP	Conference room paper	INF	Information series
L	Limited distribution	NGO	Statement by non-governmental organisations
PET	Petition	PRST	Statement by the President of the Security Council
PV	Verbatim record of meeting	R	Restricted distribution
RES	Resolution	SR	Summary record of meeting
WP	Working paper		

The following components, which indicate subsequent additions or changes to a document, often form a fourth (and final) component of a UN document number:

Abbreviation	Meaning	Abbreviation	Meaning
Add	Addendum	Amend	Amendment
Corr	Corrigendum	Rev	Revision
Summary	Summarised version	*	Reissuance of document for technical reasons

Document numbers of General Assembly resolutions prior to the 31st session (1976) include the session number (and, for special and emergency special sessions, an abbreviation for the type of session) in parentheses after the document number. Examples are '(XXV)' for the 25th regular session, '(S-VI)' for the sixth special session, and '(ES-V)' for the fifth emergency special session.

8.2.11 Full Date

Rule

The full date of the document should be included in parentheses after the UN document number.

Where there are multiple dates on a document, the date that appears directly below the document number should be included.

Where the date of adoption differs from the document date and the date of adoption is important, the date of adoption may be included after the full date as follows:

(Full Date, adopted Full Date of Adoption)
(for example, '(27 July 2001, adopted 14 June 2001)').

Where there is not a full date on the document, as much of the full date as appears should be included.

Examples

Maurice Kamto, Special Rapporteur, *Third Report on the Expulsion of Aliens*, 59th sess, UN Doc A/CN.4/581 (19 April 2007) 6 [11].

UN GAOR, 5th Comm, 51st sess, 68th mtg, UN Doc A/C.5/51/SR.68 (12 August 1997). [**Not:** … (4 June 1997).]

General and Complete Disarmament, GA Res 49/75, UN GAOR, 49th sess, 90th plen mtg, Agenda Item 62, Supp No 49, UN Doc A/RES/49/75 (9 January 1995, adopted 15 December 1994) pt K.

Rules of Procedure of the General Assembly, UN Doc A/520/Rev.17 (2008).

Note

The date of a UN document (the date of issuance) often precedes or follows the date of its adoption.

8.2.12 Annex

Rule

Where an annex is included as a pinpoint reference, 'annex' should appear as the pinpoint. Where there are multiple annexes, a reference to one annex should include its number or other designation as it appears on the document (for example, 'annex 1', '2nd annex', 'annex A').

Where an annex to a UN document is effectively a document in its own right (for example, where the annex has separate pagination or pinpoints from the rest of the document or has a separate title) and reference is made to pinpoints within the annex, the first reference to the annex should appear as follows:

Citation of UN Document Containing Annex annex ('*Title of Annex*').

Subsequent references should appear as follows:

Title of Annex, UN Doc Document Number of UN Document Containing Annex, annex Pinpoint.

Where there are multiple annexes, 'annex' should be replaced with the numbered annex as it appears on the source.

Examples

22 SC Res 1512, UN SCOR, 58th sess, 4849th mtg, UN Doc S/RES/1512 (27 October 2003) annex.

23 *United Nations Convention against Transnational Organized Crime*, GA Res 55/25, UN GAOR, 55th sess, 62nd plen mtg, Agenda Item 105, Supp No 49, UN Doc A/RES/55/25 (8 January 2001) annex II ('*Protocol to Prevent, Suppress and Punish Trafficking in Persons, Especially Women and Children, Supplementing the United Nations Convention against Transnational Organized Crime*').

…

25 *Protocol to Prevent, Suppress and Punish Trafficking in Persons, Especially Women and Children, Supplementing the United Nations Convention against Transnational Organized Crime*, UN Doc A/RES/55/25, annex II art 2(a).

8.2.13 Pinpoint Reference

Rule

Pinpoint references should appear at the end of the citation.

Where a UN document is a resolution, decision or in the nature of a treaty, pinpoint references should adhere to and appear using the abbreviations in rule 3.1.4. In particular:

- 'paragraph' should be abbreviated 'para'; and
- where multiple combinations of abbreviations and numbers form one pinpoint reference, commas should not separate them (for example, to refer to paragraph 2 in part B 'pt B para 2', not 'pt B, para 2', should be included).

Pinpoint references to operative paragraphs in resolutions and decisions should not be preceded by any designation. Pinpoint references to preambular paragraphs in resolutions and decisions should appear as follows:

Preamble para Number
(for example, 'Preamble para 3').

Where a UN document is in the nature of a report, judicial decision or secondary source, pinpoint references should adhere to rules 1.1.5–1.1.6. Where such a document has page and paragraph numbers, paragraph numbers must be included and page numbers *may* be included in addition. Where such a document has only page numbers or paragraph numbers, pinpoints should be to page numbers or paragraphs as appropriate. Paragraph numbers should appear in square brackets.

Examples

2005 World Summit Outcome, GA Res 60/1, UN GAOR, 60th sess, 8th plen mtg, Agenda Items 46 and 120, Supp No 49, UN Doc A/RES/60/1 (24 October 2005) paras 138–9.

SC Res 1717, UN SCOR, 61st sess, 5550th mtg, UN Doc S/RES/1717 (13 October 2006) Preamble paras 3–4.

Report of the Secretary-General Pursuant to General Assembly Resolution 53/35: The Fall of Srebrenica, 54th sess, Agenda Item 42, UN Doc A/54/549 (15 November 1999) 6 [3]–[4].

Committee against Torture, *Decision: Communication No 227/2003*, 37th sess, UN Doc CAT/C/37/D/227/2003 (14 December 2006) [8.6]–[8.7] ('*AAC v Sweden*').

Note

Preambular paragraphs are usually not numbered. When citing preambular paragraphs, Arabic numerals should be assigned to them in order.

8.2.14 Documents of Multiple Organs

Rule

Where a document is considered by or addressed to multiple UN organs (for example, both the General Assembly and Security Council):

- parallel citations of the *Official Records* of both organs should be included, separated by a semi-colon; and
- both document numbers should be included, separated by 'and'.

Example

Letter Dated 5 November 2001 from the Chargé d'affaires ai of the Permanent Mission of the Syrian Arab Republic to the United Nations Addressed to the Secretary-General, UN GAOR, 56th sess, Agenda Items 42, 88 and 166; UN SCOR, 56th sess, UN Docs A/56/601 and S/2001/1045 (5 November 2001).

8.3 UN Treaty Body Documents

8.3.1 Decisions of UN Treaty Bodies on Individual Communications

Rule

Decisions of UN treaty bodies on individual communications should be cited in accordance with rule 8.2. However, they should always be given a short title (in accordance with rule 8.5) as follows:

('*Complainant's Surname* v *Respondent State*')

Subsequent references should adhere to rule 8.5.

Example

[22] Human Rights Committee, *Views: Communication No 1011/2001*, 81st sess, UN Doc CCPR/C/81/D/1011/2001 (26 August 2004) 21 [9.8] ('*Madafferi v Australia*').

…

25 *Madafferi v Australia*, UN Doc CCPR/C/81/D/1011/2001, 22 [10].

8.3.2 Communications and Submissions to UN Treaty Bodies

Rule

Communications and submissions to UN treaty bodies should be cited as follows:

[Author], '[Document Title]', [Document Type] to the [UN Treaty Body] in [*Complainant's Surname*] *v* [*Respondent State*], [Full Date], [Pinpoint].

The document type should generally be 'Submission' or 'Communication' as appropriate. Pinpoint references should adhere to rules 1.1.5–1.1.6. Pinpoints should be to paragraph numbers where available, or otherwise to page numbers.

A URL may be included after the full date or any pinpoint reference where this would aid retrieval of the document. It should appear in accordance with rule 6.15.6.

Example

Human Rights Law Resource Centre, 'Individual Communication under the *Optional Protocol to the International Covenant on Civil and Political Rights* — Original Communication', Communication to the Human Rights Committee in *Nystrom v Australia*, 4 April 2007, [77]–[103] <http://www.hrlrc.org.au/files/PXB9OSNUM6/Individual%20Communication.pdf>.

8.4 United Nations Yearbooks

Rule

Where material is available as a UN document, it should be cited in accordance with rule 8.2 (even if reproduced in a UN yearbook). Where material in a UN yearbook is not otherwise available, the yearbook should be cited.

Where the yearbook is organised by year, it should be cited as follows:

'[Title]' [[Year]] [*Yearbook Title*] [Starting Page], [Pinpoint].

Where there are multiple volumes for one year, the volume number should be included in Roman numerals after the year (for example, '[2002] II'). Where a volume is split into parts, the part number should be included, enclosed in parentheses, immediately after the volume number (for example, '[1999] II(2)').

Where the yearbook is organised by volume, it should be cited as follows:

'[Title]' ([Year]) [Volume Number] [*Yearbook Title*] [Starting Page], [Pinpoint].

Where a volume is split into multiple issues or parts, the issue number should be included immediately following the volume number in parentheses (for example, '34(I)').

In citations of UN yearbooks, an author's name may be included before the document title, followed by a comma, where an individual or body is clearly identified as the author. A UN document number should *not* be included.

Examples

'National Legislation Providing for the Levying of Certain Air Travel Taxes — The United Nations Should Be Exempt from Such Taxes under Section 7(a) of the *Convention on the Privileges and Immunities of the United Nations*' [1973] *United Nations Juridical Yearbook* 132, 135.

'Report of the International Law Commission on the Work of Its Fifty-Third Session (23 April – 1 June and 2 July – 10 August 2001)' [2001] II(2) *Yearbook of the International Law Commission* 1.

'Judge Bruno Simma' (2005) 59 *International Court of Justice Yearbook* 54.

'Developments and Trends, 2007' (2007) 32(II) *United Nations Disarmament Yearbook* 3, 4.

Note UN yearbooks include the *Yearbook of the United Nations*, the *United Nations Juridical Yearbook*, the *International Court of Justice Yearbook* and the *Yearbook of the International Law Commission*.

8.5 Subsequent References

Rule

'Ibid' should be used for all materials in this chapter (in accordance with rule 1.4.1).

In other subsequent references to UN documents (see rule 8.2), citations should appear in full each time a source is referred to. However, where a UN document is frequently referred to, it may be given a short title. The short title should adhere to rule 1.4.3 (so should be italicised, and placed within single inverted commas and parentheses following the initial citation). Subsequent references should then appear as follows:

[*Short Title*], UN Doc [UN Document Number], [Pinpoint].

Other subsequent references to communications and submissions to UN treaty bodies (see rule 8.3.2) should appear in full.

In other subsequent references to UN yearbooks (see rule 8.4), 'above n' should be used (in accordance with rule 1.4.2). Otherwise, 'above n' should not be used for materials in this chapter.

Examples

22 SC Res 1325, UN SCOR, 4213th mtg, UN Doc S/RES/1325 (31 October 2000) ('*Resolution 1325*').

23 Ibid para 3.

…

27 *Resolution 1325*, UN Doc S/RES/1325, para 7.

28 'Legal Aspects of International Political Relations' [1988] *Yearbook of the United Nations* 796, 801.

…

31 'Legal Aspects of International Political Relations', above n 28, 797.

8.6 Commonly Cited Documents

Examples

The table below sets out example citations of common types of UN documents. The citations apply the rules above.

Document Type	Example
General Assembly Resolution	*Prevention of Armed Conflict*, GA Res 57/337, UN GAOR, 57th sess, 93rd plen mtg, Agenda Item 10, Supp No 49, UN Doc A/RES/57/337 (18 July 2003).
Security Council Resolution	SC Res 827, UN SCOR, 48th sess, 3217th mtg, UN Doc S/RES/827 (25 May 1993).
Meeting Record	UN GAOR, 63rd sess, 55th plen mtg, UN Doc A/63/PV.55 (19 November 2008).
Economic and Social Committee Decision	*Basic Program of Work of the Economic and Social Council for 2001*, ESC Dec 2001/203, UN ESCOR, 3rd plen mtg, Supp No 1, UN Doc E/2000/99 (4 February 2000).
Report of Principal Organ	*Report of the Economic and Social Council for 2005*, UN GAOR, 60th sess, UN Doc A/60/3/Rev.1 (11 July 2007).
Report of UN Treaty Body	Conference of the Parties, United Nations Framework Convention on Climate Change, *Report of the Conference of the Parties on Its Fifteenth Session, Held in Copenhagen from 7 to 19 December 2009 — Addendum — Part 2: Action Taken by the Conference of the Parties at Its Fifteenth Session*, UN Doc FCCC/CP/2009/11/Add.1 (30 March 2010).
Secretary-General's Report	*In Larger Freedom: Towards Development, Security and Human Rights for All — Report of the Secretary-General*, 59th sess, Agenda Items 45 and 55, UN Doc A/59/2005 (21 March 2005).
Secretariat Document	*Secretary-General's Bulletin — Organization of the Office of Central Support Services*, UN Doc ST/SGB/1998/11 (1 June 1998).
Annex	*Responsibility of States for Internationally Wrongful Acts*, GA Res 56/83, UN GAOR, 56th sess, 85th plen mtg, Supp No 49, UN Doc A/RES/56/83 (28 January 2002, adopted 12 December 2001) annex ('*Responsibility of States for Internationally Wrongful Acts*').
Draft Resolution	*Draft Resolution — International Cooperation in the Peaceful Uses of Outer Space*, 4th Comm, 62nd sess, Agenda Item 31, UN Doc A/C.4/62/L.2 (14 November 2007).

9 International Court of Justice and Permanent Court of International Justice

9.1 Constitutive and Basic Documents

Rule	The *Statute of the International Court of Justice* should be cited as follows: *Statute of the International Court of Justice* [Pinpoint]. The *Statute of the Permanent Court of International Justice* should be cited as follows: *Statute of the Permanent Court of International Justice* [Pinpoint]. The rules of the International Court of Justice should be cited as follows: International Court of Justice, *Rules of Court* (adopted [Full Date]) [Pinpoint]. The rules of the Permanent Court of International Justice should be cited as follows: Permanent Court of International Justice, *Rules of Court* (adopted [Full Date]) [Pinpoint].
Examples	*Statute of the International Court of Justice* art 24. *Statute of the Permanent Court of International Justice* art 4. International Court of Justice, *Rules of Court* (adopted 14 April 1978) art 59. Permanent Court of International Justice, *Rules of Court* (adopted 24 March 1922) art 48.

9.2 Decisions

Examples	*East Timor*	*(Portugal v Australia)*	*(Judgment)*	[1995]	ICJ Rep	90	, 93
	Western Sahara	*(Advisory Opinion)*		[1975]	ICJ Rep	12	, 17
	Mavrommatis Palestine Concessions	*(Greece v United Kingdom)*	*(Jurisdiction)*	[1924]	PCIJ (ser A)	No 2	, 10
Element	Case Name	Parties' Names or Advisory Opinion	Phase	Year	Report Series and Series Letter	Starting Page and Case Number	Pinpoint
Rule	9.2.1	9.2.2	9.2.3	9.2.4	9.2.5	9.2.6	9.2.7

9.2.1 Case Name

Rule

A citation of a decision of the International Court of Justice ('ICJ') or Permanent Court of International Justice ('PCIJ') should include the case name in italics as it appears on the first page of the report. However:

- '*The*', '*Case concerning*' and '*Case concerning the*' at the start of a case name and '*Case*' or '*Cases*' at the end of a case name should be omitted;
- punctuation should adhere to rule 1.6.1 (so full stops should not be used in abbreviations); and
- capitalisation should adhere to rule 1.7.

Examples

Certain Phosphate Lands in Nauru (Nauru v Australia) (Preliminary Objections) [1992] ICJ Rep 240.

Legality of Use of Force (Serbia and Montenegro v France) (Preliminary Objections) [2004] ICJ Rep 575. [**Not:** *Case concerning the Legality of Use of Force …*]

Fisheries Jurisdiction (Spain v Canada) (Jurisdiction) [1998] ICJ Rep 432. [**Not:** *Fisheries Jurisdiction Case …*]

9.2.2 Parties' Names or Advisory Opinion

Rule

The names of the parties should be italicised and included (after the case name) as they appear on the first page of the report (even if in an elaborate form). They should be enclosed within parentheses and separated by '*v*'.

Where parties do not appear on the first page of the report, their names should be included in the conventional shortened form (if any exists), rather than the full elaborate form (for example, 'Zimbabwe', not 'Republic of Zimbabwe'). However, the full form should be used where necessary to avoid ambiguity.

Where multiple cases are joined together, only the names of the parties to the first-listed case should be included.

For advisory opinions, '*(Advisory Opinion)*' should appear instead of party names.

Examples

Application of the Convention on the Prevention and Punishment of the Crime of Genocide (Bosnia and Herzegovina v Yugoslavia) (Preliminary Objections) [1996] ICJ Rep 595.

Factory at Chorzów (Germany v Poland) (Jurisdiction) [1927] PCIJ (ser A) No 9. [**Not:** … *(Germany v Polish Republic)* …]

North Sea Continental Shelf (Federal Republic of Germany v Denmark) (Merits) [1969] ICJ Rep 3. [**Not:** … *(Federal Republic of Germany v Denmark; Federal Republic of Germany v Netherlands)* …]

Legal Consequences of the Construction of a Wall in the Occupied Palestinian Territory (Advisory Opinion) [2004] ICJ Rep 136.

9.2.3 Phase

Rule

The phase should be italicised and appear in parentheses (after the parties' names). It should be included as it appears on the first or second page of the report, in accordance with chapter 1. However:

- any date in the phase should be omitted;
- where the phase is an order with respect to 'provisional measures', 'interim measures of protection' or similar matters, the phase should appear as '*(Provisional Measures)*';
- where the phase is an order or judgment with respect to 'preliminary objections' or similar matters, the phase should appear as '*(Preliminary Objection)*' or '*(Preliminary Objections)*' as appropriate; and
- where the phase is expressed as 'Jurisdiction of the Court', it should appear as '*(Jurisdiction)*'.

For procedural orders of the court on a particular matter, the phase should be included in the following form:

(Order on [*Name of Matter*] *)*

The name of the matter should appear as it does on the first page of the case. The name of the subject matter of the application, and not the date of the order, should be used (for example, '*(Order on Application by Malta for Permission to Intervene)*'). However, where the date is the *only* description of the order on the first page of the case, the phase should be included in the following form:

(Order of [*Full Date*] *)*

Examples

United States Diplomatic and Consular Staff in Tehran (United States of America v Iran) (Provisional Measures) [1979] ICJ Rep 7, 12 [10]–[11]. [**Not:** … *(Request for the Indication of Provisional Measures)* [1979] …]

South West Africa (Ethiopia v South Africa) (Preliminary Objections) [1962] ICJ Rep 319, 378. [**Not:** … *(Ethiopia v South Africa) (Judgment of 21 December 1962)* …]

Fisheries Jurisdiction (United Kingdom of Great Britain and Northern Ireland v Iceland) (Jurisdiction) [1973] ICJ Rep 3.

Right of Passage over Indian Territory (Portugal v India) (Merits) [1960] ICJ Rep 6.

Asylum (Colombia v Peru) (Judgment) [1950] ICJ Rep 266.

Nottebohm (Liechtenstein v Guatemala) (Second Phase) [1955] ICJ Rep 4.

Nuclear Tests (New Zealand v France) (Order on Application by Fiji for Permission to Intervene) [1973] ICJ Rep 324. [**Not:** … *(Order of 12 July 1973 — Application by Fiji for Permission to Intervene)* …]

But: *Nuclear Tests (New Zealand v France) (Order of 6 September 1973)* [1973] ICJ Rep 341.

Note

Cases before the ICJ and PCIJ may involve a number of separate decisions of the court. The 'phase' is the broad characterisation of the stage of the decision cited in the course of a case. The most common phases are:

- '*(Provisional Measures)*';
- '*(Preliminary Objections)*';
- '*(Jurisdiction)*';
- '*(Merits)*'; and
- '*(Judgment)*'.

A phase should always be included in a contentious case. Where there are not multiple phases in a particular contentious case, the phase '*(Judgment)*' will usually be appropriate.

9.2.4 Year

Rule

The year of the volume of the report series in which the case appears should be included (after the phase) in square brackets.

Examples

Certain German Interests in Polish Upper Silesia (Germany v Poland) (Judgment) [1925] PCIJ (ser A) No 6.

LaGrand (Germany v United States of America) (Judgment) [2001] ICJ Rep 466.

Note	The official report series of both the ICJ and PCIJ are organised by year. The year therefore appears in square brackets (in accordance with rule 2.2).

9.2.5 Report Series and Series Letter

Rule	The report series abbreviation should appear (unitalicised) after the year. For decisions of the PCIJ, the letter of the series ('A', 'B' or 'A/B') should also be included in the form: (ser [Letter of Series]) (for example, '(ser B)').
Examples	*Oil Platforms (Islamic Republic of Iran v United States of America) (Preliminary Objection)* [1996] ICJ Rep 803. *SS 'Lotus' (France v Turkey) (Judgment)* [1927] PCIJ (ser A) No 10.
Notes	The ICJ publishes its decisions in *Reports of Judgments, Advisory Opinions and Orders* (abbreviated 'ICJ Rep'). The PCIJ published its decisions in series A, series B and series A/B of *Publications of the Permanent Court of International Justice* (abbreviated 'PCIJ').

9.2.6 Starting Page and Case Number

Rule	For decisions of the ICJ, the starting page should be included after the report series abbreviation. For decisions of the PCIJ, the case number should be included (instead of a starting page) after the series.
Examples	*Frontier Dispute (Benin v Niger) (Judgment)* [2005] ICJ Rep 90. *Factory at Chorzów (Germany v Poland) (Merits)* [1928] PCIJ (ser A) No 17.

Notes

For decisions of the ICJ, the starting page is generally that on which the judgment begins. The page numbers of title page and the page containing information about mode of citation should not be used as the starting page. (However, the information on mode of citation indicates the correct starting page in its suggested citation of the decision.)

Decisions of the PCIJ were assigned a sequential number by the Court (for example, 'No 3'). This number should be used to cite PCIJ decisions because the page numbering of each decision (even within a series) is non-consecutive (see rule 4.4 on non-consecutive pagination).

9.2.7 Pinpoint Reference

Rule

Pinpoint references should adhere to rules 1.1.5–1.1.6 and 2.5. In particular:

- where the pinpoint reference is to the first page of the report, the page number should be repeated;
- a series of pinpoint references should be separated by commas rather than 'and';
- where cases are paginated, pinpoint references should be to pages; and
- where a report has both page numbers and paragraph numbers, page numbers should *always* be included in a pinpoint reference and paragraph numbers *may* be included *in addition*.

Examples

Railway Traffic between Lithuania and Poland (Advisory Opinion) [1931] PCIJ (ser A/B) No 42, 109.

Barcelona Traction, Light and Power Company Ltd (Belgium v Spain) (Judgment) [1970] ICJ Rep 3, 5, 9, 10–11.

Corfu Channel (United Kingdom v Albania) (Preliminary Objection) [1948] ICJ Rep 15, 26–7.

Certain Property (Liechtenstein v Germany) (Judgment) [2005] ICJ Rep 6, 19 [26], 20 [31]–[32], 21–5 [34]–[45].

9.2.8 Identifying Judges

Rule	Where a judgment of the court is referred to, neither a judge's name nor '(The Court)' should be included. Where a separate or dissenting opinion or a declaration is referred to, the name(s) of the relevant judge(s) (if not otherwise apparent) may be included in parentheses after the pinpoint reference. Judges' names should appear in accordance with rules 1.14.4 and 2.9.1, except that 'Judge(s)', 'President' and 'Vice-President' should be written out in full before judges' surnames. 'Separate Opinion', 'Dissenting Opinion' and 'Declaration' (and any abbreviations of these terms) should not be included with judges' names.
Examples	*Avena and Other Mexican Nationals (Mexico v United States of America) (Judgment)* [2004] ICJ Rep 12, 79 (Judge Vereshchetin). *Interhandel (Switzerland v United States of America) (Preliminary Objections)* [1959] ICJ Rep 6, 78 (President Klaestad). *Arrest Warrant of 11 April 2000 (Democratic Republic of the Congo v Belgium) (Judgment)* [2002] ICJ Rep 3, 63–4 [2]–[3] (Judges Higgins, Kooijmans and Buergenthal). *Elettronica Sicula SpA (ELSI) (United States of America v Italy) (Judgment)* [1989] ICJ Rep 15, 98 (Judge Schwebel). [**Not:** … (Dissenting Opinion of Judge Schwebel). **nor** … (Dis Op Judge Schwebel). **nor** … (DO Judge Schwebel).]
Note	Where it is important that a judge made a declaration or gave a separate or dissenting opinion, this should be made clear in the text.

9.3 Pleadings and Other Documents Originating in ICJ and PCIJ Proceedings

Rule	Pleadings and other material of parties and of the court originating in proceedings before the ICJ should be cited as follows:

'Document Title', *Case Name* (*Parties' Names*)
[Year] ICJ Pleadings Starting Page, Pinpoint
(Speaker's Name).

Pleadings and other material of parties and of the court originating in proceedings before the PCIJ should be cited as follows:

'Document Title', *Case Name* (*Parties' Names*) [Year]
PCIJ (ser C) No Number, Starting Page, Pinpoint
(Speaker's Name).

The title of the document should appear as it does in the source, subject to chapter 1. Case names and parties' names should adhere to rules 9.2.1–9.2.2. The year should be that of the volume cited. If the title page of a volume does not include a year, the year should be that of the decision (in the phase) to which the volume relates. Pinpoint references should adhere to rule 9.2.7, but should be to page numbers.

A speaker's name (if not otherwise apparent) may be included after a pinpoint reference. Judges' names should adhere to rule 9.2.8. Names of counsel, witnesses and other persons should adhere to rules 1.14 and 2.9.3.

For ICJ Pleadings, where more than one volume is published for a case, the volume number should precede 'ICJ Pleadings'. It should appear in Roman numerals (for example, '[1985] II ICJ Pleadings').

For PCIJ (ser C), the 'number' *and* the starting page of the document should be included (for example, 'No 76, 12'). Where there are multiple parts within a 'number', the part should follow the number, preceded by 'pt'. The part should appear in Roman numerals (for example, 'No 17 pt II').

Examples

'Written Statement of the Government of the Kingdom of Denmark', *Certain Expenses of the United Nations (Advisory Opinion)* [1962] ICJ Pleadings 137.

'Questions Put to Professor Glennon by Judge Schwebel', *Military and Paramilitary Activities in and against Nicaragua (Nicaragua v United States of America)* [1986] V ICJ Pleadings 78, 78 (Judge Schwebel), 79 (Professor Glennon).

	'Memorial Filed by the Government of His Britannic Majesty', *Treaty of Lausanne, Article 3, Paragraph 2 (Advisory Opinion)* [1925] PCIJ (ser C) No 10, 198, 200–3. 'Speech by Dr Budding', *Rights of Minorities in Upper Silesia (Germany v Poland)* [1928] PCIJ (ser C) No 14 pt II, 20, 25–7.
Notes	The ICJ publishes *Pleadings, Oral Arguments, Documents* (abbreviated 'ICJ Pleadings'), which contains documents and transmissions of the parties and the Court (such as the application instituting proceedings, submissions, minutes of oral argument and evidence). The ICJ Pleadings series is organised by case, then volume number. The PCIJ published similar documents in series C of *Publications of the Permanent Court of International Justice* (abbreviated 'PCIJ'). PCIJ (ser C) is organised by 'numbers' (for example, 'No 2'). A 'number' sometimes contains multiple 'parts'. Each 'part' is separately paginated and contains documents relating to a separate case.

9.4 Unreported Materials

9.4.1 Decisions

Rule	Decisions of the ICJ that are not reported should be cited as follows: [*Case Name*] *(*[*Parties' Names*]*) (*[*Phase*]*)* (International Court of Justice, General List No [Number], [Full Date]) [Pinpoint]. Case names and parties' names should adhere to rules 9.2.1–9.2.2. The general list number should be included as it appears on the page on which the judgment commences. The full date is that of the judgment. Pinpoint references should be to paragraphs (and should adhere to rules 1.1.5–1.1.6). Judges' names may be included after pinpoints in accordance with rule 9.2.8.

Examples

Certain Questions of Mutual Assistance in Criminal Matters (Djibouti v France) (Judgment) (International Court of Justice, General List No 136, 4 June 2008).

Dispute regarding Navigational and Related Rights (Costa Rica v Nicaragua) (Judgment) (International Court of Justice, General List No 133, 13 July 2009) [34].

Sovereignty over Pedra Branca/Pulau Batu Puteh, Middle Rocks and South Ledge (Malaysia v Singapore) (Judgment) (International Court of Justice, General List No 130, 23 May 2008) [8] (Judge Parra-Aranguren).

Notes

Paragraph numbering generally begins afresh in a separate or dissenting opinion. Paragraph references to a separate or dissenting opinion are therefore to paragraphs *within* the opinion. A judge's name must therefore be included in such references.

Decisions, pleadings and other material of the ICJ and PCIJ are available from the ICJ's website at <http://www.icj-cij.org>. There is no need to include a URL (to the ICJ's website or otherwise) after a citation of unreported ICJ decisions or other material.

9.4.2 Pleadings and Other Documents

Rule

Pleadings and other material of parties and of the court originating in proceedings before the ICJ that are not reported should be cited as follows:

> '[Document Title]', [*Case Name*] *(*[*Parties' Names*]*)*, International Court of Justice, General List No [Number], [Full Date], [Pinpoint].

The title of the document should appear as it does in the source, subject to chapter 1. Case names and parties' names should adhere to rules 9.2.1–9.2.2. The general list number should be included as it appears on the page on which the judgment commences. The full date is that of the document cited.

Pinpoint references should adhere to rules 1.1.5–1.1.6 and should be to paragraph numbers where available (and where these are continuous across an entire document). Where a document has only page numbers, pinpoints should be to page numbers. Pinpoint references to verbatim proceedings (and other transcripts) should be to page numbers.

Speakers' names may be included after pinpoint references and should adhere to rule 9.3.

Examples

'Application Instituting Proceedings', *Aerial Herbicide Spraying (Ecuador v Colombia)*, International Court of Justice, General List No 138, 31 March 2008, 28 [41].

'Request for the Indication of Provisional Measures Submitted by the Government of the Kingdom of Belgium', *Questions Relating to the Obligation to Prosecute or Extradite (Belgium v Senegal)*, International Court of Justice, General List No 144, 17 February 2009, 2.

'Memorial Submitted by Romania', *Maritime Delimitation in the Black Sea (Romania v Ukraine)*, International Court of Justice, General List No 132, 19 August 2005, [6.21]–[6.22].

'Verbatim Record', *Dispute regarding Navigational and Related Rights (Costa Rica v Nicaragua)*, International Court of Justice, General List No 133, 2 March 2009, 12 (Edgar Ugalde-Alvarez).

9.5 Subsequent References

Rule

'Ibid' should be used for all materials in this chapter (in accordance with rule 1.4.1).

In other subsequent references:

- citations of decisions of the ICJ and PCIJ should adhere to rule 2.14; and
- citations of pleadings and other documents should appear in full.

'Above n' should not be used for any materials in this chapter.

Examples

[3] *Reparation for Injuries Suffered in the Service of the United Nations (Advisory Opinion)* [1949] ICJ Rep 174, 178 ('*Reparations*').

[4] Ibid 179.

[5] 'Memorial of Nicaragua', *Border and Transborder Armed Actions (Nicaragua v Costa Rica)* [1987] ICJ Pleadings 9, 55.

[6] Ibid 56–7.

…

[9] *Reparations* [1949] ICJ Rep 174, 198 (Judge Hackworth).

[10] 'Memorial of Nicaragua', *Border and Transborder Armed Actions (Nicaragua v Costa Rica)* [1987] ICJ Pleadings 9, 17. [**Not:** 'Memorial of Nicaragua', above n 5, 7.]

10 International Arbitral and Tribunal Decisions

10.1 State–State Decisions

10.1.1 Reported Decisions

Example	*Expropriated Religious Properties*	*(France v Portugal)*	*(Awards)*	(1932) 2 Hag Crt Rep 2d (Scott)	1	, 4
Element	Case Name	Parties' Names	Phase	Year, Volume and Report Series	Starting Page	Pin-point

Rule

State–state arbitral and tribunal decisions published in a report series should be cited in accordance with rule 9.2, as shown above. In particular:

- the case name should adhere to rule 9.2.1; and
- pinpoint references should adhere to rule 9.2.7.

However:

- the parties' names should appear in the conventional shortened form, not the full elaborate form, regardless of how they appear on the decision;
- the phase should appear as it does on the decision cited, except that any date should be omitted from the phase unless it is necessary to unambiguously identify the decision;
- the year, volume and report series should adhere to rules 2.2–2.3; and
- the starting page should adhere to rule 2.4.

Judges' or arbitrators' names should be included in accordance with rule 9.2.8 (so should appear only after pinpoint references to separate or dissenting opinions or declarations). However, tribunal members

	may be referred to by a title other than 'Mr' or 'Ms' (such as 'Dr', 'Prof', etc).
Examples	*Cordillera of the Andes Boundary (Argentina v Chile) (Report of the Tribunal Appointed by the Arbitrator)* (1902) 9 RIAA 39. *Southern Bluefin Tuna (Australia v Japan) (Jurisdiction and Admissibility)* (2000) 39 ILM 1359. [**Not:** … *(Australia and New Zealand v Japan)* …] *Responsibility for the Death of Letelier and Moffitt (United States of America v Chile) (Decision)* (2005) 25 RIAA 1, 12–13 (Prof Orrego Vicuña).
Notes	Some commonly cited report series containing state–state arbitral decisions are the Arb Mat, Hague Ct Rep (Scott), Hague Ct Rep 2d (Scott), ILR and RIAA. In accordance with rule 2.3.2, the abbreviations for report series should appear as they do in the Appendix to this *Guide*. Where an otherwise unreported case is published in the *International Legal Materials* (abbreviated 'ILM'), the ILM should be cited.

10.1.2 Unreported Decisions

Example	*Hoshinmaru*	*(Japan v Russia)*	*(Judgment)*	(International Tribunal for the Law of the Sea,	Case No 14,	6 August 2007)	[1]
Element	Case Name	Parties' Names	Phase	Name of Arbitral Body or Tribunal	Case Number	Full Date	Pinpoint

Rule	Unreported state–state arbitral and tribunal decisions should be cited as shown above. The case name, parties' names and phase should adhere to rule 10.1.1. The name of the arbitral body or tribunal should appear as it does on

	the title page of the decision (or, where cumbersome, in a conventional shortened form). A case number should be included only if it appears in the decision. It should appear as it does on the title page, preceded by 'Case No' (in accordance with rule 8.2.10). If there is no full date, as much of the full date as appears should be included. Pinpoint references should adhere to rules 1.1.5–1.1.6. Where a decision has paragraph numbers, pinpoints should be to paragraph numbers. Where a decision has only page numbers, pinpoints should be to page numbers. Judges' or arbitrators' names should be included after pinpoint references in accordance with rule 9.2.8 (so should appear only after pinpoint references to separate or dissenting opinions or declarations).
Examples	*Access to Information under Article 9 of the Ospar Convention (Ireland v United Kingdom) (Final Award)* (Permanent Court of Arbitration, 2 July 2003) [146]. *Maritime Boundary (Barbados v Trinidad and Tobago) (Award)* (UNCLOS Arbitral Tribunal, 11 April 2006) [198]. [**Not:** … (Arbitral Tribunal Constituted Pursuant to Article 287, and in Accordance with Annex VII, of the United Nations Convention on the Law of the Sea, …] *Ports — Ethiopia's Claim 6 (Ethiopia v Eritrea) (Final Award)* (Eritrea Ethiopia Claims Commission, 19 December 2005) [26].

10.2 Individual–State Decisions (including Investor–State Decisions)

10.2.1 Reported Decisions

Example	*Olguín v Paraguay*	*(Jurisdiction)*	(2004) 6 ICSID Rep	154	, 158
Element	Parties' Names	Phase	Year, Volume and Report Series	Starting Page	Pinpoint

Rule	Reported individual–state arbitral and tribunal decisions should be cited as shown above. Parties' names should adhere to rule 2.1. The phase should adhere to rule 10.1.1. The year, volume and report series should adhere to rules 2.2–2.3. The starting page should adhere to rule 2.4. Pinpoint references should adhere to rule 9.2.7. Judges' or arbitrators' names should be included after pinpoint references in accordance with rule 10.1.1 (so should appear only after pinpoint references to separate or dissenting opinions or declarations).
Examples	*Chas T Main International Inc v Mahab Consulting Engineers Inc (Award)* (1983) 3 Iran–US CTR 270. *Southern Pacific Properties (Middle East) Ltd v Egypt (Decision on Jurisdiction of 27 November 1985)* (1983) 3 ICSID Rep 112, 129–30. *Azurix Corporation v Argentina (Jurisdiction)* (2004) 43 ILM 262, 282.
Notes	Some commonly cited report series containing investor–state arbitral decisions are the Iran–US CTR and ICSID Rep. In accordance with rule 2.3.2, the abbreviations for report series should appear as they do in the Appendix to this *Guide*. Disputes between individuals and international organisations (in international forums applying international law) should also be cited in accordance with this rule or rule 10.2.2.

10.2.2 Unreported Decisions

Example	*Enron Corporation v Argentina*	*(Jurisdiction)*	(ICSID Arbitral Tribunal,	Case No ARB/01/3,	14 January 2004)	[39]
Element	Parties' Names	Phase	Name of Arbitral Body or Tribunal	Case Number	Full Date	Pinpoint

Rule	Unreported individual–state arbitral and tribunal decisions should be cited as shown above.

Parties' names should adhere to rule 2.1. A phase should be included only if it appears in the decision and should adhere to rule 10.1.1. The name of the arbitral body or tribunal, case number and full date should adhere to rule 10.1.2.

Pinpoint references should adhere to rules 1.1.5–1.1.6. Where a decision has paragraph numbers, pinpoints should be to paragraph numbers. Where a decision has only page numbers, pinpoints should be to page numbers.

Judges' or arbitrators' names should be included after pinpoint references in accordance with rule 10.1.1 (so should appear only after pinpoint references to separate or dissenting opinions or declarations).

Examples

Re Polystyrene and Impact Crystal from the United States of America (United States of America v Mexico) (Panel Decision) (North American Free Trade Agreement Chapter 19 Panel, Case No MEX-94-1904-03, 12 September 1996).

Keeney v Secretary-General of the United Nations (United Nations Administrative Tribunal, Judgement No 6, 4 September 1951).

Phoenix Action Ltd v Czech Republic (Award) (ICSID Arbitral Tribunal, Case No ARB/06/5, 15 April 2009) [54].

Trans-Global Petroleum Inc v Jordan (Consent Award) (ICSID Arbitral Tribunal, Case No ARB/07/25, 8 April 2009) [12].

CMS Gas Transmission Co v Argentina (Annulment) (ICSID Arbitral Tribunal, Case No ARB/01/8, 25 September 2007) [158]–[159].

Tokelés v Ukraine (Jurisdiction) (ICSID Arbitral Tribunal, Case No ARB/02/18, 29 April 2004) [27] (President Weil).

10.3 Subsequent References

Rule

'Ibid' should be used for all materials in this chapter (in accordance with rule 1.4.1).

Other subsequent references should adhere to rule 2.14. In accordance with rule 2.14, it may be necessary to give an international arbitral or tribunal decision a short title incorporating its phase to distinguish it from other decisions with the same parties.

'Above n' should not be used for any materials in this chapter.

Examples

17 *Boundary Dispute between India and Pakistan Relating to the Interpretation of the Report of the Bengal Boundary Commission, 12 and 13 August 1947 (India v Pakistan) (Decisions)* (1997) 21 RIAA 3, 13 ('*Boundary Dispute (Decisions)*').

18 Ibid 16.

…

27 *Boundary Dispute (Decisions)* (1997) 21 RIAA 3, 15.

11 International Criminal Tribunals and Courts

11.1 Basic Documents

11.1.1 Constitutive Documents

Rule

Constitutive documents of international criminal tribunals and courts should be cited in accordance with the appropriate rules of this *Guide* for the source type.

Where the constitutive document of an international criminal tribunal or court was (partly) created by a UN Security Council resolution, an appropriate short title (usually that of the instrument or an abbreviated version, for example, '*Statute of the International Tribunal for Rwanda*') should be included in accordance with rule 8.5 (or rule 8.2.12 for an annex) after the initial citation of the resolution or the relevant annex. Subsequent references should appear in the form:

[*Short Title*] [Pinpoint].

Where an amendment is important, or where it is important to indicate the state of a constitutive document at a particular point in time, the amending instrument should be included in the form:

[Citation of Original Constitutive Document], as amended by [Citation of Amending Instrument].

Where this is the first reference to a constitutive document, the short title should appear after the citation of the amending instrument.

Pinpoint references should adhere to rule 7.5 and should generally be to articles and paragraphs.

Examples

[22] *Rome Statute of the International Criminal Court*, opened for signature 17 July 1998, 2187 UNTS 90 (entered into force 1 July 2002).

23 SC Res 955, UN SCOR, 49th sess, 3453rd mtg, UN Doc S/RES/955 (8 November 1994) annex ('*Statute of the International Tribunal for Rwanda*').

…

25 *Statute of the International Criminal Tribunal for Rwanda* art 2.

26 SC Res 827, UN SCOR, 48th sess, 3217th mtg, UN Doc S/RES/827 (25 May 1993), as amended by SC Res 1877, UN SCOR, 64th sess, 6155th mtg, UN Doc S/RES/1877 (7 July 2009) ('*ICTY Statute*').

27 *Agreement between the United Nations and the Government of Sierra Leone on the Establishment of a Special Court for Sierra Leone*, signed 16 January 2002, 2178 UNTS 137 (entered into force 12 April 2002) annex ('*Statute of the Special Court for Sierra Leone*').

11.1.2 Rules

Rule

The rules of international criminal tribunals and courts should be cited as follows:

[Name of Tribunal or Court], [*Title of Rules*], Doc No [Document Number] (adopted [Full Date]) [Pinpoint].

A document number should be included only where it appears on the rules. It should be preceded by 'Doc No' and adhere to rule 8.2.10. Where rules have been revised, the full date should be the date of adoption of the revision.

Pinpoint references should adhere to rule 7.5 and should generally be to rules and sub-rules.

Examples

International Criminal Court, *Rules of Procedure and Evidence*, Doc No ICC-ASP/1/3 (adopted 9 September 2002) r 74.

Extraordinary Chambers in the Courts of Cambodia, *Internal Rules (Ver 4)* (adopted 11 September 2009) r 23.

11.2 Cases

Example	*Prosecutor v Sesay*	*(Sentencing Judgement)*	(Special Court for Sierra Leone,	Trial Chamber I,	Case No SCSL-04-15-T,	8 April 2009)	[12]
Element	Parties' Names	Phase	Court	Chamber	Case Number	Full Date	Pin-point
Rule	11.2.1	11.2.2	11.2.3	11.2.4	11.2.5	11.2.6	11.2.7

11.2.1 Parties' Names

Rule

Parties' names should appear in italics in the form:

Prosecutor v *Surname of Defendant*

The order of the names should be reversed for appeals (if they are on the decision itself). Where there are multiple defendants or appellants, only the name of the first defendant or appellant should be included.

Examples

Prosecutor v Nikolić (Sentencing Judgement) (International Criminal Tribunal for the Former Yugoslavia, Trial Chamber II, Case No IT-94-2-S, 18 December 2003).

Prosecutor v Lubanga (Decision on the Manner of Questioning Witnesses by the Legal Representatives of Victims) (International Criminal Court, Trial Chamber I, Case No ICC-01/04-01/06-2127, 16 September 2009) [6]. [**Not**: *Situation in the Democratic Republic of the Congo in the Case of the Prosecutor v. Thomas Lubanga Dyilo …*]

Simba v Prosecutor (Judgement) (International Criminal Tribunal for Rwanda, Appeals Chamber, Case No ICTR-01-76-A, 27 November 2007) [40]–[41].

Prosecutor v Prlić (Decision on Defence Motion to Reopen Its Case) (International Criminal Tribunal for the Former Yugoslavia, Trial Chamber III, Case No IT-04-74-T, 3 July 2009). [**Not:** *The Prosecutor v Jadranko Prlić, Bruno Stojić, Slobodan Praljak, Milivoj Petković, Valentin Ćorić, Berislav Pušić …* **nor** *Prosecutor v Prlić et al …*]

11.2.2 Phase

Rule

The phase should be italicised and appear in parentheses. Capitalisation should adhere to rule 1.7. The phase should be included as it appears on the judgment (including any date in the name of the phase). However, the defendant's name should be omitted from the phase if the name is included in accordance with rule 11.2.1.

Examples

Prosecutor v Blaškič (Decision on the Prosecution and Defence Motions Dated 25 January 1999 and 25 March 1999 Respectively) (International Criminal Tribunal for the Former Yugoslavia, Trial Chamber I, Case No IT-95-14-T, 22 April 1999) 4.

Prosecutor v Al Bashir (Warrant of Arrest) (International Criminal Court, Pre-Trial Chamber I, Case No ICC-02/05-01/09-1, 4 March 2009). [**Not**: … *(Warrant of Arrest for Omar Hassan Ahmad Al Bashir)* …]

11.2.3 Court

Rule

The name of the court should be included in its commonly used shortened form (if any exists), not its full elaborate form.

Example

Prosecutor v Karadžić (Decision on Prosecution Motion Seeking Determination that the Accused Understands English for the Purposes of the Statute and Rules of Procedure and Evidence) (International Criminal Tribunal for the Former Yugoslavia, Trial Chamber III, Case No IT-95-5/18-PT-S, 26 March 2009) [6]. [**Not:** … (International Tribunal for the Prosecution of Persons Responsible for Serious Violations of International Humanitarian Law Committed in the Territory of the Former Yugoslavia since 1991, …]

11.2.4 Chamber

Rule

The name of the chamber should include both:

- the type of chamber (where an international criminal tribunal or court has multiple types of chambers); and

	• any numerical designation given to the chamber, which should appear in Roman numerals.
Examples	*Prosecutor v Tadić (Judgement)* (International Criminal Tribunal for the Former Yugoslavia, Appeals Chamber, Case No IT-94-1-A, 15 July 1999). *Prosecutor v Ntaganda (Warrant of Arrest)* (International Criminal Court, Pre-Trial Chamber I, Case No ICC-01/04-02/06-18, 22 August 2006).
Note	The International Criminal Court has three types of chambers: Pre-Trial Chambers, Trial Chambers and Appeals Chambers. Other international criminal tribunals and courts often have one or several Trial Chambers and an Appeals Chamber. Such chambers are typically numbered using Roman numerals (for example, 'Trial Chamber II').

11.2.5 Case Number

Rule	The case number should be preceded by the words 'Case No'. Otherwise, it should adhere to rule 8.2.10. In particular: • the case number should appear as it does on the judgment cited (including any component specific to that document, where available); • full stops should not be used in abbreviations, but should be reproduced if they are used within a case number; and • where there are multiple case numbers, all should be included (preceded by 'Case Nos').
Examples	*Prosecutor v Renzaho (Decision on Motion for Extension of Time for the Filing of Notice of Appeal and Brief in Reply)* (International Criminal Tribunal for Rwanda, Appeals Chamber, Case No ICTR-97-31-A, 22 September 2009) [6]. *Prosecutor v Kunarac (Judgement)* (International Criminal Tribunal for the Former Yugoslavia, Trial Chamber II, Case Nos IT-96-23-T and IT-96-23/1-T, 22 February 2001).

Note	The case number should be that assigned by the relevant international criminal tribunal or court.

11.2.6 Full Date

Rule	The full date of the judgment cited should be included.
Example	*Prosecutor v Kambanda (Decision Ordering Continued Detention)* (International Criminal Tribunal for Rwanda, Trial Chamber I, Case No ICTR-97-23-T, 1 May 1998).

11.2.7 Pinpoint Reference

Rule	Pinpoint references should adhere to rules 1.1.5–1.1.6 and should be to paragraph numbers.
Example	*Prosecutor v Jokić (Judgement on Sentencing Appeal)* (International Criminal Tribunal for the Former Yugoslavia, Appeals Chamber, Case No IT-01-42/1-A, 30 August 2005) [24]. [**Not:** … 9 [24].]

11.2.8 Identifying Judges

Rule	Judges' names should be included after pinpoint references in accordance with rule 9.2.8. In particular: • where a judgment (including a 'principal judgment') of a tribunal or court is referred to, neither the judges' names nor '(The Court)' should be included after a pinpoint reference; • judges' names should be included after pinpoint references to separate or dissenting opinions; and • 'Judge' should be written out in full before a judge's name.
Examples	*Prosecutor v Jelisić (Judgement)* (International Criminal Tribunal for the Former Yugoslavia, Trial Chamber I, Case No IT-95-10-T, 14 December 1999) [105].

Prosecutor v Erdemović (Judgement) (International Criminal Tribunal for the Former Yugoslavia, Appeals Chamber, Case No IT-96-22-A, 7 October 1997) [6] (Judge Stephen).

11.3 Reports of Cases

Rule

It is generally unnecessary to cite reports of judgments of international criminal tribunals and courts due to their wide availability. However, where a judgment is difficult to locate or where there is good reason for doing so, a report of the judgment may be cited.

Reported judgments of international criminal tribunals should be cited as follows:

[*Parties' Names*] *(*[*Phase*]*)* [Year, Volume and Report Series] [Starting Page], [Pinpoint].

Parties' names and the phase should adhere to rules 11.2.1–11.2.2. The year, report series and starting page should adhere to rules 2.2–2.4. Pinpoint references should adhere to rule 9.2.7. The inclusion of judges' names should adhere to rule 11.2.8.

The name of the international tribunal or court and the relevant chamber may be included after any pinpoint or judges' names in accordance with rule 2.6. It should appear in the form:

([Conventional Shortened Name of Tribunal or Court], [Chamber])

The name of the tribunal or court and the chamber should adhere to rules 11.2.3–11.2.4.

Example

Prosecutor v Blaškič (Objection to the Issue of Subpoenae Duces Tecum) (1997) 110 ILR 688, 693 [15] (International Criminal Tribunal for the Former Yugoslavia, Appeals Chamber).

11.4 Subsequent References

Rule

'Ibid' should be used for all materials in this chapter (in accordance with rule 1.4.1).

In other subsequent references:

- citations of the basic documents of international criminal tribunals and courts should adhere to rule 11.1 or the appropriate rules of this *Guide* for the source type; and
- citations of decisions of international criminal tribunals and courts (see rules 11.2–11.3) should adhere to rule 2.14.

In accordance with rule 2.14, it may be useful to give a decision of an international criminal tribunal or court a short title incorporating its phase or trial/appellate status to distinguish it from other decisions relating to the same parties.

'Above n' should not be used for any materials in this chapter.

Examples

24 International Criminal Tribunal for the Former Yugoslavia, *Rules of Procedure and Evidence*, Doc No IT/32/Rev.44 (adopted 10 December 2009) ('*ICTY Rules*').

…

26 *ICTY Rules* r 3(F).

27 *Serushago v Prosecutor (Reasons for Judgment)* (International Criminal Tribunal for Rwanda, Appeals Chamber, Case No ICTR-98-39-A, 6 April 2000) ('*Serushago Appeal*').

28 Ibid [21]–[22].

…

30 *Serushago Appeal* (International Criminal Tribunal for Rwanda, Appeals Chamber, Case No ICTR-98-39-A, 6 April 2000) [27].

12 International Economic Materials

12.1 World Trade Organization

12.1.1 Constitutive and Basic Documents

Rule

The *Marrakesh Agreement Establishing the World Trade Organization* should be cited in accordance with chapter 7.

The other agreements and understandings of the World Trade Organization ('WTO') are annexed to the *Marrakesh Agreement*, and should be cited as follows:

> *Marrakesh Agreement Establishing the World Trade Organization*, opened for signature 15 April 1994, 1867 UNTS 3 (entered into force 1 January 1995) [Pinpoint to Relevant Annex] ('[*Title of Agreement or Understanding*]').

The title of the relevant agreement or understanding (or a commonly used abbreviated version) should appear after the pinpoint to the annex containing it (in accordance with rule 7.6). Agreements or understandings annexed to the *Marrakesh Agreement* should *not* be cited as separate treaties.

Subsequent references should be cited as follows:

> [*Short Title of Agreement or Understanding*] [Pinpoint].

Examples

Marrakesh Agreement Establishing the World Trade Organization, opened for signature 15 April 1994, 1867 UNTS 3 (entered into force 1 January 1995).

Marrakesh Agreement Establishing the World Trade Organization, opened for signature 15 April 1994, 1867 UNTS 3 (entered into force 1 January 1995) annex 1A ('*General Agreement on Tariffs and Trade 1994*').

Marrakesh Agreement Establishing the World Trade Organization, opened for signature 15 April 1994, 1867 UNTS 3 (entered into force 1 January 1995) annex 1A ('*Anti-Dumping Agreement*').

	Marrakesh Agreement Establishing the World Trade Organization, opened for signature 15 April 1994, 1867 UNTS 3 (entered into force 1 January 1995) annex 2 ('*DSU*').
Note	Annexes 1A and 4 to the *Marrakesh Agreement* both contain more than one agreement or understanding. It is thus necessary to include the name of the relevant agreement or understanding as a short title when referring to WTO agreements or understandings other than the *Marrakesh Agreement* itself (to avoid ambiguity).

12.1.2 Official WTO Documents

Example	*Implementation of Paragraph 6 of the Doha Declaration on the TRIPS Agreement and Public Health*,	WTO Doc WT/L/540	(2 September 2003)	(Decision of 30 August 2003)	para 2(a)
Element	Document Title	Document Number	Full Date	Document Description	Pin-point

Rule

An official WTO document (except an Appellate Body report, panel report or arbitrator's decision) should be cited as shown above.

The title should appear in italics and be included as it appears in the document, subject to chapter 1. In particular:

- punctuation should adhere to rule 1.6.1 (so full stops should not be used in abbreviations); and
- capitalisation should adhere to rule 1.7.

The document number should adhere to rule 8.2.10 (so full stops should not be used in abbreviations but the document number should be reproduced *exactly* as it appears, with any punctuation).

Where there is not a full date in the document, as much of the full date as appears should be included. The date of adoption (if any) may be included in addition to the full date in the form:

([Full Date of Document], adopted [Full Date of Adoption])

	A document description should be omitted if it does not appear in the WTO document. Pinpoint references to resolutions, decisions, declarations, waivers and other documents in the nature of a treaty should adhere to rule 3.1.4 (and the pinpoint abbreviations in that rule should be used). Pinpoint references to documents in the nature of secondary sources should adhere to rules 1.1.5–1.1.6 and pinpoint references should be to paragraphs (in square brackets). Annexes and schedules may be cited in accordance with rule 8.2.12.
Examples	*India — Measures Affecting Customs Duties*, WTO Doc WT/DS150/1, G/L/266 (3 November 1998) (Request for Consultations by the European Communities). *Doha Work Programme*, WTO Doc WT/MIN(05)/DEC (22 December 2005, adopted 18 December 2005) (Ministerial Declaration) para 50(1). *Notification*, WTO Doc G/TBT/N/BHR/188 (24 February 2010) [7]. *Preferential Tariff Treatment for Least-Developed Countries*, WTO Doc WT/L/304 (17 June 1999, adopted 15 June 1999) (Decision on Waiver) paras 1–2, 4. *Past Negotiations and Consultations on Tropical Products*, WTO Doc TN/AG/S/17 (10 February 2005) (Note by the Secretariat) [32]–[33]. *Accession of the People's Republic of China*, WTO Doc WT/L/432 (23 November 2001) (Decision of 10 November 2001) annex 7 ('*Reservations by WTO Members*').
Note	The document description of a WTO document ordinarily appears below the title. It usually appears underlined and in parentheses.

12.1.3 WTO Panel, Appellate Body and Arbitration Decisions

Examples	Panel Report,	*Colombia — Indicative Prices and Restrictions on Ports of Entry*,	WTO Doc WT/DS366/R	(27 April 2009)	[7.1]
	Appellate Body Report,	*United States — Continued Existence and Application of Zeroing Methodology*,	WTO Doc WT/DS350/AB/R, AB-2008-11	(4 February 2009)	[171]
Element	Document Description	Case Name	Document Number	Full Date	Pinpoint

Rule

A WTO panel report, Appellate Body report or decision of the arbitrator should be cited as shown above.

The document description should be 'Panel Report', 'Appellate Body Report' or 'Decision by the Arbitrator' as appropriate.

The case name should appear in italics and be included as it appears in the report, subject to chapter 1. In particular:

- punctuation should adhere to rule 1.6.1 (so full stops should not be used in abbreviations); and
- capitalisation should adhere to rule 1.7.

Case names of subsequent stages in proceedings between the same parties should include the second subtitle in the report, preceded by an em-dash (for example, '— *Recourse to Article 21.5 by …*' or '— *Recourse to Arbitration by … under …*').

Appellate Body reports and arbitration decisions should include their unique document designation (the numbers commencing 'AB-' and 'ARB-' respectively) after the WTO document number, preceded by a comma.

A date of adoption may be included in accordance with rule 12.1.2. Where a report has not been adopted, 'unadopted' may be included after the full date, preceded by a comma (for example, '(12 May 2007, unadopted)').

A citation of the *Dispute Settlement Reports* ('DSR') may be included after the full date. It should appear in the form:

DSR [Year]:[Volume], [Starting Page]
(for example, 'DSR 1999:III, 1377').

Pinpoint references should adhere to rules 1.1.5–1.1.6. They should be to paragraphs and should appear in square brackets. Even where a DSR citation is included, page numbers should not be included in pinpoint references. Pinpoint references should *not* be preceded by a comma, unless a DSR citation is included.

Examples

Panel Report, *China — Measures Affecting the Protection and Enforcement of Intellectual Property Rights*, WTO Doc WT/DS362/R (26 January 2009) [7.28]–[7.50].

Panel Report, *United States — Sunset Reviews of Anti-Dumping Measures on Oil Country Tubular Goods from Argentina — Recourse to Article 21.5 of the DSU by Argentina*, WTO Doc WT/DS268/RW (30 November 2006) [7.51]–[7.52].

Appellate Body Report, *Australia — Measures Affecting Importation of Salmon*, WTO Doc WT/DS18/AB/R, AB-1998-5 (20 October 1998) [105].

Decision by the Arbitrator, *Brazil — Measures Affecting Imports of Retreaded Tyres — Arbitration under Article 21.3(c) of the Understanding on Rules and Procedures Governing the Settlement of Disputes*, WTO Doc WT/DS332/16, ARB-2008-2/23 (29 August 2008) [25]–[28].

Panel Report, *Guatemala — Anti-Dumping Investigation Regarding Portland Cement from Mexico*, WTO Doc WT/DS60/R (19 June 1998, adopted 23 November 1998) DSR 1998:IX, 3797, [4.49].

12.2 General Agreement on Tariffs and Trade

12.2.1 Official GATT Documents

Example	*Meeting of 19–20 October 1983*,	GATT Doc CG.18/W/77	(24 October 1983)	(Opening Remarks by Chairman)	[4]
Element	Document Title	Document Number	Full Date	Document Description	Pinpoint

Rule

A citation of an official document of the *General Agreement on Tariffs and Trade* ('GATT') should appear as shown above.

The title and full date (including any date of adoption) should adhere to rule 12.1.2.

The document number should adhere to rule 12.1.2, but should be included only if it appears in the document. If there is no document number, a comma should *not* follow the document title.

The document description should adhere to rule 12.1.2 (so should be included only if it appears in the document). However, if the document description includes the full date, that date should be omitted from the description.

Where a document is reproduced in *Basic Instruments and Selected Documents* (abbreviated 'GATT BISD'), a citation of GATT BISD should be included after the full date. Citations of documents in the original volumes of GATT BISD should appear as follows (with the volume number in Roman numerals):

GATT BISD [Volume No]/[Starting Page]
(for example, 'GATT BISD I/120').

Citations of GATT BISD supplements should appear as follows:

GATT BISD [Supplement No]S/[Starting Page]
(for example, 'GATT BISD 31S/114').

Pinpoint references should adhere to rule 12.1.2. However, where a document does not have paragraph numbers, pinpoint references should be to page numbers. There should be no punctuation between the full date and the pinpoint. However, where a citation of GATT BISD is included, a comma should precede the pinpoint reference.

Examples

Communication from the Republic of the Philippines — Revised Conditional Offer by the Philippines on Initial Commitments on Trade in Services, GATT Doc MTN.GNS/W/131/Rev.1/Corr.1 (16 October 1992) (Corrigendum).

Agreement on Trade in Civil Aircraft — Status of Acceptances on 1 July 1980, GATT Doc AIR/12 (2 July 1980) (Note by the Secretariat) 2–3.

Waiver in Respect of the Trust Territory of the Pacific Islands (8 September 1948) (Decision) GATT BISD II/9, para 2.

Report on the 1993 Consultation with the Republic of South Africa, GATT Doc BOP/R/211 (30 July 1993) [5].

European Communities — Transitional Measures to Take Account of the External Economic Impact of German Unification, GATT Doc L/6792 (13 December 1990) (Decision) GATT BISD 37S/296. [**Not:** … L/6792 (Decision of 13 December 1990) …]

Notes

Some early GATT documents do not have a GATT document number. Where possible, such documents should be cited in GATT BISD.

GATT BISD was first published in volumes I to IV. A revised volume of GATT BISD I (denoted 'IR') was also published. In 1952, the first Supplement (GATT BISD 1S) was published, and publication of GATT documents continued in the Supplements.

12.2.2 GATT Panel Reports

Rule

GATT Panel reports should be cited in the same manner as WTO panel reports (in accordance with rule 12.1.3). However, GATT BISD references should appear instead of DSR references where available (and should adhere to rule 12.2.1).

	In accordance with rule 12.1.3, even where a GATT BISD reference is included, pinpoint references should be to paragraph numbers, which should appear in square brackets.
Examples	GATT Panel Report, *United States — Taxes on Petroleum and Certain Imported Substances*, GATT Doc L/6175 (5 June 1987, adopted 17 June 1987) GATT BISD 34S/136, [4.1.1]–[4.1.4]. GATT Panel Report, *EEC — German Exchange Rate Scheme for Deutsche Airbus*, GATT Doc SCM/142 (4 March 1992, unadopted) [5.9].

12.3 Investment and Trade Treaties and Investor–State Arbitrations

Rule	Investment and trade treaties (such as bilateral investment treaties and free trade agreements) should be cited in accordance with chapter 7. Investor–state arbitrations should be cited in accordance with chapter 10.
Examples	*North American Free Trade Agreement*, signed 17 December 1992, [1994] CTS 2 (entered into force 1 January 1994) art 2005. *United Parcel Service of America Inc v Canada (Merits)* (North American Free Trade Agreement Chapter 11 Arbitral Tribunal, 24 May 2007) [119]–[120].

12.4 Subsequent References

Rule	'Ibid' should be used for all materials in this chapter (in accordance with rule 1.4.1). Other subsequent references to treaties should adhere to rule 7.6.

Other subsequent references to WTO and GATT documents should appear in full each time a source is referred to. However, where a WTO or GATT document is referred to frequently, it may be given a short title. The short title should adhere to rule 1.4.3 (so should be italicised and placed within single inverted commas and parentheses following the initial citation). Subsequent references should then take the form:

Short Title, WTO/GATT Doc Document Number, Pinpoint.

For subsequent references to WTO panel reports, Appellate Body reports or decisions by the arbitrator or GATT panel reports, the document description (the name of the reporting body) should be included *before* the short title, followed by a comma. The short title should be that commonly used for the report, unless there is good reason to do otherwise.

'Above n' should not be used for any materials in this chapter.

Examples

13 *Ministerial Declaration on Trade in Information Technology Products*, WTO Doc WT/MIN(96)/16 (13 December 1996) ('*Information Technology Agreement*').

…

17 *Information Technology Agreement*, WTO Doc WT/MIN(96)/16, para 2.

18 Appellate Body Report, *United States — Measures Relating to Zeroing and Sunset Reviews — Recourse to Article 21.5 of the DSU by Japan*, WTO Doc WT/DS322/AB/RW, AB-2009-2 (18 August 2009, adopted 31 August 2009) ('*US — Zeroing (Article 21.5 — Japan)*').

19 Ibid [160].

…

22 Appellate Body Report, *US — Zeroing (Article 21.5 — Japan)*, WTO Doc WT/DS322/AB/RW, [162].

13 European Supranational Materials

13.1 European Union Materials

13.1.1 Official Journal of the European Union

Example	*Council Directive 93/13/EEC of 5 April 1993 on Unfair Terms in Consumer Contracts*	[1993]	OJ	L	95	/29	, art 3(1)
Element	Document Title	Year	Official Journal	Series	Issue Number	Starting Page	Pinpoint

Rule

A reference to a document of the European Union ('EU'), European Communities ('EC') or predecessor organisations should include a citation of the *Official Journal of the European Union* (abbreviated 'OJ') where possible.

The document title should appear in italics and as it does on the document cited, subject to chapter 1. In particular:

- punctuation should adhere to rule 1.6.1 (so full stops should not be used in abbreviations); and
- capitalisation should adhere to rule 1.7.

The year is that of publication in the OJ.

For documents published from 1 January 1968, the series should be included after 'OJ', preceded by a space. Legislative acts are contained in the 'L' series (abbreviated 'OJ L'), and information and notices are contained in the 'C' series (abbreviated 'OJ C').

The issue number and starting page should be separated by an (unspaced) slash (for example, '22/34').

Part of the C series is published only in electronic format. References to documents in this part of the C series should appear as follows:

Document Title [Year] OJ C Issue Number E/ Starting Page , Pinpoint .

For documents published before 1 January 1974, a parallel citation of the English language Special Edition of the *Official Journal* ('OJ Spec Ed'), preceded by a semi-colon, should be included (where possible). It should appear in the form:

[Year] OJ Spec Ed Starting Page , Pinpoint .

Pinpoint references should adhere to rules 1.1.5–1.1.6 and be preceded by a comma. Pinpoints may be to pages, paragraphs, articles or other internal divisions of the relevant document. Abbreviations in pinpoints should adhere to rule 3.1.4.

Examples

Commission Decision of 18 December 2002 Relating to National Provisions on Limiting the Importation and Placement on the Market of Certain NK Fertilisers of High Nitrogen Content and Containing Chlorine Notified by France Pursuant to Article 95(5) of the EC Treaty [2003] OJ L 1/72, 79.

Notice for the Attention of Ghuma Abd'rabbah concerning His Inclusion in the List Referred to in Articles 2, 3 and 7 of Council Regulation (EC) No 881/2002 Imposing Certain Specific Restrictive Measures Directed against Certain Persons and Entities Associated with Usama bin Laden, the Al-Qaida Network and the Taliban [2009] OJ C 230/29, paras 3(a), 4, 6.

Regulation (EC) No 2037/2000 of the European Parliament and of the Council of 29 June 2000 on Substances That Deplete the Ozone Layer [2000] OJ L 244/1, art 3(1).

European Parliament — 2008–2009 Session — Sittings of 20 to 23 October 2008 — Strasbourg — Minutes — Proceedings of the Sitting [2009] OJ C 3 E/1.

Regulation (EEC) No 2005/70 of the Commission of 6 October 1970 on the Classification of Vine Varieties [1970] OJ L 224/1; [1970] OJ Spec Ed 623, art 2(1), annex.

Notes

The *Official Journal of the European Communities* became the *Official Journal of the European Union* on 1 February 2003. Both, as well as previous equivalent publications, are abbreviated 'OJ'.

Within the EU, legislative acts include regulations, directives and decisions of the various organs (other than EU courts).

The OJ Spec Ed is a non-binding official translation of some documents published in the OJ into the languages of non-member states or states to whom the document does not apply. From 1 January 1974, the official OJ was published in English, obviating the need to refer to the OJ Spec Ed from this date.

Until 30 June 1967, the pagination of the OJ was continuous. Thus, an issue number is not necessary to identify documents up to this date.

13.1.2 Constitutive Treaties of the European Union

Rule

The constitutive treaties of the EU and EC (and predecessor organisations) should be cited as treaties in accordance with chapter 7. However:

- a reference to the OJ (where available) should replace a reference to the UNTS or an official national treaty series; and
- a short title or amendment information *must* be included in accordance with this rule.

When referring to constitutive treaties of the EU and EC as in force (that is, as amended and renumbered from time to time):

- a citation of the latest consolidation of the treaty in the OJ should be included (if available); and
- the 'short title for current references' in the table below should be included in the first citation and used for subsequent references (in accordance with rule 7.6).

When referring to constitutive treaties of the EU and EC as made (prior to *any* amendment):

- a citation of the UNTS or the OJ containing the treaty as made should be included; and
- the 'short title for historical references' should be included in the first citation and used for subsequent references (in accordance with rule 7.6).

Treaty	Short Title for Current References	Short Title for Historical References
Treaty on European Union	*EU*	*Treaty on European Union*
Treaty on the Functioning of the European Union	*FEU*	*Treaty on the Functioning of the European Union*
Treaty Establishing the European Community	*EC*	*EC Treaty*
Treaty Establishing the European Atomic Energy Community	*EA*	*EAEC Treaty*
Treaty Instituting the European Coal and Steel Community	*CS*	*ECSC Treaty*

Where the fact of amendment is important, or when referring to a foundational EU treaty after amendment by a specific intermediate amending treaty, amendment information may be included (in accordance with rule 3.8) in the form:

[Citation of Foundational EU Treaty], as amended by [Citation of Amending Treaty].

The dates of opening for signature and entry into force for all foundational EU treaties should adhere to rule 7.3 (so should be those of the treaty as made), regardless of whether the treaty is referred to as in force or historically.

Examples

Treaty on European Union, opened for signature 7 February 1992, [2009] OJ C 115/13 (entered into force 1 November 1993) ('*EU*'). [**cited as amended**]

Treaty on the Functioning of the European Union, opened for signature 7 February 1992, [2009] OJ C 115/199 (entered into force 1 November 1993) ('*FEU*'). [**cited as amended**]

Treaty Establishing the European Atomic Energy Community, opened for signature 25 March 1957, 298 UNTS 167 (entered into force 1 January 1958) ('*EA*'). [**cited as amended**]

Treaty on European Union, opened for signature 7 February 1992, [1992] OJ C 191/1 (entered into force 1 November 1993) ('*Treaty on European Union*'). [**cited historically**]

Treaty Establishing the European Community, opened for signature 7 February 1992, [1992] OJ C 224/6 (entered into force 1 November 1993) ('*EC Treaty*'). [**cited historically**]

Treaty Establishing the European Economic Community, opened for signature 25 March 1957, 298 UNTS 11 (entered into force 1 January 1958) ('*EEC Treaty*').

Treaty Instituting the European Coal and Steel Community, signed 18 April 1951, 261 UNTS 140 (entered into force 23 July 1952) ('*ECSC Treaty*'). [**cited historically**]

Treaty on European Union, opened for signature 7 February 1992, [1992] OJ C 191/1 (entered into force 1 November 1993), as amended by *Treaty of Amsterdam Amending the Treaty on European Union, the Treaties Establishing the European Communities and Certain Related Acts*, opened for signature 2 October 1997, [1997] OJ C 340/1 (entered into force 1 May 1999).

Treaty Establishing the European Community, opened for signature 7 February 1992, [1992] OJ C 224/6 (entered into force 1 November 1993), as amended by *Treaty of Nice Amending the Treaty on European Union, the Treaties Establishing the European Communities and Certain Related Acts*, opened for signature 26 February 2001, [2001] OJ C 80/1 (entered into force 1 February 2003).

	Treaty on European Union, opened for signature 7 February 1992, [1992] OJ C 191/1 (entered into force 1 November 1993) art 2, as amended by *Treaty of Lisbon Amending the Treaty on European Union and the Treaty Establishing the European Community*, opened for signature 13 December 2007, [2007] OJ C 306/1 (entered into force 1 December 2009) art 1(4).
Notes	The system of short titles used in this rule is adapted from that used by the European Court of Justice, due to the amendment and renumbering of the provisions in the various constitutive EU treaties. The *Treaty of Amsterdam* (with effect from 1 May 1999) renumbered several provisions of the *Treaty on European Union* and the *EC Treaty*. The *Treaty of Nice* (with effect from 1 February 2003) inserted several new provisions into both treaties. The *Treaty of Lisbon* (with effect from 1 December 2009) recast the *EC Treaty* as the *Treaty on the Functioning of the European Union* and substantially amended and renumbered the *Treaty on European Union*. The *ECSC Treaty* is commonly known as the '*Treaty of Paris*'. The *EEC Treaty* is commonly known as the '*Treaty of Rome*'. The *Treaty on European Union* is commonly known as the '*Treaty of Maastricht*'.

13.1.3 Courts of the European Union

Examples	*Costa v ENEL*	(C-6/64)	[1964]	ECR	585	, 594
	Vainker v European Parliament	(T-48/01)	[2004]	ECR-SC	II-197	, II-207
Element	Parties' Names	Case Number	Year	Report Series	Starting Page	Pinpoint

Rule	Reported decisions of the Court of Justice of the European Union ('ECJ'), the General Court of the European Union ('General Court') and the European Union Civil Service Tribunal should be cited as shown above. The parties' names, including those of EU organs, should be included as they appear on the first page of the report, subject to chapter 1. They should be italicised and separated by '*v*'.

The case number (including the prefixes 'C-' for cases decided by the ECJ, 'T-' for cases decided by the General Court, and 'F-' for cases decided by the European Union Civil Service Tribunal) should be included after the parties' names in parentheses. It should *not* be italicised.

Pinpoint references should adhere to rule 9.2.7. However, the starting page and page pinpoint references for decisions in the ECR since 1990 should include the prefix 'I-' (for decisions of the ECJ) and 'II-' (for decisions of the General Court). Page references to judgments in the ECR-SC should include the prefix 'II-'. Spans of page numbers should adhere to rule 1.12.1. The prefixes 'I-' or 'II-' should *not* be repeated in the second number of a page span.

Decisions not reported in the ECR or ECR-SC should be cited as follows:

[*Parties' Names*] ([Name of Court/Tribunal], [Case Number], [Full Date]) [Pinpoint].

The name of the court should be included as it appears on the decision. Pinpoint references should be to paragraphs.

Examples

Grad v Finanzamt Traunstein (C-9/70) [1970] ECR 825, 833.

Ireland v Council of the European Communities (C-151/73) [1974] ECR 285, 298 [21]–[23].

Germany v Commission of the European Communities (C-301/96) [2003] ECR I-9919, I-9949–51. [**Not:** … I-9919, I-9949–I-9951.]

O'Casey v Commission of the European Communities (T-184/94) [1998] ECR-SC II-565, II-577–8 [52]–[54].

Commission of the European Communities v Luxembourg (Court of Justice of the European Communities, C-34/07, 29 November 2007) [14]–[15].

Clearwire Corp v Office for Harmonisation in the Internal Market (Court of First Instance of the European Communities, T-399/08, 19 November 2009).

Vinci v European Central Bank (European Union Civil Service Tribunal, F-130/07, 16 September 2009) [58].

Notes

The Court of Justice of the European Union is commonly referred to as the 'European Court of Justice'. The General Court was the Court of First Instance of the European Communities ('CFI') until December 2009.

Decisions of the Court of Justice are published in *Reports of Cases before the Court* and, since 1990, *Reports of Cases before the Court of Justice and the Court of First Instance* (both abbreviated 'ECR'). Decisions of the General Court are published (from 1990) in *Reports of Cases before the Court of Justice and the Court of First Instance.*

Since 1995, cases between staff and EU institutions heard by the CFI and (since its creation in 2005) the European Union Civil Service Tribunal are reported in *European Court Reports — Reports of European Community Staff Cases* (abbreviated 'ECR-SC'). Judgments are printed in Section II of the ECR-SC. (Section I summarises decisions and orders. It is thus preferable to cite to Section II, unless the case in Section II is not in an accessible language.)

Other report series (such as the CMLR) that contain reports of cases decided by EU courts and tribunals should be used where a case is not reported in the ECR or ECR-SC (in preference to citing a case as unreported).

13.2 Council of Europe

13.2.1 Basic Documents of the Council of Europe

Rule

The *Statute of the Council of Europe* should be cited (in accordance with chapter 7) as follows:

Statute of the Council of Europe, opened for signature 5 May 1949, 8 UNTS 103 (entered into force 3 August 1949).

The *Convention for the Protection of Human Rights and Fundamental Freedoms* (commonly known as the '*European Convention on Human Rights*' or '*ECHR*') should be cited as follows:

Convention for the Protection of Human Rights and Fundamental Freedoms, opened for signature 4 November 1950, 213 UNTS 221 (entered into force 3 September 1953), as amended by Relevant Amending Protocol.

Citations of substantive protocols should include details of amendments in the same manner. Citations of amending protocols should adhere to chapter 7 (and the ETS should be the treaty series cited, where available).

Examples

Convention for the Protection of Human Rights and Fundamental Freedoms, opened for signature 4 November 1950, 213 UNTS 222 (entered into force 3 September 1953), as amended by *Protocol No 14bis to the Convention for the Protection of Human Rights and Fundamental Freedoms*, opened for signature 27 May 2009, CETS No 204 (entered into force 1 September 2009).

Protocol to the Convention for the Protection of Human Rights and Fundamental Freedoms, opened for signature 20 March 1952, ETS No 9 (entered into force 18 May 1954), as amended by *Protocol No 11 to the Convention for the Protection of Human Rights and Fundamental Freedoms*, opened for signature 11 May 1994, ETS No 155 (entered into force 1 November 1998).

Protocol No 14 to the Convention for the Protection of Human Rights and Fundamental Freedoms, Amending the Control System of the Convention, opened for signature 13 May 2004, CETS No 194 (not yet in force).

Notes

The *European Treaty Series* (abbreviated 'ETS'), which included Nos 1 to 193, is continued from 2004 (No 194) by the *Council of Europe Treaty Series* (abbreviated 'CETS').

The most recent amending protocol to the *ECHR* is *Protocol No 14bis*. However, when referring to the *ECHR* as in force *for a particular state party*, it may be necessary to refer to a less recent amending protocol. All states parties have ratified *Protocol No 11*.

13.2.2 European Court of Human Rights

Examples	*Wemhoff v Federal Republic of Germany*	(1968)	7	Eur Court HR (ser A)		23
	Bouchelkia v France	[1997]	I	Eur Court HR	47	, 67
Element	Parties' Names	Year	Volume	Report Series	Starting Page	Pin-point

Rule

Reported decisions of the European Court of Human Rights should be cited as shown above.

The parties' names should appear in the form:

Complainant's Surname v *Respondent State*

Where there are multiple complainants or respondents, only the first-named party should be included. The name of the respondent state should appear as it does on the first page of the report. If it does not appear on the first page of the report, the conventional shortened form (if any exists), rather than the full elaborate form, should be included. However, the full form should be used where this is necessary to avoid ambiguity.

Where there are multiple reported phases in a case, the phase should be included. It should be italicised and appear in parentheses after the parties' names (for example, '*(Preliminary Objections)*', '*(Revision)*' and '*(Just Satisfaction)*').

Citations of decisions until the end of 1995 (that is, decisions reported in Eur Court HR (ser A)) should *not* include a starting page. Where there are multiple decisions in one volume, the letter of the case should be included in the volume number, preceded by a hyphen (for example, '320-B').

Citations of decisions from 1996 (that is, decisions reported in Eur Court HR) should include a volume number (in Roman numerals) after the year and a starting page.

Pinpoint references should adhere to rule 9.2.7. Judges should be identified after pinpoint references in accordance with rule 9.2.8.

Decisions of the Court not reported in Eur Court HR (ser A) or Eur Court HR should be cited in an unofficial report series (where available).

Unreported decisions of the Court should be cited as follows:

Parties' Names (European Court of Human Rights, Chamber, Application No Number, Full Date) Pinpoint.

The 'Chamber' of the Court refers to the manner of its configuration for a case (as the 'Grand Chamber' or a 'Chamber'). Pinpoint references should be to paragraphs.

Citations of pleadings reported in Eur Court HR (ser B) should appear as follows:

'Document Title', *Complainant's Surname* v *Respondent State* [Year] Eur Court HR (ser B) Starting Page, Pinpoint.

Examples

Campbell v United Kingdom (1992) 233 Eur Court HR (ser A).

Boujlifa v France [1997] VI Eur Court HR 2250, 2264.

The Observer v United Kingdom (1992) 216 Eur Court HR (ser A) 10–11. [**Not:** *The Observer and The Guardian v United Kingdom* …]

Leander v Sweden (1987) 116 Eur Court HR (ser A) 32 [84]. [**Not:** *Leander Case* (1987) …]

Loizidou v Turkey (Preliminary Objections) (1995) 310 Eur Court HR (ser A).

Beldjoudi v France (1992) 234-A Eur Court HR (ser A).

Slivenko v Latvia [2003] X Eur Court HR 229, 237–8 [15]–[21].

Nasri v France (1995) 320-B Eur Court HR (ser A) 28 (Judge Pettiti).

S v United Kingdom (European Court of Human Rights, Grand Chamber, Application Nos 30562/04 and 30566/04, 4 December 2008) [125].

'The Case of Gerard Richard Lawless — Memorial Submitted by the European Commission of Human Rights', *Lawless v Ireland* [1960–61] Eur Court HR (ser B) 193, 201.

Notes	Until the end of 1995, judgments of the European Court of Human Rights were published in *Series A: Judgments and Decisions* (abbreviated 'Eur Court HR (ser A)'), which is organised by volume. The pagination begins again for each case (that is, in each volume or in each part of a volume denoted by a letter). From 1996, judgments of the Court have been published in *Reports of Judgments and Decisions* (abbreviated 'Eur Court HR'), which is organised by year. Because the pagination is not consecutive across a volume, the volume number should be included in citations of Eur Court HR. Decisions of the European Court of Human Rights are also published in the unofficial *European Human Rights Reports* ('EHRR'), which should be cited if a case does not appear in Eur Court HR (ser A) or Eur Court HR. Until 1988, the Court published *Series B: Pleadings, Oral Arguments and Documents* (abbreviated 'Eur Court HR (ser B)').

13.2.3 European Commission of Human Rights

Example	*Klass v Federal Republic of Germany*	(1974)	1	Eur Comm HR	20	, 29
Element	Parties' Names	Year	Volume	Report Series	Starting Page	Pin-point

Rule	Reported decisions of the European Commission of Human Rights should be cited as shown above. The parties' names should adhere to rule 13.2.2. The year should be that of the decision. A volume number and starting page should always be included. Pinpoints should adhere to rules 1.1.5–1.1.6 and be to pages.
Example	*X v Austria* (1979) 17 Eur Comm HR 80, 85–6.
Notes	Decisions of the European Commission of Human Rights were published between 1960 and 1974 in *Collection of Decisions* and from 1974 to 1998 in *Decisions and Reports* (both abbreviated 'Eur Comm HR').

Until 1998, complaints under the *European Convention on Human Rights* were sometimes heard by the European Commission of Human Rights. *Protocol 11* to the *European Convention on Human Rights* abrogated the Commission.

13.3 Subsequent References

Rule

'Ibid' should be used for all materials in this chapter (in accordance with rule 1.4.1).

Other subsequent references to treaties should adhere to rule 7.6. Other subsequent references to judicial decisions should adhere to rule 2.14. Other subsequent references to EU documents (that are not treaties or judicial decisions) should appear in full each time a source is referred to. However, where an EU document is referred to frequently, it may be given a short title. The short title should adhere to rule 1.4.3 (so should be italicised and placed within single inverted commas and parentheses following the initial citation). Subsequent references should then take the form:

[*Short Title*] [OJ Citation], [Pinpoint].

The OJ citation should adhere to rule 13.1.1.

'Above n' should not be used for any materials in this chapter.

Examples

2 *Convention for the Protection of Human Rights and Fundamental Freedoms*, opened for signature 4 November 1950, 213 UNTS 222 (entered into force 3 September 1953), as amended by *Protocol No 11 to the Convention for the Protection of Human Rights and Fundamental Freedoms*, opened for signature 11 May 1994, ETS No 155 (entered into force 1 November 1998) ('*ECHR*').

…

5 *ECHR* art 6.

6 *El Boujaïdi v France* [1997] VI Eur Court HR 1980, 1994 (Judge Foighel) ('*El Boujaïdi*').

…

9 *El Boujaïdi* [1997] VI Eur Court HR 1980, 1992–3.

[10] *Directive 2003/71/EC of the European Parliament and of the Council of 4 November 2003 on the Prospectus to Be Published When Securities Are Offered to the Public or Admitted to Trading and Amending Directive 2001/34/EC* [2003] OJ L 345/64 ('*European Prospectus Directive*').

...

[13] *European Prospectus Directive* [2003] OJ L 345/64, art 3(2).

PART V

FOREIGN DOMESTIC MATERIALS

Part V
Foreign Domestic
Materials

14 Canada

14.1 Cases

14.1.1 General Rule

Rule	Canadian cases should be cited in accordance with chapter 2.
Example	*R v Sharpe* [2001] 1 SCR 45.
Note	When citing cases from Canada, it may be useful to include the name of the court in a citation (in accordance with rule 2.6) where the court is not otherwise apparent. However, this is unnecessary for references to the *Supreme Court Reports* (abbreviated 'SCR') and other report series specific to a particular court.

14.1.2 Official and Unofficial Report Series

Rule	In accordance with rule 2.3, citations of Canadian cases should include a citation of an authorised report series where possible. Where a decision is not reported in an official report series, a semi-official provincial report series or an unofficial report series, such as the *Dominion Law Reports* (abbreviated 'DLR'), should be cited.
Examples	*AB v Minister of Citizenship and Immigration* [2003] 1 FC 3. *Eli Lilly Canada Inc v Apotex Inc* [2008] 2 FC 636. *The Coca-Cola Co of Canada Ltd v The Pepsi-Cola Co of Canada Ltd* [1938] Ex CR 263. *Bangoura v Washington Post* (2005) 258 DLR (4th) 341 (Ontario Court of Appeal).

Notes

Only federal Canadian reports are authorised. Those series are:

Court	Abbreviation	Years
Supreme Court of Canada	SCR	1876–
Canadian Federal Courts	FC	1971–
Exchequer Court of Canada	Ex CR	1875–1970

Semi-official provincial report series are published under the auspices of a provincial law society or Bar association. Commonly cited semi-official state report series include the AR, BCR, Nfld & PEIR, NWTR, OR, RJQ and YR (or various series of them).

14.2 Legislation

Example	*Copyright Act*,	RSC	1985,	c C-42	, s 25
Element	Title	Statute Volume and Jurisdiction	Year	Chapter	Pinpoint
Rule	14.2.1	14.2.2	14.2.3	14.2.4	14.2.5

14.2.1 Title

Rule

Canadian statute titles should adhere to rule 3.1.1, but should be followed by a (non-italic) comma. '*The*' should be omitted from the beginning of a statute title.

Example

Agri-Food Amendment Act, SS 1997, c 27. [**Not:** *The Agri-Food Amendment Act*, …]

14.2.2 Statute Volume and Jurisdiction

Rule

An abbreviated form of the statute volume and jurisdiction should be included as follows:

Statute Volume	Jurisdiction

The statute volume and jurisdiction should *not* be separated by a space or any punctuation.

For the statute volume, a citation of the *Revised Statutes* or the *Re-enacted Statutes* (both abbreviated 'RS') should be included where available (for example, 'RSC'). Otherwise, a citation of the sessional or annual volumes (abbreviated 'S') should be included (for example, 'SC').

An abbreviated version of the jurisdiction should be included (for example, 'RSO'). The following abbreviations should be used:

Jurisdiction	Abbreviation
Canada (federal)	C
Alberta	A
British Columbia	BC
Lower Canada	LC
Manitoba	M
New Brunswick	NB
Newfoundland	N
Newfoundland and Labrador	NL
Northwest Territories	NWT
Nova Scotia	NS
Nunavut	Nu
Ontario	O
Prince Edward Island	PEI
Province of Canada	Prov C
Quebec	Q
Saskatchewan	S
Upper Canada	UC
Yukon Territory	Y

Examples

Criminal Code, RSC 1985, c C-46, s 515.

Controlled Drugs and Substances Act, SC 1996, c 19, s 4.

Escheats Act, RSO 1980, c 142. [**Not:** … RS O 1980, …]

14.2.3 Year

Rule

The year (or span of years) of the statute volume should be followed by a comma.

A session number (for example, '3rd Sess') should be included after the year if more than one parliamentary session occurred in that year and the statute volume is divided by session (with non-consecutive chapter numbering). A supplement number (for example, '2nd Supp') should be included after the year where a statute appears only in a supplement to the RS.

Session and supplement numbers should be ordinal and should adhere to rule 1.12.1 (so letters in ordinal numbers should be superscript). Session or supplement numbers should appear in parentheses. If a session or supplement number is included, the year should *not* be followed by a comma. Instead, the session or supplement number *should* be followed by a comma.

Examples

Clean Air Act, SNB 1997, c C-5.2.

Criminal Law Amendment Act, RSC 1985 (1st Supp), c 27.

An Act to Amend the Essential Services Emergency Act 1966, SS 1970 (2nd Sess), c 1.

Note

Statutes generally appear in a supplement to the RS where they are passed in the year of a consolidation too late to be included in that consolidation.

14.2.4 Chapter

Rule

The chapter number of the statute (including any letters) should be included. Letters and numbers forming the chapter number should be separated by a hyphen.

'Chapter' should be abbreviated 'c'.

Examples

Arthur Wishart Act (Franchise Disclosure), SO 2000, c 3.

Interpretation Act, RSC 1985, c I-21.

14.2.5 Pinpoint Reference

Rule	Pinpoint references should be preceded by a comma. They should adhere to (and use the abbreviations in) rules 3.1.4–3.1.6.
Example	*Tobacco Act*, SQ 1998, c 33, s 58.

14.3 Constitutions

14.3.1 Federal

Rule

The federal Canadian constitutional statutes should be cited as shown below. The short titles should be used for subsequent references in accordance with rules 3.9.1–3.9.2 (and should be included regardless of whether there are subsequent references):

Canada Act 1982 (UK) c 11, sch B ('*Constitution Act 1982*').

Constitution Act 1867 (Imp), 30 & 31 Vict, c 3 ('*Constitution Act 1867*').

Subsequent references should be cited as follows:

Constitution Act 1982 [Pinpoint].

Constitution Act 1867 [Pinpoint].

The *Canadian Charter of Rights and Freedoms* should be cited (in accordance with rule 3.9.2) as follows:

Canada Act 1982 (UK) c 11, sch B pt I ('*Canadian Charter of Rights and Freedoms*').

Subsequent references should be cited as follows:

Canadian Charter of Rights and Freedoms [Pinpoint].

Note

The Canadian constitution is contained in both the *Constitution Act 1982* (itself a schedule to a UK statute) and the *Constitution Act 1867* (an imperial statute). The *Canadian Charter of Rights and Freedoms* is part I of the *Constitution Act 1982*.

14.3.2 Provincial and Territorial

Rule	Provincial and territorial Canadian constitutions should be cited as regular legislation (in accordance with rule 14.2).
Example	*Constitution Act*, RSBC 1996, c 66.

14.4 Delegated Legislation (Regulations)

14.4.1 Revised Federal Regulations

Rule	Revised federal regulations are published in the *Consolidated Regulations of Canada* (abbreviated 'CRC'). They should be cited as follows: [*Title*], CRC, c [Chapter Number], [Pinpoint]. Pinpoint references should adhere to rules 3.1.4–3.1.6 and 3.3.2. When referring to a consolidation other than the latest version, a year should be included in parentheses after the chapter number or any pinpoint reference.
Examples	*Maple Products Regulations*, CRC, c 289, s 9. *Air Regulations*, CRC, c 2, s 201 (1955).
Note	The *Consolidated Regulations of Canada* is a consolidation of important federal regulations. There have been five consolidations to date (in 1874, 1889, 1949, 1955 and 1978).

14.4.2 Unrevised Federal Regulations

Rule	Unrevised federal regulations are published in the *Statutory Orders and Regulations* (abbreviated 'SOR'). They should be cited as follows: [*Title*], SOR/[Year]-[Regulation Number], [Pinpoint].

	Until 1999, only the last two digits of the year should be included. From 2000, the full year should be included. Pinpoint references should adhere to rules 3.1.4–3.1.6 and 3.3.2.
Examples	*Regulations Amending the Food and Drug Regulations*, SOR/98-580. *Sex Offender Information Registration Regulations (Canadian Forces)*, SOR/2008-247, s 2.

14.4.3 Provincial and Territorial Regulations

Rule

Provincial and territorial regulations should be cited as follows:

[*Title*], [Citation of Regulation], [Pinpoint].

The title may be omitted. Pinpoint references should adhere to rules 3.1.4–3.1.6 and 3.3.2.

The citation of the regulation should appear as shown in the table below for the relevant jurisdiction (examples appear in parentheses):

Jurisdiction	Unrevised Regulations	Revised Regulations
Alberta	Alta Reg [Regulation No]/[Year] (Alta Reg 62/2009)	
British Columbia	BC Reg [Regulation No]/[Year] (BC Reg 278/2008)	
Manitoba	Man Reg [Regulation No]/[Year*] (Man Reg 351/87)	Man Reg [Regulation No]/[Year*]R (Man Reg 401/88R)
New Brunswick	NB Reg [Year*]-[Regulation No] (NB Reg 2006-23)	

Newfoundland (until 5 December 2000)	Nfld Reg Regulation No / Year[*] (Nfld Reg 19/97)	
Newfoundland and Labrador (from 6 December 2000)	NLR Regulation No / Year[†] (NLR 4/09)	CNLR Regulation No / Year of Consolidation[*] (CNLR 1195/96)
Northwest Territories	NWT Reg Regulation No - Year[*] (NWT Reg 26-2008)	RRNWT Year of Revision, c Chapter No (RRNWT 1990, c P-26)
Nova Scotia	NS Reg Regulation No / Year (NS Reg 235/2007)	
Nunavut (from 1 April 1999)	Nu Reg Regulation No - Year[†] (Nu Reg 040-99)	
Ontario	O Reg Regulation No / Year[†] (O Reg 361/08)	RRO Year of Revision, Reg Regulation No (RRO 1990, Reg 469)
Prince Edward Island	PEI Reg EC Year - Regulation No (PEI Reg EC2002-249)	
Quebec	OC Regulation No - Year[*], Full Date, GOQ Gazette Citation (OC 764-97, 25 June 1997, GOQ 1997.II.2737)	RRQ 1981, c Chapter No, r Rule No (RRQ 1981, c V-5, r 1)
Saskatchewan	Sask Reg Regulation No / Year[*] (Sask Reg 444/67)	RRS, c Chapter No, Reg Regulation No (RRS, c C-4.01, Reg 1)

Yukon Territory	YOIC Year / Regulation No (YOIC 1995/87)	

* Only the last two digits of the year should be used for regulations prior to 2000.

† Only the last two digits of the year should be used.

Unless otherwise indicated, the year should appear in full.

Where nothing is shown in the 'revised regulations' column, there are no revised regulations for that jurisdiction.

Example *Elevating Devices Codes Regulation*, Alta Reg 62/2009, s 3.

14.5 Other

Rule For further information on the citation of Canadian materials, see the latest edition of the *Canadian Guide to Uniform Legal Citation*.

15 China

Note

The rules in this chapter should be used when citing Chinese language materials. Published translations of Chinese primary materials should be cited in accordance with rule 25.1.2 and rule 15.1 in this chapter.

15.1 Specific Rules for Chinese Language Materials

Rule

In citations of Chinese primary materials, translations of elements appearing in Chinese should adhere to rule 25.1.1 (so should appear in square brackets after the element translated).

Where text in Chinese is included in a citation, it should appear as it does in the source (in simplified or traditional Chinese characters or pinyin). To avoid ambiguity, Chinese characters that appear in the source should *not* be transliterated into pinyin.

Chinese characters should not be italicised, in titles or otherwise. Instead, where an element of a citation would ordinarily be italicised according to the relevant rule of this *Guide*, Chinese characters forming that element should appear between guillemets (« »).

Examples

In the document, the word 'interior' ('内地') is used instead of 'Chinese' to reflect the fact that Hong Kong and Macau are part of the People's Republic of China. [**Not:** … the word 'interior' ('*neidi*') … — **Original:** 内地]

---

12 «中华人民共和国循环经济促进法» [Circular Economy Promotion Law of the People's Republic of China] (People's Republic of China) National People's Congress Standing Committee, Order No 4, 29 August 2008, art 2.

13 «中华人民共和国护照法» [Passport Law of the People's Republic of China] (People's Republic of China) National People's Congress Standing Committee, Order No 50, 29 April 2006.

15.2 Cases

15.2.1 General Rule

Rule

Reported Chinese cases should be cited as follows:

Case Name [Year of Decision] Issue Number Official Gazette or Report Series Starting Page in Report Series, Pinpoint.

Only those elements that appear in the report should be included.

A translation of parties' names into English should be included where possible. Chinese names of natural persons should be transliterated into pinyin. Where the case name includes both the parties' names and a description of the case, the translation of the case name should appear as follows:

[Parties' Names — Case Description]

(for example, '[Xinjiang Yinhai Real Property Development Co Ltd v Xinjiang Hop Joint Stock Co Ltd — Company Transfer Contract Dispute Appeal Case]').

The title of the report series should be translated into English where possible. Otherwise, it should be transliterated into pinyin.

Examples

«兴业银行广州分行与深圳市机场股份有限公司借款合同纠纷案» [Industrial Bank Guangzhou Branch v Shenzhen Airport Co Ltd — Case of Loan Contract Dispute] [2009] 11 中华人民共和国最高人民法院公报 [Gazette of the Supreme People's Court of the People's Republic of China] 30, 36.

«施忠荣受贿案» [Shi Zhongrong — Case of Taking Bribes] [2009] 4 中华人民共和国最高人民检察院公报 [Gazette of the Supreme People's Procuratorate of the People's Republic of China] 28, 29.

Notes

When citing Chinese cases, it may be useful to include the name of the court at the end of a citation in parentheses where it is not otherwise apparent (in accordance with rule 2.6).

Chinese courts include the following (in order of hierarchy):

Court Name in English	Simplified Chinese	Pinyin
Supreme People's Court	最高人民法院	Zui Gao Ren Min Fa Yuan
High People's Court	高级人民法院	Gao Ji Ren Min Fa Yuan
Intermediate People's Court	中级人民法院	Zhong Ji Ren Min Fa Yuan
Basic People's Court	基层人民法院	Ji Ceng Ren Min Fa Yuan

15.2.2 Report Series

Rule

Decisions of the Supreme People's Court (最高人民法院 [Zui Gao Ren Min Fa Yuan]) should be cited from an official government gazette where available.

Other Chinese decisions should be cited from a report series where available.

Examples

«家园公司诉森得瑞公司合同纠纷案» [Jiayuan Co v Senderui Co — Contract Dispute Case] [2007] 2 中华人民共和国最高人民法院公报 [Gazette of the Supreme People's Court of the People's Republic of China] 39, 41.

«杨建立，魏铃故意杀人案» [Yang Jianli, Wei Ling — Intentional Homicide Case] [2002] 4 人民法院案例选 [Selected Cases of the People's Courts] 7 (Zheng Zhou City, He Nan Province Intermediate People's Court, People's Republic of China).

Notes

The official report series of the Supreme People's Court is 中华人民共和国最高人民法院公报 [Zhong Hua Ren Min Gong He Guo Zui Gao Ren Min Fa Yuan Gong Bao — Gazette of the Supreme People's Court of the People's Republic of China].

A commonly used report series is 人民法院案例选 [Ren Min Fa Yuan An Li Xuan — Selected Cases of the People's Courts].

15.2.3 Unreported Judgments

Rule

Unreported Chinese judgments should be cited as follows:

Case Name, Court Name, Case Number, Full Date, Pinpoint.

The case name should adhere to rule 15.2.1.

'People's Republic of China', 'Republic of China' or 'Macau' should be included in the translation of the court name if it is not otherwise apparent that the court is Chinese.

Example

«焦其铸与重庆市信心农牧科技有限公司租赁合同纠纷案» [Jiao Qizhu v Confidence Farming Technology Co Ltd of Chongqing Municipality — Lease Contract Dispute Case], 重庆市第五中级人民法院 [Fifth Intermediate People's Court of Chongqing Municipality, People's Republic of China], 渝五中民终字第93号 [Economic Appeal No 93], 24 April 2008.

15.3 Legislative Materials

15.3.1 Chinese Legislative Acts

Rule

Chinese legislative acts should be cited as follows:

Title of Law (Jurisdiction) Promulgating Body, Order/Decree/Opinion No Number, Full Date of Promulgation, Pinpoint.

Only those elements that appear on the source should be included.

Generally, only the title of a legislative act should appear in Chinese with a translation. However, if there is good reason, the name of the promulgating body or the order, decree or opinion number may be included in Chinese with a translation.

The jurisdiction should be 'People's Republic of China', 'Republic of China' or 'Macau' as appropriate.

To aid retrieval of the law, a citation of an official gazette or

	publication may be included after the full date of promulgation and before any pinpoint reference.
Examples	«中华人民共和国合同法» [Contract Law of the People's Republic of China] (People's Republic of China) National People's Congress, 15 March 1999. «中华人民共和国物权法» [Property Law of the People's Republic of China] (People's Republic of China) National People's Congress, Order No 62, 16 March 2007. «劳动部关于企业职工流动若干问题的通知» [Notice of Ministry of Labour on Several Issues Concerning the Movement of Employees of Enterprises] (People's Republic of China) Ministry of Labour, 31 October 1996. «著作權法» [Copyright Act] (Republic of China) Legislative Yuan, 10 February 2010, art 10. «第225/2002號行政長官批示» [Order No 225/2002 of the Chief Executive] (Macau) 9 October 2002, 澳門特別行政區公報—第一組 [Macau Special Administrative Region Gazette — Part 1], No 41, 15 October 2002, 1088.
Notes	Legislative materials can take the form of codes, national laws, regulations, notices, guidelines or other governmental determinations. Older legislative acts often do not have an order, decree or opinion number. Materials from Hong Kong should be cited in English in accordance with chapter 18.

15.3.2 Constitutions

Rule	The constitution of the People's Republic of China should be cited as follows: «中华人民共和国宪法» [Constitution of the People's Republic of China] [Pinpoint].

	The constitution of the Republic of China should be cited as follows: «中華民國憲法» [Constitution of the Republic of China] Pinpoint. The constitution of Macau should be cited as follows: «中華人民共和國澳門特別行政區基本法» [Basic Law of the Macau Special Administrative Region of the People's Republic of China] Pinpoint.
Examples	«中华人民共和国宪法» [Constitution of the People's Republic of China] art 3. «中華民國憲法» [Constitution of the Republic of China] art 129. «中華人民共和國澳門特別行政區基本法» [Basic Law of the Macau Special Administrative Region of the People's Republic of China] ch III.
Note	Where it is relevant or important, more information (such as a date of adoption or promulgating body) can be included in citations of constitutional documents. Such citations should adhere to rule 15.3.1.

15.4 Chinese Language Secondary Sources

15.4.1 General Rules

Rule	Citations of Chinese language secondary sources should adhere to rules 25.4 and 15.1. In particular: • materials should be cited in accordance with the relevant rules of this *Guide* for the source type; • a translation of a citation element should be included in square brackets after that element; • where Chinese characters are used in a source, they should be reproduced in a citation (and where a source uses pinyin, this should be reproduced in a citation); and

- Chinese characters should not be italicised in titles or otherwise (and should appear between guillemets as appropriate).

Where a source includes a Chinese title and an English title, both should be included in a citation. The English title should be italicised where appropriate.

Examples

胡克, 张卫, 胡智锋 [Hu Ke, Zhang Wei and Hu Zhifeng], «当代电影理论文选» [Selected Works of Contemporary Film Theory] (北京广播学院出版社 [Beijing Broadcasting Institute Press], 2000) 22.

蔡永彤 [Cai Yongtong], «WTO服务市场开放研究及相关法律问题探析—以法律服务市场开放为视角» [Research on the Opening Up of the Services Market under WTO and Analysis of Relevant Legal Questions — From the Perspective of the Opening Up of the Legal Services Market] (2004) 12(2) 山西经济管理干部学院学报 *Journal of Shanxi Institute of Economic Management* 60, 63.

15.4.2 Author Names and Subsequent 'Above n' References

Rule

Author names should be included as they appear on the source (in simplified or traditional Chinese characters or pinyin). The capitalisation and order of surnames and given names should not be changed from that in the source.

If a name appears in Chinese characters, a transliteration into pinyin should be included in square brackets after the characters.

Subsequent 'above n' references should adhere to rule 1.4.2. However, the *full* name of the author should always be included. If the name appears in Chinese characters, both the characters and the pinyin transliteration should be included in subsequent references.

Examples	卫铄 [Wei Shuo] … [**Original:** 卫铄] Cai Yuanpei … [**Original:** Cai Yuanpei] ——— 17 方建伟 [Fang Jianwei], «试论入世后中国法律服务业的开放» Examining the Opening Up of China's Legal Services Sector after WTO Accession] [2004] 行政与法 *Public Administration and Law* 21, 122. … 20 方建伟 [Fang Jianwei], above n 17, 124.
Note	In Chinese characters, the surname of an author always appears first. In names transliterated into pinyin, the surname sometimes appears first and sometimes last. The order of the names in a citation should replicate the order in the source.

16 France

Note

The rules in this chapter should be used when citing French language primary materials. Published translations of French primary materials should be cited in accordance with rule 25.1.2.

16.1 Cases

Rule

Decisions of the Cour de cassation should be cited as follows:

Cour de cassation [French Court of Cassation], [Appeal Number], [Full Date] reported in ([Year of Publication]) [Abbreviation of Publication] n° [Number of Volume/Issue], [Pinpoint].

Cases from the Conseil constitutionnel should be cited as follows:

Conseil constitutionnel [French Constitutional Court], decision n° [Number of Decision], [Full Date] reported in JO, [Full Date of Publication], [Pinpoint].

Cases from the Conseil d'État should be cited as follows:

Conseil d'État [French Administrative Court], [Full Date] reported in [[Year of Publication]] Rec Lebon [Pinpoint].

Other cases should be cited as follows:

[Name of Court (Including City)], [Case Number], [Full Date] reported in [Report Series Citation], [Pinpoint].

The words 'reported in' and a citation of a report series or publication should be included only where available.

A popular or commonly used name of a case may be included before the name of the court. It should appear italicised and be followed by a (non-italic) comma.

Translations of elements appearing in French should adhere to rule 25.1.1 (so should appear in square brackets after the element translated).

Examples

Cour de cassation [French Court of Cassation], 06-81968, 5 December 2006 reported in (2006) Bull crim n° 304, 1095.

Conseil constitutionnel [French Constitutional Court], decision n° 2005-527 DC, 8 December 2005 reported in JO, 13 December 2005, 19162.

Demoiselle X, Conseil d'État [French Administrative Court], 28 May 1971 reported in [1971] Rec Lebon 409.

Cour d'appel de Toulouse [Toulouse Court of Appeal], 2003/05292, 7 March 2005.

Notes

Official report series of the French Cour de cassation [Court of Cassation], Conseil constitutionnel [Constitutional Court] and Conseil d'État [Administrative Court] are set out in the table below:

Court	Report Series	Abbreviation
Cour de cassation — civil matters	*Bulletin des arrêts de la Cour de cassation, Chambres civiles*	Bull civ
Cour de cassation — criminal matters	*Bulletin des arrêts de la Cour de cassation, Chambre criminelle*	Bull crim
Conseil constitutionnel	*Journal officiel de la République française*	JO
Conseil d'État	*Recueil des arrêts du Conseil d'État statuant au contentieux*	Rec Lebon

For decisions of the Cour de cassation, the 'appeal number' is generally the number following 'n° de pourvoi' in the decision.

16.2 Legislative Materials

16.2.1 Individual Laws

Rule

French legislation and delegated legislation should be cited as follows:

[*Title of Law*] (France) JO, [Full Date of Publication], [Pinpoint].

	The title of the law generally includes a number (preceded by '*n°*') and a date (preceded by '*du*'). Laws are gazetted in the *Journal officiel* (abbreviated 'JO'). Translations of elements appearing in French should adhere to rule 25.1.1 (so should appear in square brackets after the element translated).
Examples	*Loi n° 91-662 du 13 juillet 1991* [Law No 91-662 of 13 July 1991] (France) JO, 19 July 1991, 9521. *Décret n° 95-221 du 27 février 1995* [Decree No 95-221 of 27 February 1995] (France) JO, 2 March 1995, 3350.

16.2.2 Codes

Rule	French codes should be cited as follows: *Title of Code* (France) Pinpoint. Translations of elements appearing in French should adhere to rule 25.1.1 (so should appear in square brackets after the element translated).
Examples	*Code civil* [Civil Code] (France) art 147. *Code de procédure pénale* [Code of Criminal Procedure] (France) art 689.

16.2.3 Constitution

Rule	The French Constitution should be cited as follows: *La Constitution du 4 octobre 1958* [French Constitution of 4 October 1958] Pinpoint.
Example	*La Constitution du 4 octobre 1958* [French Constitution of 4 October 1958] art 2.

17 Germany

Note	The rules in this chapter should be used when citing German language primary materials. Published translations of German primary materials should be cited in accordance with rule 25.1.2.

17.1 Cases

Rule

Cases should be cited as follows:

[Court Name], [Case Number], [Full Date] reported in ([Year of Decision]) [Volume Number] [Abbreviation of Report Series] [Starting Page], [Pinpoint].

A popular or commonly used name of a case may be included before the name of the court. It should appear italicised and be followed by a (non-italic) comma.

The words 'reported in' and a citation of a report series should be included only where available.

Translations of elements appearing in German should adhere to rule 25.1.1 (so should appear in square brackets after the element translated).

Examples

Bundesverfassungsgericht [German Constitutional Court], 1 BvR 131/96, 24 March 1998 reported in (1998) 97 BVerfGE 391.

Bundesgerichtshof [German Federal Court of Justice], VII ZR 110/83, 19 January 1984 reported in (1984) 89 BGHZ 376, 378.

Solange II, Bundesverfassungsgericht [German Constitutional Court], 2 BvR 197/83, 22 October 1986 reported in (1986) 73 BVerfGE 271.

Pumuckl, Oberlandesgericht München [Munich Court of Appeal], 29 U 4743/02, 4 September 2003.

Note

The preferred report series of German final courts of appeal are as follows:

Court	Name of Court in English	Report Series Abbreviation
Bundesverfassungsgericht	Federal Constitutional Court	BVerfGE
Bundesgerichtshof — Strafsachen	Federal Court of Justice — Criminal Matters	BGHSt
Bundesgerichtshof — Zivilsachen	Federal Court of Justice — Civil Matters	BGHZ
Bundessozialgericht	Federal Social Court	BSGE
Bundesfinanzhof	Federal Finance Court	BFHE
Bundesarbeitsgericht	Federal Labour Court	BAGE

17.2 Legislative Materials

17.2.1 Individual Laws

Rule

Legislation and delegated legislation should be cited as follows:

[*Title of Law*] (Germany) [Full Date of Enactment], [Abbreviated Gazette Name], [Year], [Starting Page], [Pinpoint].

Translations of elements appearing in German should adhere to rule 25.1.1 (so should appear in square brackets after the element translated).

Example

Sozialversicherungs-Rechnungsverordnung [Social Security Calculation Regulation] (Germany) 27 April 2009, BGBl I, 2009, 951.

17.2.2 Codes

Rule

German codes should be cited as follows:

[*Title of Code*] (Germany) [Pinpoint].

Where a code has a commonly used abbreviation, this abbreviation may be included in the first citation of the code as a short title and used in subsequent references, in accordance with rule 3.9.

	Translations of elements appearing in German should adhere to rule 25.1.1 (so should appear in square brackets after the element translated).
Example	[1] *Bürgerliches Gesetzbuch* [Civil Code] (Germany) § 823(1) ('*BGB*'). … [3] *BGB* § 826.

17.2.3 Constitution

Rule	The German Constitution should be cited as follows: *Grundgesetz für die Bundesrepublik Deutschland* [Basic Law of the Federal Republic of Germany] Pinpoint.
Example	*Grundgesetz für die Bundesrepublik Deutschland* [Basic Law of the Federal Republic of Germany] art 8(1).

18 Hong Kong

18.1 Cases

Rule	Hong Kong cases should be cited accordance with chapter 2. However, names of individuals (both parties and judicial officers) should generally appear in full.
Examples	*Ng Ka Ling v Director of Immigration* [1999] 1 HKLRD 337. *Victor Chandler (International) Ltd v Zhou Chu Jian He* (2007) 12 HKPLR 595, 601 [24] (Court of First Instance). *Penny's Bay Investment Co Ltd v Director of Lands* [2009] 1 HKC 391. *Hong Kong Special Administrative Region v Lau Wai Wo* (2003) 6 HKCFAR 624. *Discovery Bay Services Management Ltd v David Buxhaum* [1995] HKDCLR 7, 9 (Downey J). *Faithway Enterprise Ltd v Lee Wan* [2007] HKCA 175 (25 April 2007).
Notes	The *Hong Kong Law Reports and Digest* (abbreviated 'HKLRD') and the *Hong Kong Court of Final Appeal Reports* (abbreviated 'HKCFAR') are authorised report series, so should be cited where available. Commonly cited unauthorised law report series are the HKC and HKLR, which should be cited where no authorised series is available. When citing cases from Hong Kong, it may be useful to include the name of the court in a citation (in accordance with rule 2.6). Names of individuals should generally appear in full in Hong Kong decisions to ensure that individuals are unambiguously identified. If given names are not necessary to identify an individual, they may be omitted.

18.2 Legislative Materials

18.2.1 Principal and Delegated Legislation

Rule

Hong Kong principal and delegated legislation should be cited in accordance with rules 3.1–3.4. However:

- no year should be included;
- the jurisdiction should appear as '(Hong Kong)'; and
- a chapter number should be included after the jurisdiction.

The chapter number should appear as follows:

cap [Chapter Number]
(for example, 'cap 3').

Where a pinpoint reference is included, the chapter number should be followed by a comma.

Where principal or delegated legislation has not been allocated a chapter number (or when citing principal or delegated legislation historically, as enacted), the year should be included.

Examples

Evidence Ordinance (Hong Kong) cap 8, s 4.

Dogs and Cats Regulations (Hong Kong) cap 167A, reg 22.

Rules of the High Court (Hong Kong) cap 4A.

Telephone Ordinance 1925 (Hong Kong).

Note

A piece of primary legislation in Hong Kong is usually called an 'ordinance'.

18.2.2 Constitution

Rule

The Hong Kong Constitution should be cited as follows:

Basic Law of the Hong Kong Special Administrative Region of the People's Republic of China [Pinpoint].

Example

Basic Law of the Hong Kong Special Administrative Region of the People's Republic of China art 4.

19 Malaysia

19.1 Cases

19.1.1 General Rule

Rule

Malaysian cases should be cited in accordance with chapter 2. However:

- the names of individuals (both parties and judicial officers) should generally appear in full; and
- abbreviations of judicial titles should appear as they do in the case cited (but should adhere to rule 1.6.1, so full stops should not be used in abbreviations).

'Sendirian Berhad' (an expression indicating incorporation) should be abbreviated '*Sdn Bhd*' in parties' names. 'Datuk' (approximately equivalent to 'Sir') and 'Haji' (a religious status) should always be omitted from parties' names.

Examples

Ratna Ammal v Tan Chow Soo (1964) 30 MLJ 24.

Achieva Technology Sdn Bhd v Lam Yen Ling [2009] 8 MLJ 625 (High Court).

Notes

When citing cases from Malaysia, it may be useful to include the name of the court in a citation (in accordance with rule 2.6).

Names of individuals should generally appear in full in Malaysian decisions to ensure that individuals are unambiguously identified. If given names are not necessary to identify an individual, they may be omitted.

19.1.2 Report Series

Rule

In Malaysia, the most commonly used and authoritative law report series is the *Malayan Law Journal* (abbreviated 'MLJ'), which should be cited where possible.

	Where a case is not reported in the MLJ, the *Current Law Journal* (abbreviated 'CLJ') should be cited where possible.
Examples	*Polygram Records Sdn Bhd v The Search* [1994] 3 MLJ 127, 140 (Visu Sinnadurai J) (High Court of Malaya). *TAM Abdul Aziz & Co v Shamsudeen* (1951) 17 MLJ 141, 141 (Murray-Aynsley CJ) (Court of Appeal). *PP v Segaran S Mathavan* [2010] 2 CLJ 121 (High Court of Malaya).
Note	The *Malayan Law Journal* contains both journal articles and cases from the Federal Court, Court of Appeal and High Court. Until 1965, volumes of the *Malayan Law Journal* were organised by volume. From 1966, the volumes are organised by year.

19.1.3 Unreported Cases

Rule	Unreported Malaysian decisions should be cited in accordance with rule 2.8.2.
Example	*Mohamed Musa bin Amanullah v Public Prosecutor* (Unreported, Malaysian Court of Appeal, Hasan Lah, Sulong Matjeraie and Mohd Hishamudin Yunus JJCA, 1 March 2010) [45]–[46].
Note	Although some online databases do so, Malaysian courts do not allocate medium neutral citations. Medium neutral citations should thus *not* be used for unreported Malaysian cases, in accordance with rule 2.8.1.

19.2 Legislative Materials

19.2.1 Statutes and Delegated Legislation

Rule	Malaysian statutes and delegated legislation should be cited in accordance with chapter 3. The jurisdiction should appear as '(Malaysia)'.

Examples	*Copyright Act 1987* (Malaysia) s 7. *Digital Signature Regulations 1998* (Malaysia) reg 58(a).

19.2.2 Constitution

Rule	The Malaysian Constitution should be cited as follows: *Federal Constitution* (Malaysia) [Pinpoint].
Example	*Federal Constitution* (Malaysia) art 5.

20 New Zealand

20.1 Cases

20.1.1 General Rule

Rule	New Zealand cases should be cited in accordance with chapter 2.
Example	*Haylock v Patek* [2009] 1 NZLR 351.
Note	When citing cases from New Zealand, it may be useful to include the name of the court in a citation (in accordance with rule 2.6).

20.1.2 Official and Unofficial Report Series

Rule	The *New Zealand Law Reports* (abbreviated 'NZLR'), which are authorised, should be cited where possible in accordance with rule 2.3.1. Where a case is not reported in the NZLR, an unofficial report series should be cited (where available).
Examples	*Buchanan v Jennings* [2000] NZAR 113 (Randerson and Neazor JJ) (High Court). *Gloken Holdings Ltd v CDE Co Ltd* (1997) 6 NZBLC ¶99-418, 102 272.

20.1.3 Unreported Cases

Rule

Where a case is unreported and has been assigned a medium neutral citation by the court, it should be cited in accordance with rule 2.8.1. The following medium neutral unique court identifiers should be used from the years indicated:

Court	Unique Court Identifier	Years
New Zealand Supreme Court	NZSC	2005–
New Zealand Court of Appeal	NZCA	2007–

	Other unreported New Zealand decisions (including unreported decisions of the High Court of New Zealand) should be cited in accordance with rule 2.8.2.
Examples	*Ludgater Holdings Ltd v Gerling Australia Insurance Co Pty Ltd* [2009] NZSC 131 (16 December 2009) [1]. *Lowe v New Zealand Police* (Unreported, High Court of New Zealand, Clifford J, 2 March 2010) [11]–[12].
Note	Some New Zealand tribunals also assign medium neutral citations to their decisions. Such medium neutral citations should be used only where the tribunal itself has assigned that citation.

20.1.4 Māori Land Court and Māori Appellate Court

Rule

Decisions of the Māori Land Court and the Māori Appellate Court should be cited as follows:

[*Parties' Names*] — [*Block Name*] ([Year]) [Case Number] [Registry] [Minute Book Abbreviation] [Starting Page], [Pinpoint].

Parties' names should be separated by '*v*'. The block name should be included only where it appears in the decision. The following abbreviations should be used for the minute book abbreviation:

Type of Minute Book	Abbreviation
Minute Book	MB
Appellate Court Minute Book	ACMB
Chief Judge's Minute Book	CJMB

Where minute book references are unavailable, Māori Land Court and Māori Appellate Court decisions should be cited as unreported decisions (in accordance with rule 2.8).

Pinpoint references should adhere to rule 2.5. Judges' names should adhere to rule 2.9.1.

Examples

O'Rorke v Hohaia — Pukekohatu 7B Block (2006) 173 Aotea MB 114, 117 [12]–[13] (Judge Harvey).

Taipari v Hauraki Maori Trust Board (2008) 114 Hauraki MB 75.

Notes	The block name is usually preceded by the words 'In the matter of' in Māori Land Court and Māori Appellate Court decisions (and those words should be omitted in citations). Minute books are divided according to registry.

20.1.5 Waitangi Tribunal

Rule	Reports of the Waitangi Tribunal should be cited as follows: Waitangi Tribunal, *Title of Report* (Year). The 'Wai number' (sometimes used to identify reports of the Waitangi Tribunal) should not be included.
Example	Waitangi Tribunal, *Maori Electoral Option Report* (1994).

20.2 Legislative Materials

20.2.1 Statutes

Rule	New Zealand statutes should be cited in accordance with rule 3.1. The jurisdiction should be abbreviated 'NZ'.
Example	*Habeas Corpus Act 2001* (NZ).

20.2.2 Delegated Legislation

Rule	New Zealand delegated legislation should be cited in accordance with rule 3.3. However, the statutory rule number should be included after the jurisdiction and followed by a comma. It should appear in the form: SR Year/Instrument Number (for example, 'SR 2004/225').
Example	*Electronic Transactions Regulations 2003* (NZ) SR 2003/288, reg 4.

20.3 Other

Rule

For further information on the citation of New Zealand materials, see the latest edition of the *New Zealand Law Style Guide*.

21 Singapore

21.1 Cases

21.1.1 General Rule

Rule	Singaporean cases should be cited in accordance with chapter 2. However: • names of individuals (both parties and judicial officers) should generally appear in full; and • 'Proprietary Limited' is abbreviated 'Pte Ltd' (not 'Pty Ltd') for Singaporean companies.
Examples	*Re Econ Corp Ltd* [2004] 1 SLR 273. *Lim Choo Suan v Goh Kok Hwa* [2009] 4 SLR 193, 201–2 [15]–[16] (Woo Bih Li J) (High Court). *Virtual Map (Singapore) Pte Ltd v Singapore Land Authority* [2009] 2 SLR 558, 563 (Court of Appeal).
Notes	When citing cases from Singapore, it may be useful to include the name of the court in a citation (in accordance with rule 2.6). Names of individuals should generally appear in full in Singaporean decisions to ensure that individuals are unambiguously identified. If given names are not necessary to identify an individual, they may be omitted.

21.1.2 Report Series

Rule	The most commonly used and authoritative report series for cases from 1965 is the *Singapore Law Reports* (abbreviated 'SLR'), which should be cited where available. For cases prior to 1965, the *Malayan Law Journal* (abbreviated 'MLJ') should be cited where available.
Examples	*PT Garuda Indonesia v Birgen Air* [2002] 1 SLR 393. *Loo Seong Thye v Goh Teik Yah* (1964) 30 MLJ 346.

21.1.3 Unreported Cases

Rule

Where a decision is unreported and has been assigned a medium neutral citation by the court, it should be cited in accordance with rule 2.8.1. The following unique court identifiers should be used:

Court	Unique Court Identifier	Years
Supreme Court of Singapore — Court of Appeal	SGCA	2003–
Supreme Court of Singapore — High Court	SGHC	2003–
Singapore District Court	SGDC	2001–
Singapore Magistrates' Court	SGMC	2001–
Singapore Juvenile Court	SGJC	2001–
Singapore Small Claims Tribunal	SGSCT	2001–

Other unreported Singaporean decisions should be cited in accordance with rule 2.8.2.

Examples

Orient Centre Investments Ltd v Société Générale [2007] SGCA 24 (9 May 2007).

Ong v Lim Lie Hoa [2008] SGHC 44 (25 March 2008) [8] (Choo Han Teck J).

Public Prosecutor v Zhang Jing [2006] SGDC 82 (3 May 2006) [17]–[19].

Note

The Supreme Court of Singapore consists of the High Court and the Court of Appeal.

21.2 Legislative Materials

21.2.1 Statutes and Subsidiary Legislation

Rule

Singaporean legislation and subsidiary legislation that has been assigned a chapter number should be cited as follows:

[*Title*] (Singapore, cap [Chapter Number], [Year] rev ed) [Pinpoint].

The title should adhere to rule 3.1.1. Where a statute or subsidiary legislation is cited as in force, the year is that of the most recent revision. For historical references, the appropriate year of revision should be included. Pinpoint references should adhere to rules 3.1.4–3.1.6 and 3.3.2.

Legislation and subsidiary legislation that has not been assigned a chapter number or been revised (as well as historical statutes and subsidiary legislation that preceded chapter numbering) should be cited as follows:

[*Title*] [*Year*] (Singapore) [Pinpoint].

The year is that in which the statute was passed or the subsidiary legislation was promulgated originally (and should adhere to rule 3.1.2).

Examples

Adoption of Children Act (Singapore, cap 4, 1985 rev ed) s 5.

Land Titles Act (Singapore, cap 157, 1994 rev ed) pt III.

Rules of Court (Singapore, cap 322, 2006 rev ed) O 10 r 1.

Road Traffic (Motor Vehicles, Driving Licences) (Amendment) Rules 2010 (Singapore).

Land Titles Ordinance 1956 (Singapore) ss 28(2)(b)–(e).

Notes

In Singapore, all forms of delegated legislation are called 'subsidiary legislation'.

The chapter number (abbreviated 'cap') refers to a statute or piece of subsidiary legislation as first passed or promulgated. Singaporean Acts and subsidiary legislation are regularly revised by the Law Revision Commission with the assent of the President and become official revised editions (abbreviated 'rev ed').

21.2.2 Constitutional Documents

Rule

Singaporean constitutional documents should be cited in accordance with rule 21.2.1. These documents do not have chapter numbers, but revision or reprint information should be indicated.

Examples

Constitution of the Republic of Singapore (Singapore, 1999 reprint) ss 9–16.

Republic of Singapore Independence Act (Singapore, 1985 rev ed) s 5.

21.3 Other

Rule

For further information on the citation of Singaporean materials, see the latest edition of *The Singapore Academy of Law Style Guide*.

22 South Africa

22.1 Cases

22.1.1 General Rule

Rule	South African cases should be cited in accordance with chapter 2. Where a judicial officer is identified (in accordance with rule 2.9.1), 'Judge President' should be abbreviated 'JP' and appear after a judge's name. In accordance with rule 2.6, the name of the court (for example, 'Constitutional Court') or name of the division of the Supreme Court or High Court (for example, 'Appellate Division') may be included. However, the location of a Supreme Court or High Court division should be omitted (for example, 'Provincial Division', not 'Transvaal Provincial Division').
Examples	*Christian Education South Africa v Minister of Education* [1999] 2 SA 83 (Constitutional Court). *Mahlangu v De Jager* [2000] 3 SA 145 (Land Claims Court). *Belvedere Sugar Co (Pty) Ltd v Sugar Industry Central Board* [1962] 1 SA 221, 230 (Williamson JP). *S v Zinn* [1969] 2 SA 537, 540 (Rumpff JA) (Appellate Division). *Soller No v G* [2003] 5 SA 430, 437–8 [22]–[27] (Satchwell J) (Local Division). [**Not:** … (Witwatersrand Local Division).]
Notes	'*S*' is commonly used as an abbreviation for 'State' where the state is a party to a criminal case. The High Court of South Africa replaced the local and provincial divisions of the Supreme Court of South Africa in 1997. The Supreme Court of Appeal replaced the Appellate Division of the Supreme Court in 1996. The Constitutional Court deals only with constitutional matters. Accordingly, the following court names may be included in accordance with rule 2.6:

Court(s)	Court Name for Citations
Constitutional Court	(Constitutional Court)
The current Supreme Court of Appeal	(Supreme Court of Appeal)
The former Appellate Division of the Supreme Court	(Appellate Division)
All current locations of the High Court (for example, 'North West High Court, Mafikeng')	(High Court)
All former Supreme Court local and provincial divisions (for example, 'Cape Provincial Division')	(Local Division)/(Provincial Division)
All former Supreme Court divisions not designated 'local' or 'provincial' (for example, 'Eastern Cape Division')	(Supreme Court)

The names of other courts (such as the Magistrates' Court, Land Claims Court, Labour Court, Labour Appeal Court and Competition Appeal Court) may be included as appropriate. Specific geographical locations should be omitted from such names.

22.1.2 Report Series

Rule

South Africa does not have authorised reports of judicial decisions. The most commonly used report series is the *South African Law Reports* (abbreviated 'SA'), which should be cited where possible.

Example

S v Manamela [2000] 3 SA 1 (Constitutional Court).

Note

Decisions of the Supreme Court and High Court of Namibia and the Supreme Court and High Court of Zimbabwe are reported in the SA, and should be cited in accordance with this rule.

22.2 Legislative Materials

22.2.1 Statutes and Delegated Legislation

Rule

South African legislation and delegated legislation should be cited in accordance with chapter 3.

The following abbreviations and phrases should be used to indicate South African jurisdictions:

Jurisdiction	Abbreviation/Phrase
South Africa	South Africa
Eastern Cape	EC
Free State	FS
Gauteng	G
KwaZulu-Natal	KZN
Limpopo	LP
Mpumalanga	MP
North West	NW
Northern Cape	NC
Western Cape	WC

In provincial legislation, where the jurisdiction appears at the beginning of the title of an Act, it should be omitted from the title and included in abbreviated form in accordance with rule 3.1.3.

Examples

Local Government Transition Act 1993 (South Africa).

Digital Terrestrial Television Regulations 2009 (South Africa) reg 5.

Land Administration Act 2003 (KZN). [**Not:** *KwaZulu-Natal Land Administration Act 2003*.]

22.2.2 Constitutions

Rule

The constitutions of South Africa and its provinces should be cited as regular legislation (in accordance with rule 22.2.1).

Example

Constitution of the Republic of South Africa Act 1996 (South Africa) ch 8.

22.3 Truth and Reconciliation Commission

Rule	Reports of the Truth and Reconciliation Commission of South Africa should be cited as books (in accordance with chapter 5).
Example	Truth and Reconciliation Commission of South Africa, *Report* (1998–2003) vol 3, 155.

23 United Kingdom

23.1 Cases

23.1.1 General Rule

Rule

United Kingdom cases should be cited in accordance with chapter 2.

'Public Limited Company' should be abbreviated '*plc*' in parties' names.

In judicial review cases from 2001 where the Crown is a party (often described as '*R on the application of X*' in the report), the Crown and the party seeking judicial review should appear in the form:

R (*Name of Party Seeking Judicial Review* *)*

(for example, '*R (Anderson)*').

Examples

CAS Nominees Ltd v Nottingham Forest FC plc [2001] 1 All ER 954.

R (Amin) v Secretary of State for the Home Department [2004] 1 AC 653, 673–4 [39] (Lord Bingham).

23.1.2 Modern English Reports

Rule

The *Law Reports*, published by the Incorporated Council of Law Reporting for England and Wales, should be cited where available.

The abbreviations for commonly used series in the *Law Reports* (and predecessor series) are in the table below. Where 'LR' appears in an abbreviation, the volume number should be included between 'LR' and the rest of the abbreviation (for example, 'LR 7 QB', not '7 LR QB').

Jurisdiction	Abbreviation	Years
Admiralty and Ecclesiastical Cases	LR Adm & Eccl	1865–75
Appeal Cases	AC	1890–
	App Cas	1875–90

Chancery	Ch	1891–
	Ch D	1875–90
Chancery Appeal Cases	LR Ch App	1865–75
Common Pleas	CPD	1875–80
	LR CP	1865–75
Crown Cases Reserved	LR CCR	1865–75
English and Irish Appeals and Peerage Claims	LR HL	1865–75
Equity	LR Eq	1865–75
Exchequer	Ex D	1875–80
	LR Ex	1865–75
Family	Fam	1972–
Privy Council	LR PC	1865–75
Probate and Divorce	P	1891–1971
	PD	1875–90
	LR P & D	1865–75
Queen's and King's Bench	QB	1952–
	KB	1901–51
	QB	1891–1900
	QBD	1875–90
	LR QB	1865–75
Restrictive Practices	LR RP	1957–72
Scotch and Divorce Appeals	LR Sc & Div	1865–75

Examples

Beevis v Dawson [1957] 1 QB 195.

Astley v Micklethwait (1880) 15 Ch D 59.

Skinner v Orde (1871) LR 4 PC 60.

23.1.3 Nominate Reports

Rule

Citations of nominate reports should include a parallel citation of the *English Reports* (abbreviated 'ER') or the *Revised Reports* (abbreviated 'RR') where available, after the citation of the nominate report (including any pinpoint references). The ER should be cited in preference to the RR.

	Where necessary to avoid ambiguity, judges' names should be repeated after both the nominate report and the ER or RR pinpoints.
Examples	*Russel v Lee* (1661) 1 Lev 86; 83 ER 310. *Janvrin v De La Mare* (1861) 14 Moo 334, 345; 15 ER 332, 336 (Lord Kingsdown). *Peters v Fleming* (1840) 6 M & W 42, 47 (Parke B), 48 (Alderson B), 49 (Rolfe B); 151 ER 314, 315 (Parke B), 316 (Alderson B), 316 (Rolfe B).
Note	The nominate reports, published between 1537 and 1865, are reports that were published under the name of the reporter. Many of the nominate reports have been compiled and reprinted. The first reprint was published as the RR. The subsequent (and preferred) reprint is the ER.

23.1.4 Scottish Reports

Rule	Scottish cases should be cited in accordance with rule 23.1. However, in report series organised by year, square brackets should *not* enclose the year.
Example	*Logan v Harrower* 2008 SLT 1049.

23.1.5 Unreported Cases

Rule

UK unreported decisions should be cited in accordance with rule 2.8.

Where a decision is unreported and has been assigned a medium neutral citation by the court, it should be cited in accordance with rule 2.8.1. The following are medium neutral unique court identifiers for important UK courts:

Court	Unique Court Identifier	Years
Supreme Court of the United Kingdom	UKSC	2009–
United Kingdom House of Lords	UKHL	2001–09

United Kingdom Privy Council	UKPC	2001–
England and Wales Court of Appeal — Civil Division	EWCA Civ	2001–
England and Wales Court of Appeal — Criminal Division	EWCA Crim	2001–
England and Wales High Court — Administrative Court	EWHC Admin	2001–02
	EWHC (Admin)*	2002–
England and Wales High Court — Admiralty Court	EWHC (Admlty)*	2002–
England and Wales High Court — Chancery Division	EWHC (Ch)*	2002–
England and Wales High Court — Commercial Court	EWHC (Comm)*	2002–
England and Wales High Court — Family Division	EWHC (Fam)*	2002–
England and Wales High Court — Patents Court	EWHC (Pat)*	2002–
England and Wales High Court — Queen's Bench Division	EWHC (QB)*	2002–
England and Wales High Court — Technology and Construction Court	EWHC (TCC)*	2002–
Scotland High Court of Justiciary — Appeal Court	HCJAC	2005–
Scotland High Court of Justiciary — Trial Court	HCJT	2005–
Scotland Court of Session — Inner House	CSIH	2005–
Scotland Court of Session — Outer House	CSOH	2005–
Northern Ireland Court of Appeal	NICA	2001–
Northern Ireland High Court — Chancery Division	NICh	2001–
Northern Ireland High Court — Family Division	NIFam	2001–
Northern Ireland High Court — Queen's Bench Division	NIQB	2001–
Northern Ireland Crown Court	NICC	2001–

* The part of the unique court identifier in parentheses appears *after* the judgment number (for example, '[2010] EWHC 64 (Fam)').

Other unreported UK decisions should be cited in accordance with rule 2.8.2.

Examples

Martin v Her Majesty's Advocate (Scotland) [2010] UKSC 10 (3 March 2010) [5] (Lord Hope DP).

Cavell USA Inc v Seaton Insurance Co [2009] EWCA Civ 1363 (16 December 2009) [24]–[25] (Longmore LJ).

Trajer v Lord Advocate [2008] HCJAC 78 (19 December 2008) [11] (Lord Osborne).

R (Pounder) v HM Coroner for the North and South Districts of Durham and Darlington [2009] EWHC 76 (Admin) (22 January 2009) [40], [51].

Training for Tomorrow (Holdings) Ltd v The Corporate Services Group plc (Unreported, England and Wales High Court, Langley J, 28 February 2000) 7–8.

23.1.6 Identifying Judicial Officers

Rule

Judicial officers' names should be included in accordance with rule 2.9.1 (so may be included after a pinpoint reference where the judicial officer's name is not otherwise apparent). The abbreviations of judicial titles in the table below should be used in addition to or instead of those in rule 2.9.1. However, those titles marked with an asterisk should always appear before the judicial officer's name.

Judicial Title	Abbreviation/Title
Baron of the Exchequer	B
Baroness	Baroness*
Chief Baron	CB
Circuit Judge	Judge*
District Judge	DJ
Deputy President of the Supreme Court of the United Kingdom	DP
Justice of the High Court	J
Lord Chancellor	LC

Lord Chief Justice, Chief Justice of the Common Pleas, Chief Justice of the King's Bench, Chief Justice of the Queen's Bench	CJ
Lord Commissioner	Lord Commissioner*
Lord of Appeal	Lord*
Lord/Lady Justice of Appeal	LJ
Master	Master*
Master of the Rolls	MR
President of the Supreme Court of the United Kingdom, President of the Family Division of the High Court	P
Recorder	Recorder*
Registrar	Registrar*
Justice of the Supreme Court of the United Kingdom	SCJ
Vice-Chancellor	V-C

Examples

Lord Cozens-Hardy MR	Kindersley V-C	Lord Diplock
Lord Hope DP	Lord Brown SCJ	Hoffmann J
James, Baggallay and Bramwell LJJ	Lord Thurlow LC	Arden LJ

23.2 Legislation

Examples	*Patents Act 2004*	(UK)		c 16	, s 5
	Artificers and Apprentices Act 1562,		5 Eliz 1,	c 4	, s 3
Element	Title and Year	Jurisdiction	Regnal Year	Chapter, Act or Measure Number	Pin-point
Rule	23.2.1	23.2.2	23.2.3	23.2.4	23.2.5

23.2.1 Title and Year

Rule

UK statute titles and years should adhere to rules 3.1.1–3.1.2. In particular, the year in which the statute was passed should be included in the title regardless of whether it appears in the original short or long title.

'*The*' should be omitted from the beginning of a statute title.

For pre-19th century statutes that do not include a short title, the short title given in Great Britain, *Chronological Table of the Statutes* (Stationery Office, 2007) or equivalent online publications should be included (instead of the long title appearing in the statute itself).

Examples

Human Rights Act 1998 (UK) c 42, s 6(1).

Government of Wales Act 1998 (UK) c 38. [**Not:** *Government of Wales Act* (UK) …]

Staple Act 1435, 14 Hen 6, c 2. [**Not:** *The Staple Act 1435*, …]

Private (See of Dublin) Act 1705, 4 & 5 Anne, c 13. [**Not:** *An Act for Making Effectual a Grant of Their Late Majesties King William and Queen Mary of the Town and Lands of Seatown to the Archbishoprick of Dublin and for Restoring the Same to the Said See 1705*, …]

Note

Long titles were commonly the only title included in UK statutes until the 19th century. The UK Office of Public Sector Information maintains an online version of the *Chronological Table of the Statutes*, accessible at <http://www.opsi.gov.uk/chron-tables/chron-index>.

23.2.2 Jurisdiction

Rule

The jurisdiction of a statute should be included or omitted according to the table below:

Parliament/Assembly	Jurisdiction
United Kingdom Parliament (from 1 January 1963)	'(UK)' should be included
United Kingdom Parliament (before 1 January 1963)	Omit jurisdiction

United Kingdom Parliament sitting as the Imperial Parliament (before 1 January 1963)	'(Imp)' may be included
Northern Ireland Assembly	'(NI)' should be included
Scottish Parliament	'(Scot)' should be included
National Assembly for Wales	'(Wales)' should be included

Where the jurisdiction is omitted in a citation, the statute title should be followed by a (non-italic) comma.

Examples

Factories Act 1961, 9 & 10 Eliz 2, c 34.

Colonial Laws Validity Act 1865 (Imp) 28 & 29 Vict, c 63.

Appropriation Act 2004 (UK) c 9.

Libraries Act (Northern Ireland) 2008 (NI) c 8.

Dog Fouling (Scotland) Act 2003 (Scot) asp 12.

Learner Travel (Wales) Measure 2008 (Wales) nawm 2.

23.2.3 Regnal Year

Rule

For statutes enacted before 1 January 1963, the regnal year should be included. It should *not* be included for statutes enacted from this date.

Regnal years should appear (using Arabic numerals) as follows:

Year(s) of Reign	Monarch's Name	Regnal Number of Monarch

(for example, '2 & 3 Will 4').

The year of reign is the number of years for which the monarch had reigned when the statute was enacted (for example, '1 Geo' indicates the first year of reign). The monarch's name should be abbreviated according to the table below. The regnal number of the monarch is the sequential number of monarchs of the same name (for example, 'Geo 6' indicates George VI). (A session of Parliament during the first year of reign of George VI would thus be indicated '1 Geo 6'.)

Where there are multiple sessions of Parliament in a given year of reign, the session number should be included after the regnal year for subsequent sessions. 'Session' should be abbreviated 'sess' (for example, '1 Wm & M sess 2').

The following abbreviations for monarchs' names should be used:

Monarch's Name	Abbreviation	Monarch's Name	Abbreviation
Anne	Anne	Charles	Car
Edward	Edw	Elizabeth	Eliz
George	Geo	Henry	Hen
James	Jac	John	John
Mary	Mary	Philip and Mary	Ph & M
Richard	Ric	Victoria	Vict
William	Wm	William and Mary	Wm & M

Examples

Workmen's Compensation Act 1906, 6 Edw 7, c 58.

Statute of Westminster 1931 (Imp) 22 & 23 Geo 5, c 4.

East India Company Act 1784, 24 Geo 3 sess 2, c 2.

Note

Regnal years are listed in Mick Woodley (ed), *Osborn's Concise Law Dictionary* (Sweet and Maxwell, 11th ed, 2009) and Peter Butt (ed), *Butterworths Concise Australian Legal Dictionary* (LexisNexis Butterworths, 3rd ed, 2004).

23.2.4 Chapter, Act or Measure Number

Rule

For statutes enacted by the United Kingdom Parliament after 1 January 1963 or by the Northern Ireland Assembly, the chapter number (abbreviated 'c') should be included after the jurisdiction.

For Scottish statutes, the Act of the Scottish Parliament number (abbreviated 'asp') should be included.

For measures enacted by the National Assembly for Wales, the National Assembly of Wales Measure number (abbreviated 'nawm') should be included.

Examples	*Racial and Religious Hatred Act 2006* (UK) c 1. *Learning and Skills (Wales) Measure 2009* (Wales) nawm 1.

23.2.5 Pinpoint Reference

Rule	Pinpoint references should adhere to rules 3.1.4–3.1.6. However, they should be preceded by a comma. The pinpoint abbreviations in rule 3.1.4 should be used.
Example	*Welfare Reform Act 2007* (UK) c 5, s 4.

23.3 Delegated Legislation

Example	*Undersized Bass Order 2007*	(UK)	SI 2007/809	, O 6.
Element	Title	Jurisdiction	Instrument Number	Pinpoint

Rule

UK subordinate legislation should appear in accordance with rules 3.3–3.4. However:

- the title and year should adhere to rule 23.2.1;
- the jurisdiction should adhere to rule 23.2.2; and
- the instrument number should be included between the jurisdiction and any pinpoint reference.

The instrument number should appear in the form:

[Abbreviation of Instrument Type] [Year]/[Number]

(for example, 'SR 2009/138').

The abbreviation of instrument type should appear according to the table below:

Jurisdiction	Abbreviation
United Kingdom (1890–1947)	SR & O
United Kingdom (1947–)	SI
Northern Ireland	SR
Scottish Parliament	SI

If a pinpoint reference is included, the instrument number should be followed by a comma.

Examples

Fertilisers (Amendment) Regulations 1998 (UK) SI 1998/2024. [**Not**: *The Fertilisers (Amendment) Regulations 1998* …]

Aden Colony Order 1936 (UK) SR & O 1936/1031.

Outer Space Act 1986 (Gibraltar) Order 1996 (UK) SI 1996/1916.

Work at Height Regulations (Northern Ireland) 2005 (NI) SR 2005/279.

Scottish Register of Tartans Fees Order 2009 (Scot) SI 2009/6.

Magistrates' Courts (International Criminal Court) (Forms) Rules 2001 (UK) SI 2001/2600, r 4.

23.4 Government Publications

23.4.1 Parliamentary Debates

Rule

Modern UK parliamentary debates should be cited as follows:

United Kingdom, *Parliamentary Debates*, [Chamber], [Full Date], vol [Volume Number], col [Column Number].

Historical UK parliamentary debates (appearing in *Cobbett's Parliamentary History of England* and equivalent publications) should be cited as follows:

United Kingdom, *Cobbett's Parliamentary History of England*, [Year], vol [Volume Number], col [Column Number].

'United Kingdom' should be replaced with the appropriate polity shown in the volume of parliamentary debates.

In all such citations, a speaker's name may be included in accordance with rule 6.1.1. Speakers' names should adhere to rule 1.14.

Examples

United Kingdom, *Parliamentary Debates*, House of Commons, 16 February 1998, vol 306, col 778 (Jack Straw).

United Kingdom, *Parliamentary Debates*, House of Lords, 3 May 2007, vol 691, col 1158 (Baroness Morgan).

England, *Cobbett's Parliamentary History of England*, 1558, vol 1, col 633.

23.4.2 Command Papers

Rule

Command papers should be cited as follows:

[Author], [*Title*], [Command Paper Series] [Number of Paper] ([Year]) [Pinpoint].

Command papers are numbered in five series as follows:

Date of Publication	Series
1833–69	No 1 – No 4222
1870–99	C 1 – C 9550
1900–18	Cd 1 – Cd 9239
1918–56	Cmd 1 – Cmd 9889
1956–86	Cmnd 1 – Cmnd 9927
1986–	Cm 1 –

Examples

United Kingdom, *Report of the Commissioners of Prisons for the Year 1949*, Cmd 8088 (1950) 16.

Department for Transport (UK), *Low Carbon Transport: A Greener Future — A Carbon Reduction Strategy for Transport*, Cm 7682 (2009) 18.

23.4.3 Parliamentary Papers

Rule

Parliamentary papers should be cited as follows:

[Author], [*Title*], [House] Paper No [Number], Session [Year(s) of Session] ([Year]) [Pinpoint].

	Where a parliamentary paper is presented to both Houses of Parliament, both paper numbers should be included. They should be separated by a comma.
Examples	National Audit Office, *Regenerating the English Coalfields*, House of Commons Paper No 84, Session 2009–10 (2009) 11. Joint Committee on Human Rights, *Prisoner Transfer Treaty with Libya*, House of Lords Paper No 71, House of Commons Paper No 398, Session 2008–09 (2009) 5.

23.5 Other

Rule	For further information on the citation of UK materials, see the latest edition of Derek French, *How to Cite Legal Authorities* (Oxford University Press).

24 United States of America

24.1 Cases

Example	*Bush v Schiavo*,	885	So 2d	321	, 336	(Fla,	2004)
Element	Parties' Names	Volume	Report Series and Series Number	Starting Page	Pin-point	Jurisdiction and Court Name	Year
Rule	24.1.1	24.1.2	24.1.3	24.1.4	24.1.4	24.1.5	24.1.6

24.1.1 Parties' Names

Rule	Parties' names should adhere to rule 2.1. However, they should be followed by a (non-italic) comma. Commas within company names before 'Inc', 'Corp' and other words indicating incorporation should be omitted.
Examples	*Roper v Simmons*, 543 US 551, 567 (Kennedy J) (2005). *Zapatha v Dairy Mart Inc*, 408 NE 2d 1370, 1375 (Mass, 1980). [**Not:** *Zapatha v Dairy Mart, Inc*, …]

24.1.2 Volume

Rule	The volume number of the report series should appear after the case name.
Example	*Brearley School Ltd v Ward*, 94 NE 1001, 1002 (NY, 1911).
Note	US report series are generally organised by volume, not by year (see rule 2.2).

24.1.3 Report Series and Series Number

Rule

The name of the report series should adhere to rule 2.3 (so should be abbreviated using the list of abbreviations in the Appendix). Any series number (for example, '2d', '3d', '4th') should be included as it appears in the Appendix.

For federal decisions, an authorised (or 'official') report series should be cited where available. For state decisions, a regional reporter should be cited where available. Otherwise, the state authorised report series or an unofficial report series should be cited.

For citations of US Supreme Court decisions prior to 1875 (that is, pre-'90 US'), a parallel citation of the early American report series in which the decision appears should be included as follows:

[Volume in US Series] US ([Volume in Early American Reporter] [Name of Early American Reporter]) [Starting Page]
(for example, '17 US (4 Wheat) 316').

Examples

Bush v Gore, 531 US 98 (2000). [**Not:** *Bush v Gore*, 121 S Ct 525 (2000).]

Loveladies Harbor Inc v United States, 28 F 3d 1171 (Fed Cir, 1994).

Stevenson v Shalcross, 205 F 286 (3rd Cir, 1913).

Tracy v Beaufort County Board of Education, 335 F Supp 2d 675 (D SC, 2004).

Freightliner LLC v Whatley Contract Carriers LLC, 932 So 2d 883 (Ala, 2005).

City of Sedan v Church, 29 Kan 190 (1883).

Winchester v Hackley, 6 US (2 Cranch) 342 (1804).

Notes

Authorised reports of the US Supreme Court are published in the 'US' series. Early American reports were reproduced in that series. The pagination of the early American report series is the same as that of the US series.

Authorised reports of the federal United States Courts of Appeals are published in the 'F' series ('F', 'F 2d', 'F 3d', etc).

Authorised reports of the federal United States District Courts (federal courts of first instance) are published in the 'F Supp' series ('F Supp', 'F Supp 2d', etc).

Regional reporters, which are published by West, are the various series of the *Atlantic Reporter* (abbreviated 'A'), the *North Eastern Reporter* (abbreviated 'NE'), the *North Western Reporter* (abbreviated 'NW'), the *Pacific Reporter* (abbreviated 'P'), the *South Eastern Reporter* (abbreviated 'SE'), the *Southern Reporter* (abbreviated 'So') and the *South Western Reporter* (abbreviated 'SW').

State authorised report series usually have as their abbreviation the abbreviation of their state listed in rule 24.1.5.2.

24.1.4 Starting Page and Pinpoint Reference

Rule

The first page of the case should be included after the report series abbreviation.

Pinpoint references should adhere to rule 2.5. In particular:

- a comma should precede any pinpoint reference;
- where the pinpoint reference is to the first page of the case, the page number should be repeated; and
- for reported cases, pinpoint references should be to page numbers and *may* include paragraph references *in addition*.

Examples

Kansas v Hendricks, 521 US 346, 356–7 (1996).

State v Aponte, 738 A 2d 117, 134 (McDonald J) (Conn, 1999).

24.1.5 Jurisdiction and Court Name

Rule

Where an abbreviated form of the jurisdiction and/or the abbreviated name of the court must be included (in accordance with rules 24.1.5.1–24.1.5.2), they should appear in parentheses after the starting page and any pinpoint reference.

If both the jurisdiction and the court name are included, they should not be separated by any punctuation. A comma should separate the jurisdiction and/or court name from the year.

Examples

Garshman Co Ltd v General Electric Co, 176 F 3d 1 (1st Cir, 1999).

McDonald v Bauman, 433 P 2d 437 (Kan, 1967).

24.1.5.1 Federal Courts

Rule

A citation of a decision of the US Supreme Court should not include the name of the court.

The Courts of Appeals should be referred to by their numbered circuit ('1st Cir', '2nd Cir', etc). The United States Court of Appeals for the District of Columbia Circuit should be abbreviated 'DC Cir'. The United States Court of Appeals for the Federal Circuit should be abbreviated 'Fed Cir'.

For district court cases, an abbreviated form of the district (abbreviated 'D'), but not the division, should be included. Each US state is either an entire federal district, abbreviated:

D [State Abbreviation]
(for example, 'D Del')

or divided into multiple districts, abbreviated:

[Abbreviation of District Type] D [State Abbreviation]
(for example, 'CD Cal').

Common abbreviations of district types are:

District Type	Abbreviation	District Type	Abbreviation
Northern District	ND	Western District	WD
Southern District	SD	Central District	CD
Eastern District	ED	Middle District	MD

State names should be abbreviated according to rule 24.1.5.2.

The names of other federal courts should be included using their customary abbreviation (which is usually indicated on the decision). Full stops in abbreviations should be omitted (in accordance with rule 1.6.1).

Examples

Tinker v Des Moines Independent Community School District, 393 US 503 (1969). [**Not:** … (Sup Ct, 1969).]

SunTrust Bank v Houghton Mifflin Co, 268 F 3d 1257 (11th Cir, 2001).

Air Line Pilots Association v Federal Express Corporation, 402 F 3d 1245, 1248 (DC Cir, 2005).

Abbott v Moore Business Forms Inc, 439 F Supp 643 (D NH, 1977).

Huggins v Fulton, 505 F Supp 7 (MD Tenn, 1980).

Sheppard v Union Pacific Railroad Co, 357 F Supp 2d 1180 (ED Mo, 2005). [**Not:** … (ED Mo ED, 2005) **nor** (ED Mo Eastern Division, 2005).]

Note

The US Supreme Court sits at the apex of the federal court structure. Circuit courts are intermediate appellate courts. Each 'circuit' contains a number of 'districts'. District courts are federal courts of first instance. Districts are sometimes divided into 'divisions', the abbreviation of which appears after the district abbreviation (for example, 'CD Cal ED' is 'Central District of California Eastern Division'). It is not necessary to include the division in a citation.

24.1.5.2 State Courts

Rule

An abbreviated form of the jurisdiction (that is, the name of the state) followed by the conventional abbreviated name of the court ('Sup Ct', 'Ct App', etc) should be included. However:

- the jurisdiction should *not* be included if it is apparent from the title of the report series; and
- the name of the court should *not* be included if it is the highest court in the state.

(Neither the jurisdiction nor the name of the court should therefore be included if the jurisdiction is apparent from the report series and the court is the highest court in the state.)

The abbreviations for US states (that is, the jurisdiction) and the name of the highest court in each state are:

State	Highest Court	Abbreviation
Alabama	Supreme Court	Ala
Alaska	Supreme Court	Alaska

Arizona	Supreme Court	Ariz
Arkansas	Supreme Court	Ark
California	Supreme Court	Cal
Colorado	Supreme Court	Colo
Connecticut	Supreme Court	Conn
Delaware	Supreme Court	Del
Florida	Supreme Court	Fla
Georgia	Supreme Court	Ga
Hawaii	Supreme Court	Haw
Idaho	Supreme Court	Idaho
Illinois	Supreme Court	Ill
Indiana	Supreme Court	Ind
Iowa	Supreme Court	Iowa
Kansas	Supreme Court	Kan
Kentucky	Supreme Court	Ky
Louisiana	Supreme Court	La
Maine	Supreme Judicial Court	Me
Maryland	Court of Appeals	Md
Massachusetts	Supreme Judicial Court	Mass
Michigan	Supreme Court	Mich
Minnesota	Supreme Court	Minn
Mississippi	Supreme Court	Miss
Missouri	Supreme Court	Mo
Montana	Supreme Court	Mont
Nebraska	Supreme Court	Neb
Nevada	Supreme Court	Nev
New Hampshire	Supreme Court	NH
New Jersey	Supreme Court	NJ
New Mexico	Supreme Court	NM
New York	Court of Appeals	NY
North Carolina	Supreme Court	NC
North Dakota	Supreme Court	ND
Ohio	Supreme Court	Ohio
Oklahoma	Supreme Court	Okla
Oregon	Supreme Court	Or
Pennsylvania	Supreme Court	Pa
Rhode Island	Supreme Court	RI

South Carolina	Supreme Court	SC
South Dakota	Supreme Court	SD
Tennessee	Supreme Court	Tenn
Texas	Supreme Court	Tex
Utah	Supreme Court	Utah
Vermont	Supreme Court	Vt
Virginia	Supreme Court	Va
Washington	Supreme Court	Wash
West Virginia	Supreme Court of Appeals	W Va
Wisconsin	Supreme Court	Wis
Wyoming	Supreme Court	Wyo

Examples

Brogdon v State, 467 SE 2d 598 (Ga Ct App, 1996).

Poire v CL Peck/Jones Brothers Construction Corporation Inc, 46 Cal Rptr 2d 631 (Ct App, 1995).

Burr v Maclay Rancho Water Co, 98 P 260 (Cal, 1908).

24.1.6 Year

Rule

The year of the decision should appear after the jurisdiction and court name in the parentheses.

If neither the jurisdiction nor the court name is included, the year should appear in parentheses after the starting page or any pinpoint reference.

Examples

People v Eaves, 512 NW 2d 1 (Mich Ct App, 1994).

Felder v Casey, 487 US 131, 142 (Brennan J) (1987).

24.1.7 Unreported Cases

Rule

Unreported US cases should be cited as follows:

[*Parties' Names*] ([Jurisdiction and Court/District], [Docket or Reference No], [Full Date]) slip op [Pinpoint].

	The full docket or reference number, including any letters and punctuation, should be included as it appears in the decision. However, punctuation should adhere to rule 1.6.1 (so full stops should not be used in abbreviations). For state courts, both the abbreviated jurisdiction and court name should be included (using the abbreviations in rule 24.1.5.2). For federal courts, the abbreviated form of the circuit or district should be included (in accordance with rule 24.1.5.1). The words 'slip op' (indicating a 'slip opinion') should precede pinpoint references. If the judgment does not begin on the first page of the slip opinion, a starting page should be included before the pinpoint reference, followed by a comma. Pinpoint references should generally be to page numbers (and should adhere to rules 1.1.5–1.1.6). Paragraph numbers *may* be included *in addition* to page numbers.
Examples	*Red Hat Inc v The SCO Group Inc* (D Del, Civ No 03-772-SLR, 6 April 2004). *Torres v Oklahoma* (Okla Ct Crim App, No PCD-04-442, 13 May 2004) slip op 7. *Charlesworth v Mack* (1st Cir, No 90-567, 19 January 1991) slip op 3458, 3464.
Note	A 'slip opinion' is a judgment of a court as handed down. Sometimes the pagination across slip opinions for a particular court is continuous for a period, in which case a starting page should be included.

24.1.8 Identifying Judges

Rule	Judges' names should be included in accordance with rule 2.9 (so should appear immediately after a pinpoint reference in parentheses). For judges in federal courts, 'Judge', 'Assistant Justice' and 'Circuit Judge' are all abbreviated 'J' (which appears after the judge's name).
Examples	*Re Gault*, 387 US 1, 13–14, 27–8 (Fortas J) (1967). *City of Birmingham v Citigroup Inc* (ND Ala, No CV-09-BE-467-S, 19 August 2009) slip op 3 (Bowdre J).

24.2 Legislation: Code

Examples	*Trade Act of 2002*,	19	USC	§§ 3803–5		(2006)
	An Act Relating to Tobacco Master Settlement Agreement Compliance,		Ky Rev Stat Ann	§ 15.300	(West	2009)
Element	Statute Title	Title, Chapter or Volume Number	Abbreviated Code Name	Pinpoint	Publisher's Name	Year of Code and Supplement
Rule	24.2.1	24.2.2	24.2.3	24.2.4	24.2.5	24.2.6

Note

Both federal and state laws in the US are compiled into codes (collections of statute arranged according to subject matter). In accordance with rule 24.3, codes should generally be cited in preference to session laws (statutes as enacted).

24.2.1 Statute Title and Original Pinpoint

Rule

Generally, the title of a statute should not be included if the statute is reported in a code. The title (as it appeared in the session laws) may be included where:

- the statute is usually cited with its title;
- the title would assist in identifying the statute; or
- the title is otherwise important.

Where a statute title is included, it should be italicised and followed by a (non-italic) comma. Where the title of the statute includes a year, this should be retained in the title. '*The*' should be omitted from the beginning of a statute title.

	If a statute title is included, an original pinpoint (that is, the title, chapter, volume or section number cited in the session laws) may also be included after the statute name. If an original pinpoint is included, there should be no comma between the statute title and the original pinpoint, and the original pinpoint should be followed by a comma.
Examples	35 USC § 102. *Federal Deposit Insurance Act*, 12 USC §§ 1811–35a (2006). *Securities Exchange Act of 1934*, 15 USC §§ 78a–78jj (1934). *National Environmental Policy Act of 1969* § 102, 42 USC § 4332 (2000).

24.2.2 Title, Chapter or Volume Number in Code

Rule	If the code is divided into titles, chapters, volumes, etc, that contain non-consecutively numbered sections, paragraphs, articles, etc, the number of the title, chapter, volume, etc, should be included. Where the numbering of sections, articles, paragraphs, etc, across an entire code is continuous, the title, chapter, volume, etc, number should be omitted. For the federal USC and unofficial federal codes, the title number should precede the abbreviated code name (for example, '14 USC'). For state codes, the title, chapter, volume, etc, number should appear as it does in the code cited. Generally, it appears after the abbreviated code name as part of a decimal pinpoint reference (for example, '§ 63.155' refers to section 155 within chapter 63). However, it may also appear before the abbreviated code name (for example, '1 Pa Con Stat § 1991' refers to section 1991 within title 1).
Examples	5 USC § 6 (1958). Wis Stat § 944.21(2)(c) (2005). [**Not**: 944 Wis Stat § 21(2)(c) (2005).] Mass Gen Laws ch 10 § 64 (2006). 735 Ill Comp Stat 5/2-201 (2009). 11 Del Code Ann § 464 (2010).

Notes

The federal *United States Code* (abbreviated 'USC') is divided into titles. It is necessary to indicate the title number (before the abbreviated code name) when citing the USC, because the section numbers are non-consecutively numbered (that is, they begin again in each title). For example, 42 USC and 36 USC each contain a (different) § 3.

Title, chapter, volume, etc, numbers in state codes are generally included *after* the abbreviated code name as part of the pinpoint reference where the code is a subject matter code (dealing with only one area of law) or is organised by, for example, title, but contains chapters, volumes or sections that are numbered consecutively throughout the code.

24.2.3 Abbreviated Code Name

Rule

An abbreviation of the name of the code should be included.

An official code, such as the *United States Code* (abbreviated 'USC'), should be cited where available. Where an official code is not available, an unofficial code, such as the *United States Code Annotated* (abbreviated 'USCA') or the *United States Code Service* (abbreviated 'USCS') should be cited.

The name of the code should be abbreviated according to the commonly used abbreviation for that code. The abbreviations of some official or preferred codes are in the table below. (Where a publisher's, editor's or compiler's name appears in the table, it should be included before the year in accordance with rule 24.2.5.)

Jurisdiction	Abbreviated Code Name	Publisher/Editor/ Compiler
Federal	USC	
Alabama	Ala Code	
Alaska	Alaska Stat	
Arizona	Ariz Rev Stat Ann	
Arkansas	Ark Code Ann	
California	Cal [Subject] Code	West
	Cal [Subject] Code	Deering
Colorado	Colo Rev Stat	

Connecticut	Conn Gen Stat	
Delaware	Del Code Ann	
District of Columbia	DC Code	
Florida	Fla Stat	
Georgia	Ga Code Ann	
Hawaii	Haw Rev Stat	
Idaho	Idaho Code Ann	
Illinois	Ill Comp Stat	
Indiana	Ind Code	
Iowa	Iowa Code	
Kansas	Kan Stat Ann	
Kentucky	Ky Rev Stat Ann	West
	Ky Rev Stat Ann	LexisNexis
Louisiana	La Rev Stat Ann	
Maine	Me Rev Stat Ann	
Maryland	Md Code Ann [Subject]	LexisNexis
	Md Code Ann [Subject]	West
Massachusetts	Mass Gen Laws	
Michigan	Mich Comp Laws	
Minnesota	Minn Stat	
Mississippi	Miss Code Ann	
Missouri	Mo Rev Stat	
Montana	Mont Code Ann	
Nebraska	Neb Rev Stat	
Nevada	Nev Rev Stat	
New Hampshire	NH Rev Stat Ann	
New Jersey	NJ Stat Ann	West
New Mexico	NM Stat	
New York	NY [Subject] Law	McKinney
	NY [Subject] Law	Consol
	NY [Subject] Law	Gould
North Carolina	NC Gen Stat	
North Dakota	ND Cent Code	
Ohio	Ohio Rev Code Ann	LexisNexis
	Ohio Rev Code Ann	West
Oklahoma	Okla Stat	
Oregon	Or Rev Stat	

Pennsylvania	Pa Cons Stat	
Rhode Island	RI Gen Laws	
South Carolina	SC Code Ann	
South Dakota	SD Codified Laws	
Tennessee	Tenn Code Ann	
Texas	Tex Code Ann	
Utah	Utah Code Ann	
Vermont	Vt Stat Ann	
Virginia	Va Code Ann	
Washington	Wash Rev Code	
West Virginia	W Va Code	
Wisconsin	Wis Stat	
Wyoming	Wyo Stat Ann	

When citing the federal *Internal Revenue Code*, '26 USC' may be replaced with 'IRC'.

For subject matter codes, the subject area should be included as it appears (and using any abbreviation) in the code itself.

Examples

7 USC § 852 (2006).

40 USCA § 6134 (2010).

Haw Rev Stat § 281-32.

Ga Code Ann § 3-2-11 (West 2009).

IRC § 25A(a) (2006).

Cal Evid Code § 312 (Deering 2008).

Note

An official code is one published by a government or by a statutorily authorised publisher.

24.2.4 Pinpoint Reference

Rule

Any section, chapter, article, paragraph or other pinpoint reference should be included after the abbreviated code name.

Pinpoint references should adhere to rule 3.1.4. However, the following abbreviations should be used in addition to and instead of the abbreviations in rule 3.1.4:

Designation	Abbreviation	Plural	Abbreviation
Amendment	amend	Amendments	amends
Section	§	Sections	§§
Title	tit	Titles	tits

When citing an entire statute within a code, the span of sections (or, for state codes, the chapter, volume, etc) containing the statute should be included.

Examples

19 USC § 58 (1970).

Alaska Stat §§ 4.06.010–4.06.110 (2009).

Or Rev Stat ch 153 (2007).

Occupational Safety and Health Act of 1970, 29 USC §§ 651–78 (2000).

Note

In state codes, pinpoint references are commonly decimal, with full stops (for example, '§ 4.4.2'), hyphens (for example, '§ 722-124') or colons (for example, '§ 18:203') between the component numbers making up the pinpoint.

24.2.5 Publisher's Name

Rule

When citing an unofficial state code, the name of the publisher, editor or compiler of the code should appear before the year (and any supplement information) in parentheses. In addition, when citing the codes listed in the table in rule 24.2.3, the publisher's name should be included if it appears in the table.

There should be no punctuation between the publisher's name and the year.

Examples

W Va Code Ann §19-11-8 (LexisNexis 2008).

NJ Stat Ann § 6:1-2 (West 2009).

24.2.6 Year of Code and Supplement

Rule

The year in which the version of the code cited was published (not necessarily the year of enactment of the relevant provision) should appear in parentheses.

When referring to electronic versions of codes, the year should be that in which the provision cited was last updated (on that electronic service).

When referring to printed versions of codes, the year should be (in order of preference):

- the year appearing on the spine of the volume;
- the year appearing on the title page of the volume; or
- the copyright year in the publication details of the volume.

If a statute appears wholly in a supplement to a bound volume, the year in which the supplement was published should be cited and should be preceded by 'Supp' (for example, '(Supp 1991)'). If the statute appears partly in a bound volume and partly in a supplement (that is, both are needed to access the text of the statute), the years of publication of both should be included in the form:

(Year of Code & Supp Year of Supplement)
(for example, '(1994 & Supp 1999)').

In accordance with rule 24.2.5, where a publisher's name is included, the year (and any supplement) should appear after the publisher's name and should not be preceded by any punctuation.

Examples

14 USCA § 706 (2010).

Iowa Code § 331.101 (2008).

14 USC § 663 (Supp 2009).

21 USC §§ 331–4 (2006 & Supp 2009).

Ind Code Ann § 1-2-4-1 (West 2000).

Note	A new version of the USC is published every six years, and supplements are published at the end of each intervening year. Unofficial codes (such as the USCS and USCA) are updated more frequently.

24.3 Legislation: Session Laws

Examples	*Freedom to Display the American Flag Act of 2005*,	Pub L No 109-243,	§ 4,	120	Stat	572, 573	(2006)
	An Act to Amend the Indiana Code concerning Pensions,	Pub L No 5-2008,	§ 2,	2008	Ind Acts	889, 890	
Element	Statute Title	Public Law, Private Law or Chapter Number	Original Pinpoint	Volume or Year	Abbre-viated Session Laws Name	Session Laws Starting Page and Pinpoint	Year
Rule	24.3.1	24.3.2	24.3.3	24.3.4	24.3.5	24.3.6	24.3.7

Notes

Session laws are a collection of all statutes passed by a particular federal or state legislature in a legislative session. They are arranged in order of enactment.

Generally, a code should be cited in preference to a session law. However, a session law should be cited where:

- the statute has not yet been included in any official or unofficial code;
- the statute is no longer in force and not included in the latest version of the code;

- the statute makes changes to many scattered sections of a code;
- it is important to refer to the enactment, amendment or repeal of a provision or statute; or
- a private law is cited.

24.3.1 Statute Title

Rule

The title of the statute (or a title by which the statute is commonly known) should be included. The statute title should adhere to rule 24.2.1. In particular:

- the statute title should be italicised and followed by a (non-italic) comma; and
- a year that appears in the title of the statute should be included.

If no short title is included and no commonly used short title exists, the statute should be identified by the date of enactment or, if that is unavailable, by the date on which the statute came into force. The long title of the statute should *not* be used. Where a statute is identified in this manner, its title should *not* be italicised and should appear in the form:

Act of [Full Date]
(for example, 'Act of 3 March 1925').

Examples

Detainee Treatment Act of 2005, Pub L No 109-148, 119 Stat 2739.

Act of 29 January 1937, Pub Law No 75-3, 50 Stat 5. [**Not:** *An Act to Provide for Loans to Farmers for Crop Production and Harvesting during the Year 1937, and for Other Purposes* …]

24.3.2 Public Law, Private Law or Chapter Number

Rule

The public law number (abbreviated 'Pub L No'), private law number (abbreviated 'Priv L No') or chapter number (abbreviated 'ch') of the statute should be included after the statute title and should be followed by a comma.

Examples	*1997 Emergency Supplemental Appropriations Act for Recovery from Natural Disasters, and for Overseas Peacekeeping Efforts, Including Those in Bosnia*, Pub L No 105-18, 111 Stat 158. *Railroad Right-of-Way Conveyance Validation Act of 2004*, Priv L No 108-2, 118 Stat 4025. Act of 7 June 1897, ch 4, arts 2–5, 30 Stat 96, 96–7. [**Not:** *An Act to Adopt Regulations for Preventing Collisions upon Certain Harbors, Rivers, and Inland Waters of the United States*, …]
Notes	From the 60th US Congress (that is, from '35 Stat'), statutes were given public or private law numbers that continued across all sessions of that Congress. These numbers comprise the number of the Congress (without its ordinal letters) followed by the sequential number of the particular law (for example, 'Pub L No 108-37' indicates the 37th Public Law passed by the 108th Congress). Even if the public or private law number is not present on the statute in this form, it should be included in this manner in a citation. For statutes passed before the 60th Congress, the chapter number should be included. The year and the chapter number are sufficient to identify the law because the chapter number is the sequential number of a law (or resolution) as passed, restarting each year.

24.3.3 Original Pinpoint Reference

Rule	Any pinpoint reference should be followed by a comma. Pinpoint references should adhere to rule 24.2.4.
Examples	*Voting Rights Act of 1965*, Pub L No 89-110, § 2, 79 Stat 437, 437. *An Act to Incorporate the Girl Scouts of the United States of America, and for Other Purposes*, Pub L No 81-460, §§ 2–4, 64 Stat 22, 22–3 (1950).

24.3.4 Volume or Year

Rule

The volume number of the session laws should be included after the public law number, private law number or chapter number or after any pinpoint reference to the original statute.

For state session laws, where there is no volume number, the year of the volume should be included instead.

Examples

Unborn Victims of Violence Act of 2004, Pub L No 108-212, 118 Stat 568.

School Bus Enhanced Safety Inspection Act, ch 5, 1999 NJ Laws 23.

24.3.5 Abbreviated Name

Rule

An abbreviated form of the name of the session laws should be included.

The abbreviations of the official session laws for each jurisdiction are as follows:

Jurisdiction	Abbreviated Session Laws Name
Federal	Stat
Alabama	Ala Laws
Alaska	Alaska Sess Laws
Arizona	Ariz Sess Laws
Arkansas	Ark Acts
California	Cal Stat
Colorado	Colo Sess Laws
Connecticut	Conn Acts
Delaware	Del Laws
District of Columbia	Stat
Florida	Fla Laws
Georgia	Ga Laws
Hawaii	Haw Sess Laws
Idaho	Idaho Sess Laws
Illinois	Ill Laws
Indiana	Ind Acts
Iowa	Iowa Acts

Kansas	Kan Sess Laws
Kentucky	Ky Acts
Louisiana	La Acts
Maine	Me Laws
Maryland	Md Laws
Massachusetts	Mass Acts
Michigan	Mich Pub Acts
Minnesota	Minn Laws
Mississippi	Miss Laws
Missouri	Mo Laws
Montana	Mont Laws
Nebraska	Neb Laws
Nevada	Nev Stat
New Hampshire	NH Laws
New Jersey	NJ Laws
New Mexico	NM Laws
New York	NY Laws
North Carolina	NC Sess Laws
North Dakota	ND Laws
Ohio	Ohio Laws
Oklahoma	Okla Sess Laws
Oregon	Or Laws
Pennsylvania	Pa Laws
Rhode Island	RI Pub Laws
South Carolina	SC Acts
South Dakota	SD Sess Laws
Tennessee	Tenn Pub Acts
	Tenn Priv Acts
Texas	Tex Gen Laws
Utah	Utah Laws
Vermont	Vt Acts & Resolves
Virginia	Va Acts
Washington	Wash Sess Laws
West Virginia	W Va Acts
Wisconsin	Wis Sess Laws
Wyoming	Wyo Sess Laws

Where an unofficial session laws is cited, the name of the publisher, editor or compiler of the code should be included before the year in parentheses after the starting page or any pinpoint reference.

Examples

Telemarketing Fraud Prevention Act of 1998, Pub L No 105-184, 112 Stat 520.

Act of 10 April 1862, c 173, § 7, 1862 NY Stat 343, 345.

An Act to Amend Section 3303 of the Government Code, Relating to Public Safety Officers, c 1259, § 1, 1994 Cal Legis Serv 6486, 6486–7 (West).

24.3.6 Starting Page and Pinpoint Reference

Rule

The page of the session laws on which the statute begins should be included after the abbreviated name of the session laws.

Where a pinpoint reference to the original statute is included in accordance with rule 24.3.3, the page(s) on which the pinpoint appears in the session laws volume should be included after the starting page and should be preceded by a comma.

Examples

Paperwork Reduction Act of 1980, Pub L No 96-511, 94 Stat 2812.

Animal Disease Risk Assessment, Prevention, and Control Act of 2001, Pub L No 107-9, §§ 2–3, 115 Stat 11, 11–16. [**Not:** … 115 Stat 11.]

24.3.7 Year

Rule

The year in which the statute was enacted (or, if that information is unavailable, the year in which the statute came into force) should appear in parentheses after the session laws starting page (or any pinpoints). However, the year should not be included where:

- the same year is part of the title of the statute; or
- for state laws, the year of the session laws volume is included (in accordance with rule 24.3.4).

Examples	*Smithsonian Facilities Authorization Act*, Pub L No 108-72, §§ 4–5, 117 Stat 888, 889 (2003). *Child Citizenship Act of 2000*, Pub L No 106-395, tit II, 114 Stat 1631, 1633–6. [**Not:** … 114 Stat 1631, 1633–6 (2000).] *An Act to Amend the Indiana Code concerning Corrections*, Pub L No 102-2002, 2002 Ind Acts 1597. [**Not:** 2002 Inc Acts 1597 (2002).]

24.3.8 Legislative History: Amendments, Repeals and Insertions

Rule	Where a session law inserts, repeals or amends a provision of a code (or another session law), this may be indicated in accordance with rule 3.8.
Examples	*Sarbanes-Oxley Act of 2002*, Pub L No 107-204, § 201, 116 Stat 745, 771 (2002), inserting 15 USC § 78j-1(g) (2006). 42 USC § 2473(c)(2)(A), as amended by *NASA Flexibility Act of 2004*, Pub L 108-201, § 2(a), 118 Stat 461, 461.

24.4 Constitutions

Rule	The titles of US federal and state constitutions should be italicised. Pinpoint references should adhere to rule 24.2.4.
Examples	*United States Constitution* art IV § 3. *United States Constitution* amend XXI. *Texas Constitution* art 1 § 8.

24.5 Delegated Legislation

24.5.1 Federal

Rule

Where subordinate legislation appears in the *Code of Federal Regulations* (abbreviated 'CFR'), it should be cited as follows:

[*Title of Regulation*], [Title] CFR [Pinpoint] ([Year]).

The title of the regulation may (but need not) be included. A 'part' in the CFR is designated '§'. Paragraphs and sections are separated from the part number by a decimal point (for example, '§ 101.2' refers to part 101 section 2). The year should be that of the CFR consulted (not necessarily the year of promulgation of the regulation).

Where subordinate legislation does not appear in the CFR (or there is good reason to cite the subordinate legislation as gazetted), it should be cited in the *Federal Register* (abbreviated 'Fed Reg') as follows:

[*Title of Regulation*], [Volume] Fed Reg [Starting Page], [Pinpoint] ([Full Date]).

Examples

8 CFR § 101.1 (1986).

Whaling Provisions — Consolidation and Revision of Regulations — Collection-of-Information Approval, 50 CFR § 230 (2009).

Enhancing Airline Passenger Protections, 74 Fed Reg 68 983, 68 985 (30 December 2009).

Note

US federal delegated legislation is initially gazetted in the Fed Reg. Important pieces of delegated legislation are then compiled into the CFR. For the same reasons that a session law may be cited instead of a code (see rule 24.3), it may be appropriate to cite the Fed Reg even though a piece of delegated legislation appears in the CFR.

24.5.2 State

Rule

Where state subordinate legislation appears in a code of regulation, this should be cited where available. Otherwise, subordinate legislation should be cited as gazetted. Citations should appear in

	accordance with rule 24.5.1. However, the usual abbreviation of the state code or gazette should replace 'CFR' or 'Fed Reg' as appropriate.
Examples	220 Ind Admin Code 1.1-2-2 (2007). *Submetering of Natural Gas Service by General Motors Corporation*, 30 NY Reg 18 (29 May 2008).
Note	State codes of regulation are often referred to as 'administrative codes' (usually abbreviated 'Admin Code').

24.6 Federal Congressional Materials

24.6.1 Debates

Rule

Congressional debates should be cited as follows:

[Volume] *Congressional Record* [Pinpoint] ([Year]).

Where it is not otherwise apparent, the chamber ('Senate' or 'House of Representatives') may be included after the year in the parentheses, preceded by a comma.

Where only a Daily Edition of the *Congressional Record* is available, it should be cited as follows:

[Volume] *Congressional Record* [Pinpoint] (daily ed, [Full Date]).

Pinpoint references to the Daily Edition should include 'H' for House of Representatives and 'S' for Senate, and should appear in the form:

[S/H][Page Number]
(for example, 'H1987').

In citations of the bound *Congressional Record* and the Daily Edition, the speaker's name may be included between the pinpoint and the year. It should appear in parentheses and adhere to rule 6.1.1 (so the speaker's first and last names should be included and positions should only be included after the name if they are relevant).

Examples

1 *Congressional Record* 10 (James Garfield) (1874, House of Representatives).

156 *Congressional Record* H148 (Ann Kirkpatrick) (daily ed, 19 January 2010).

24.6.2 Bills and Resolutions

Rule

Congressional Bills should be cited as follows:

[Bill Title], [Abbreviated Name of Chamber] [Number of Bill], [Ordinal Number of Congress] Congress ([Year]).

The House of Representatives should be abbreviated 'HR', and the Senate should be abbreviated 'S'.

Congressional resolutions should be cited as follows:

[Resolution Title], [Abbreviated Type of Resolution] Res [Resolution Number], [Ordinal Number of Congress] Congress ([Year]).

The resolution title may be omitted. The following abbreviations should be used for the relevant type of resolution:

Type of Resolution	Abbreviation
House Resolution	HR Res
Senate Resolution	S Res
House Concurrent Resolution	HR Con Res
Senate Concurrent Resolution	S Con Res
House Joint Resolution	HRJ Res
Senate Joint Resolution	SJ Res
Senate Executive Resolution	S Exec Res

Where congressional resolutions are not easily accessible, a citation of *Statutes at Large* (in accordance with rules 24.3.4–24.3.6) or the *Congressional Record* (in accordance with rule 24.6.1) may be included between the number of the Congress and the year. If a citation of the Daily Edition of the *Congressional Record* is included, the year should be omitted (but the full date included in accordance with rule 24.6.1).

Examples

Guam Commonwealth Act, HR 100, 105th Congress (1997).

Resolution Condemning the Taliban Regime and Supporting a Broad Based Government in Afghanistan, H Con Res 336, 105th Congress (1998).

Authorization for Use of Military Force against Iraq: Resolution of 2002, HRJ Res 114, 107th Congress (2002).

Joint Resolution Providing for the Acquisition of Certain Lands in the State of California, HRJ Res 10, 56th Congress, 31 Stat 711 (1900).

HR Res 1010, 111th Congress, 156 *Congressional Record* H139 (daily ed, 13 January 2010).

Note

US Bills are referred to as 'Acts' before and after enactment.

24.7 Restatements

Rule

Restatements of law published by the American Law Institute should be cited as books authored by the Institute (in accordance with chapter 5). However, where the restatement is a subsequent restatement (that is, where the restatement is not the first restatement), the title should appear as follows:

Restatement (*Ordinal Number of Restatement in Words* *) of* *Subject Area*

(for example, '*Restatement (Third) of Trusts*').

Pinpoint references should always include a section number. References to comments, reporter's notes and other subdivisions of the sections should be included after the section number. The word 'comment' should be abbreviated 'cmt' (and 'comments' should be abbreviated 'cmts').

Examples

American Law Institute, *Restatement (Second) of Contracts* (1981) § 176.

American Law Institute, *Restatement (Third) of the Foreign Relations Law of the United States* (1987) § 465 cmt (a).

Note

The restatements are effectively codifications of US common law principles by groups of experts. They are commissioned by the American Law Institute and generally regarded as authoritative.

24.8 Other

Rule

For further information on the citation of United States materials, see the latest edition of *The Bluebook: A Uniform System of Citation*.

25 Other Foreign Domestic Materials

Note

This chapter contains general guidelines for the citation of foreign legal materials (including non-English language materials) that are not otherwise covered in this *Guide*.

Where specific rules for a jurisdiction are included in the preceding chapters of this Part, those rules should be used. Where foreign legal materials are similar to materials in jurisdictions for which specific chapters are included, the rules for the similar jurisdiction should be adapted as appropriate.

25.1 Translations of Legislation and Decisions

25.1.1 Non-English Primary Materials Translated by Author

Rule

Where the author of a document (or another person on behalf of the author) translates non-English primary materials:

- translations of elements in citations should appear in square brackets, following the translated element (for example, '*Undang-Undang Dasar Republik Indonesia 1945* [Constitution of the Republic of Indonesia 1945]'); and
- translations of titles should not be italicised, even where the titles themselves are.

Where the author has made the translation, this should be indicated at the end of the citation in the appropriate footnote by including '[author's trans]'.

Where another person has translated materials on behalf of the author, this should be indicated at the end of the citation in the appropriate footnote as follows:

[Translator's Name trans]

Alternatively, a statement that all translations are by the author (or another person on behalf of the author) should be included in the text, in the author's note or in the first footnote containing a translation. In that case, it is not necessary to indicate the translator in each footnote.

Examples

The legislation provides that a person 'born in the Kingdom or who arrived before the age of 12 and who has regularly and principally resided there since'[7] may not be deported.

---

7 *Loi du 15 décembre 1980 sur l'accès au territoire, le séjour, l'établissement et l'éloignement des étrangers* [Law of 15 December 1980 on the Access to the Territory, the Stay, the Establishment and the Removal of Foreigners] (Belgium) art 21(1) [Nawaar Hassan trans].

8 *Code civil* [Civil Code] (France) art 147 [author's trans].

---

* All translations are by the author, except where otherwise indicated.

1 *Urheberrechtsgesetz* [Copyright Law] (Switzerland) 9 October 1992, SR 231, art 29(2)(a).

25.1.2 Foreign Primary Materials Consulted in English (Published Translations)

Rule

Where a published translation of legislative materials or judicial decisions is cited, a citation to the primary source should be included in English (and in accordance with rules 25.2–25.3), followed by a citation to the published translation in square brackets.

The published translation should be cited in accordance with the applicable rules of this *Guide* for the type of source (for example, in accordance with chapters 4 or 5 or rule 6.15). However:

- the name of the author or editor of the published translation should be followed by 'trans'; and

- where the published translation is a book, the citation should adhere to rules 5.1–5.5 (and *not* the form prescribed by rule 5.6 for translations of books).

Any year included in the citation of the published translation should be the year of publication of the translation (not the year of enactment of the foreign law or of a foreign decision).

If a pinpoint reference is included in the citation of the primary source, the citation of the published translation should include the corresponding pinpoint reference (that is, the page on which the relevant provision appears in the translation) where available. If the translation begins on a certain page of the published translation, a starting page and pinpoint (as appropriate) should be included.

Examples

Civil Code (France) [John H Crabb trans, *The French Civil Code* (Rothman, revised ed, 1995)].

Act on Special Measures concerning the Handling of Legal Services by Foreign Lawyers (Japan) Act No 66 of 1986 [Ministry of Justice (Japan) trans, *English Translation of Act on Special Measures concerning the Handling of Legal Services by Foreign Lawyers* (2008) <http://www.cas.go.jp/jp/seisaku/hourei/data/hls.pdf>].

Criminal Code (People's Republic of China) Fifth People's Congress, 1 July 1979, art 2 [Chin Kim trans, *The Criminal Code of the People's Republic of China* (Sweet and Maxwell, 1982) 25].

Jand'heur I, French Court of Cassation, 21 February 1927 [Edward A Tomlinson trans, 'Tort Liability in France for the Act of Things: A Study of Judicial Lawmaking' (1988) 48 *Louisiana Law Review* 1299, 1366].

Note

Translation information should always be included where a translation has been relied upon.

25.2 Judicial and Administrative Decisions

Rule

Foreign judicial, quasi-judicial and administrative decisions from common law systems should be cited as consistently as possible with chapter 2. In particular:

- where a case is reported, it should be cited in the report series (the name of which, if not in the Appendix, should be written out in full but not italicised in accordance with rule 2.3.2);
- in accordance with rule 2.6, the name of the court may be included in parentheses after any pinpoint references; and
- abbreviations of judicial titles should appear as they do in the case or decision cited (and otherwise in accordance with rule 2.9.1).

Citations of other foreign decisions should include the following elements where available and appropriate:

- the case name (the parties' names or any name by which a case is commonly referred to);
- the name of the court or body deciding the matter (to which the jurisdiction should be added if it is not apparent from the name);
- the case or decision number;
- the full date of the decision;
- the details of any report series in which the case is contained, preceded by 'reported in'; and
- a pinpoint reference (where necessary).

These elements should be separated by commas. However, a comma should not precede 'reported in'. These elements should appear in the order in which they are listed above, unless convention in the relevant legal system is to do otherwise.

Where it would assist in retrieval, a URL may be included after the first citation to a decision. The URL should adhere to rule 6.15.6.

Examples

Asuquo v State [1967] 1 All Nigeria Law Reports 123, 126–7 (Bairamian JSC) (Supreme Court of Nigeria).

ALCC Brown Enterprises Ltd v Savaiinaea [2009] WSSC 2 (30 January 2009) [41]–[43] (Sapolu CJ) (Supreme Court of Samoa).

Idecheel v Uludong (Unreported, Supreme Court of Palau, Appellate Division, Beattie, Miller and Hoffmann AsJJ, 1 August 1994) 2.

Verfassungsgerichtshof [Constitutional Court of Austria], G 48/06, 6 October 2006, 9.

Corte costituzionale [Italian Constitutional Court], No 239, 29 December 1982 reported in [1983] I *Il Foro Italiano: Raccolta Generale di Giurisprudenza* 2, 4–5.

Hamburg Intermediate Appellate Court, 1 U 59/48, 7 December 1948 [Hans Ballreich et al trans, *Decisions of German Superior Courts Relating to International Law: 1949–1949* (Carl Heymanns Verlag, 1956) 90].

25.3 Legislative Materials

Rule

Foreign judicial, quasi-judicial and administrative decisions from common law systems should be cited as consistently as possible with chapters 3, rule 23.2 or rule 24.2 (as appropriate). However, the jurisdiction should not be abbreviated.

Other foreign legislative materials (including delegated legislation) should be cited as follows:

[*Title of Foreign Law*] ([Jurisdiction]) [Other Information], [Pinpoint].

The title of the foreign law should be italicised. However, if the title appears in a foreign language and italicisation is not used in that language, the conventional equivalent of italicisation (if any) should be used.

The jurisdiction should not be abbreviated.

Elements of other information, which should be separated by commas, may include:

- the name of the body (other than a Parliament) responsible for promulgating the law;
- the number of the law (for example, 'Act No 3 of 1982');
- the full date on which the law was enacted or took effect; and
- a citation of an official government publication in which the law is contained.

Where elements of other information are included in the title of the law, they should not be repeated.

Where it would assist in retrieval, a URL may be included after the first citation to a foreign law. The URL should adhere to rule 6.15.6.

Examples

Passports Act 1982 (Papua New Guinea).

Sexual Offences Act 2006 (Kenya) ss 3, 5(1)(a)(i).

Penal Code (Kiribati) c 67, s 161.

Änderung der Lebensmittelkennzeichnungsverordnung 1993 [Amendment of the Grocery Labelling Regulation 1993] (Austria) 9 January 2008, BGBl II, 8/2008.

Undang-Undang Nomor 1 Tahun 1974 Tentang Perkawinan [Law No 1 of 1974 on Marriage] (Indonesia) art 2(1).

Aliens Act (Sweden) No 2005:716, ch 8 s 12 para 3 [Ministry for Foreign Affairs (Sweden) trans, *Aliens Act (2005:716)* (2006) <http://www.sweden.gov.se/sb/d/5805/a/66122>].

Criminal Code (Germany) § 80 [Michael Bohlander trans, *Übersetzung des Strafgesetzbuches* (Juris, 2009) 49].

Note

When citing foreign codes, it is generally not necessary to include other information. However, where there is good reason for inclusion, for example in order to refer to the law as at a certain date, other information may be included.

25.4 Other Non-English Language Materials

Rule	Non-English secondary or other sources should be cited in accordance with the relevant rules of this *Guide* for the source type. A translation of any non-English citation element should follow that element in square brackets, where appropriate.
Examples	Jürgen Schwarze, *Der Reformvertrag von Lissabon* [The Reform Treaty of Lisbon] (Nomos, 2009) 181. 'Quelques vices de procédure' [Some Procedural Flaws] on *Le blog du droit européen des brevets* [Blog of European Patent Law] (13 September 2009) <http://europeanpatentcaselaw.blogspot.com/2009/09/quelques-vices-de-procedure.html>.
Note	Published translations of books should be cited in accordance with rule 5.6.

PART VI

APPENDIX

Part VI
Appendix

Appendix: Law Report Abbreviations

Abbreviation	Title*	Jurisdiction	Year(s) of Coverage
A	Atlantic Reporter*	USA	1885–1938
A 2d	Atlantic Reporter, Second Series*	USA	1938–
A Crim R	Australian Criminal Reports	Australia	1979–
A Jur Rep	Australian Jurist Report	Australia (Vic)	1870–74
A'Beck Res	A'Beckett's Reserved Judgments, District of Port Phillip, New South Wales	Australia (NSW)	1846–51
A'Beck RJ NSW	A'Beckett's Reserved Judgments, New South Wales	Australia (NSW)	1845
AALR	Australian Argus Law Reports	Australia	1959–73
AAR	Administrative Appeals Reports	Australia	1984–
ABA	Australian Business and Assets Planning Reporter	Australia	1986–91
ABC	Australian Bankruptcy Cases	Australia	1928–64
ABE	Australian Business and Estate Planning Reporter	Australia	1979–86
ABL	Business Law Cases for Australians	Australia	1978–80
AC	Law Reports, Appeal Cases*	UK	1890–
ACA	Australian Corporate Affairs Reporter	Australia	1971–82
ACLC	Australian Company Law Cases	Australia	1970–
ACLR	Australian Company Law Reports	Australia	1974–89
ACLR	Australian Construction Law Reporter	Australia	1982–97
ACP	Australian Company Law and Practice	Australia	1981–91
ACSR	Australian Corporations and Securities Reports	Australia	1989–
ACTLR	Australian Capital Territory Law Reports*	Australia (ACT)	2007–
ACTR	Australian Capital Territory Reports*	Australia (ACT)	1973–2008
ACTR	Australian Capital Territory Reports	Australia (ACT)	2009–
AD	Appellate Division Reports, New York Supreme Court	USA	1896–1955
AD 2d	Appellate Division Reports, New York Supreme Court, Second Series	USA	1956–2003
AD 3d	Appellate Division Reports, New York Supreme Court, Third Series	USA	2004–
Ad & El	Adolphus and Ellis' Reports, King's Bench and Queen's Bench	UK	1834–56
Ad & El NS	Adolphus and Ellis' Reports, Queen's Bench, New Series	UK	1841–52

* An asterisk next to the title of a report series indicates that it is an authorised, official or preferred series.

Adam	Adam's Justiciary Reports	Scotland	1893–1916
Add	Addam's Ecclesiastical Reports	UK	1822–26
Admn	Administrative Appeals Tribunal Decisions	Australia	1984–85
ADR	Australian De Facto Relationships Cases	Australia	1985–
AEG	Australian Estate and Gift Duty Reporter	Australia	1971–80
AFTR	Australian Federal Tax Reporter	Australia	1969–
AILR	Australian Industrial Law Reports	Australia	1997–
AILR	Australian Industrial Law Review	Australia	1959–96
AIPC	Australian Intellectual Property Cases	Australia	1982–
AITR	Australian Income Tax Reports	Australia	1940–48
AITR	Australian and New Zealand Income Tax Reports	Australia, NZ	1951–68
Ala	Alabama Reports	USA	1820–1975
ALD	Administrative Law Decisions†	Australia	1976–
ALJ	Australian Law Journal	Australia	1927–58
ALJR	Australian Law Journal Reports	Australia	1958–
All ER	All England Law Reports	UK	1936–
All ER (Comm)	All England Law Reports (Commercial Cases)	UK	1998–
All ER (Eur)	All England Law Reports (European Cases)	EU	1995–
All ER Rep	All England Law Reports Reprint	UK	1558–1935
All ER Rep Ext	All England Law Reports Reprint Australian Extension Volumes	UK	1895–1935
ALLR	Australian Labour Law Reporter	Australia	1977–
ALMD	Australian Legal Monthly Digest	Australia	1967–93
ALMD Adv	Australian Legal Monthly Digest Advance	Australia	1993–
ALR	Australian Law Reports	Australia	1973–
ALR	American Law Reports	USA	1915–48
ALR 2d	American Law Reports, Second Series	USA	1947–64
ALR 3d	American Law Reports, Third Series	USA	1965–80
ALR 4th	American Law Reports, Fourth Series	USA	1980–91
ALR 5th	American Law Reports, Fifth Series	USA	1992–2005
ALR 6th	American Law Reports, Sixth Series	USA	2005–
ALR Fed	American Law Reports, Annotated, Federal	USA	1964–2004
ALR Fed 2d	American Law Reports, Annotated, Federal, Second Series	USA	2001–
ALT	Australian Law Times	Australia (Vic)	1879–1928
Alta LR	Alberta Law Reports*	Canada	1908–32
Alta LR (2d)	Alberta Law Reports, Second Series	Canada	1976–92
Alta LR (3d)	Alberta Law Reports, Third Series	Canada	1992–2002
Alta LR (4th)	Alberta Law Reports, Fourth Series	Canada	2002–09
Alta LR (5th)	Alberta Law Reports, Fifth Series	Canada	2009–
Am R	American Reports	USA	1869–87

† This report series contains the authorised reports of the Australian Administrative Appeals Tribunal.

Amb	Ambler's Reports, Chancery	UK	1737–84
AMC	American Maritime Cases	USA	1923–
ANC	New South Wales Conveyancing Cases	Australia (NSW)	1983–
And	Anderson's Reports, Common Pleas	England	1534–1605
Andr	Andrew's Reports, King's Bench	UK	1737–38
Ann Tax Cas	Annotated Tax Cases	UK	1922–
ANRU	New South Wales Revenue Rulings	Australia	1985–89
Anst	Anstruther's Reports, Exchequer	UK	1792–97
ANZ Conv R	Australian and New Zealand Conveyancing Reports	Australia, NZ	1979–
ANZ Ins Cas	Australia and New Zealand Insurance Cases	Australia, NZ	1979–
ANZ IR	Australia and New Zealand Insurance Reporter	Australia, NZ	1979–
AOHS	Australian Occupational Health and Safety Law, Selected Cases	Australia	1979–
APAD	Australian Planning Appeal Decisions	Australia	1980–92
App Cas	Law Reports, Appeal Cases*	UK	1875–90
APR	Atlantic Provinces Reports	Canada	1975–
AQC	Queensland Conveyancing Law and Practice	Australia	1982–
AR	Alberta Reports*	Canada	1976–
AR (NSW)	Industrial Arbitration Reports	Australia (NSW)	1902–
Arb Mat	Arbitration Materials	International	1989–93
Arg LR	Argus Law Reports	Australia (Vic)	1895–1959
Ariz	Arizona Reports	USA	1866–
Ark	Arkansas Reports	USA	1837–
Arkley	Arkley's Justiciary Reports	Scotland	1846–48
Arm M & O	Armstrong, Macartney and Ogle's Reports, Nisi Prius	Ireland	1840–42
Arn	Arnold's Reports, Common Pleas	UK	1838–39
Arn & H	Arnold and Hodges' Reports, Queen's Bench	UK	1840–41
ASC	Australian Consumer Sales and Credit Law Case Reports	Australia	1977–79
ASC	Australian Consumer Sales and Credit Law Reporter	Australia	1979–82
ASC	Consumer Sales and Credit Law Cases	Australia	1982–97
ASC	Consumer Credit Law Cases	Australia	1997–
ASH	Australian Industrial Safety, Health and Welfare, Selected Cases	Australia	1984–88
ASLC	Australian Securities Law Cases	Australia	1971–91
Asp	Aspinall's Maritime Law Cases	UK	1870–1940
ASSC	Australian Social Security Cases	Australia	1984–
ATC	Australian Tax Cases	Australia	1969–
ATD	Australian Tax Decisions	Australia	1930–42
ATD	Australasian Tax Decisions	Australia	1943–69
Atk	Atkyns' Reports, Chancery	UK	1736–55
ATPR	Australian Trade Practices Reports	Australia	1974–

ATR	Australasian Tax Reports	Australia, NZ	1970–90
ATR	Australian Tax Reports	Australia	1991–
ATRU	Australian Income Tax Rulings	Australia	1983–
Aust Contract Reports	Australian Contract Reports	Australia	1991–
Aust Torts Reports	Australian Torts Reports	Australia	1984–
Av Cas	Aviation Cases	USA	1822–
B & Ad	Barnewall and Adolphus' Reports, King's Bench	UK	1830–34
B & Ald	Barnewall and Alderson's Reports, King's Bench	UK	1817–22
B & C	Barnewall and Cresswell's Reports, King's Bench	UK	1822–30
B & CR	Bankruptcy and Companies (Winding-Up) Cases	UK	1918–42
B & I	Bankruptcy and Insolvency Reports	UK	1853–55
B & PI	Bankruptcy and Personal Insolvency Reports	UK	1996–
B & S	Best and Smith's Reports, Queen's Bench and Exchequer	UK	1862–71
B D & O	Blackham, Dundas, and Osborne's Reports, Nisi Prius	Ireland	1846–48
BAGE	Entscheidungen des Bundesarbeitsgerichts	Germany	1954–
Ball & B	Ball and Beatty's Reports, Chancery	Ireland	1807–14
Barb NY	Barbour's Supreme Court Reports, New York	USA	1847–77
Barn Ch	Barnardiston's Reports, Chancery	UK	1740–41
Barn KB	Barnardiston's Reports, King's Bench	UK	1726–34
Barnes	Barnes' Notes of Cases in Points of Practice, Common Pleas	UK	1732–60
Barr & Arn	Barron and Arnold's Election Cases	UK	1843–46
Barr & Aust	Barron and Austin's Election Cases	UK	1844
Batt	Batty's Reports, King's Bench	Ireland	1825–26
BCC	British Company Law Cases	UK	1983–89
BCC	British Company Cases	UK	1990–
BCLC	Butterworths' Company Law Cases	UK	1983–
BCLR	British Columbia Law Reports, First Series*	Canada	1976–86
BCLR (2d)	British Columbia Law Reports, Second Series*	Canada	1986–95
BCLR (3d)	British Columbia Law Reports, Third Series*	Canada	1995–2002
BCLR (4th)	British Columbia Law Reports, Fourth Series*	Canada	2002–
BCR	British Columbia Reports*	Canada	1867–1947
Beat	Beatty's Reports, Chancery	Ireland	1818–29
Beav	Beavan's Reports, Rolls Court	UK	1836–66
Beav & Wal	Beavan and Walford's Railway Parliamentary Cases	UK	1846
Bell	S S Bell's Scotch Appeals, House of Lords	UK	1842–50
Bell CC	T Bell's Crown Cases Reserved	UK	1858–60
Bell Dict Dec	S S Bell's Dictionary of Decisions, Court of Session	Scotland	1808–33
Bell Fol Case	R Bell's Decisions, Court of Session	Scotland	1794–95
Bell Oct Cas	R Bell's Decisions, Court of Session	Scotland	1790–92

Ben & D	Benloe and Dalison's Reports	England	1486–1580
Bend	Bendlowe's Reports, Common Pleas	England	1534–79
Benl	Benloe's Reports, King's Bench	England	1531–1628
BFHE	Entscheidungen des Bundesfinanzhofs	Germany	1952–
BGHSt	Entscheidungen des Bundesgerichtshofes in Strafsachen	Germany	1951–
BGHZ	Entscheidungen des Bundesgerichtshofes in Zivilsachen	Germany	1951–
BILC	British International Law Cases	UK	1964–
Bing	Bingham's Reports, Common Pleas	UK	1822–34
Bing NC	Bingham's New Cases, Common Pleas	UK	1834–40
Bitt Cha Cas	Bittleston's Reports in Chambers, Queen's Bench Division	UK	1883–84
Bl R	William Blackstone's Reports, King's Bench and Common Pleas	UK	1746–79
Black	Black's Supreme Court Reports	USA	1861–62
Bli	Bligh's Reports, House of Lords	UK	1819–21
Bli NS	Bligh's Reports, House of Lords, New Series	UK	1827–37
BLR	Building Law Reports	UK	1976–
BLR	Business Law Reports	Canada	1977–91
BLR (2d)	Business Law Reports, Second Series	Canada	1991–2000
BLR (3d)	Business Law Reports, Third Series	Canada	2000–05
BLR (4th)	Business Law Reports, Fourth Series	Canada	2005–
BNC	Sir R Brooke's New Cases	England	1514–58
Bos & P	Bosanquet and Puller's Reports, Common Pleas	UK	1796–1804
Bos & P NR	Bosanquet and Puller's New Reports, Common Pleas	UK	1804–07
BPR	Butterworths' Property Reports	Australia	1950–
BR	Bankruptcy Reporter	USA	1980–
BR	Broadcasting Reports	Australia	1979–91
BR	Rapports judiciaires officiels de Québec, Cour du Banc de la Reine/du Roi*	Canada	1892–1966
BR	Recueils de jurisprudence du Québec, Cour du Banc de la Reine/du Roi*	Canada	1967–69
Br & Col Pri Cas	British and Colonial Prize Cases	UK	1914–19
Br & Lush	Browning and Lushington's Reports, Admiralty	UK	1863–65
BRA	Butterworths' Ratings Appeals	UK	1913–31
Bro CC	W Brown's Chancery Cases	UK	1778–94
Bro Parl Cas	J Brown's Parliamentary Cases	UK	1701–79
Brod & Bing	Broderip and Bingham's Reports, Common Pleas	UK	1819–22
Brod & F	Brodrick and Fremantle's Ecclesiastical Reports, Privy Council	UK	1840–64
Brooke	W G Brookes' Ecclesiastical Reports, Privy Council	UK	1850–72
Broun	Broun's Justiciary Reports	Scotland	1842–45

Brownl	Brownlow and Goldesbrough's Reports, Common Pleas	England	1569–1624
Bruce	Bruce's Decisions	Scotland	1714–15
BSGE	Entscheidungen des Bundessozialgerichts	Germany	1955–
BTLC	Butterworths' Trading Law Cases	UK	1986–89
Buch	Buchanan's Remarkable Cases	Scotland	1806–13
Buch	Buchanan's Supreme Court Reports, Cape of Good Hope	South Africa	1868–79
Buck	Buck's Cases in Bankruptcy	UK	1816–20
Bull civ	Bulletin des arrêts de la Cour de cassation, Chambres civiles	France	1792–
Bull crim	Bulletin des arrêts de la Cour de cassation, Chambre criminelle	France	1798–
Bunb	Bunbury's Reports, Exchequer	UK	1713–41
Burr	Burrow's Reports, King's Bench	UK	1756–72
Burr SC	Burrow's Settlement Cases, King's Bench	UK	1732–76
Bus LR	Business Law Reports	UK	2007–
BVerfGE	Entscheidungen des Bundesverfassungsgerichts	Germany	1952–
BWCC	Butterworths' Workmen's Compensation Cases	UK	1907–49
C Rob	Christopher Robinson's Admiralty Reports	UK	1798–1808
CA	Recueils de jurisprudence du Québec, Cour d'appel*	Canada	1970–85
CAA	Commonwealth Arbitration Awards and Determinations	Australia	1923–76
Cab & El	Cababé and Ellis's Reports, Queen's Bench	UK	1882–85
Cal	California Reports	USA	1850–1934
Cal 2d	California Reports, Second Series	USA	1934–69
Cal 3d	California Reports, Third Series	USA	1969–91
Cal 4th	California Reports, Fourth Series	USA	1991–
Cal App	California Appellate Reports	USA	1905–34
Cal App 2d	California Appellate Reports, Second Series	USA	1934–69
Cal App 3d	California Appellate Reports, Third Series	USA	1969–91
Cal App 4th	California Appellate Reports, Fourth Series	USA	1991–
Cal Rptr	California Reporter	USA	1960–92
Cal Rptr 2d	California Reporter, Second Series	USA	1992–
CAR	Commonwealth Arbitration Reports	Australia	1905–
Car & P	Carrington and Payne's Reports, Nisi Prius	UK	1823–41
Cas Sett	Cases and Resolutions concerning Settlements and Removals	UK	1685–1733
Cas t Hard	T Lee's Cases tempore Hardwicke, King's Bench	UK	1733–38
Cass Dig	Cassels' Digest, Supreme Court of Canada	Canada	1875–93
CB	Common Bench Reports, Common Pleas	UK	1845–56
CB NS	Common Bench Reports, Common Pleas, New Series	UK	1856–65
CBR	Canadian Bankruptcy Reports	Canada	1920–60
CBR NS	Canadian Bankruptcy Reports, New Series	Canada	1960–90

CBR (3d)	Canadian Bankruptcy Reports, Third Series	Canada	1991–98
CBR (4th)	Canadian Bankruptcy Reports, Fourth Series	Canada	1998–2004
CBR (5th)	Canadian Bankruptcy Reports, Fifth Series	Canada	2004–
CCC	Canadian Criminal Cases	Canada	1898–1962
CCC NS	Canadian Criminal Cases, New Series	Canada	1963–70
CCC (2d)	Canadian Criminal Cases, Second Series	Canada	1971–83
CCC (3d)	Canadian Criminal Cases, Third Series	Canada	1983–
CCC Sess Pap	Central Criminal Court Sessions Papers	UK	1834–1913
CCD	Commonwealth Employees' Compensation Decisions	Australia	1974–81
CCLI	Canadian Cases on the Law of Insurance	Canada	1983–91
CCLI (2d)	Canadian Cases on the Law of Insurance, Second Series	Canada	1991–98
CCLI (3d)	Canadian Cases on the Law of Insurance, Third Series	Canada	1998–2003
CCLI (4th)	Canadian Cases on the Law of Insurance, Fourth Series	Canada	2004–
CCPA	Court of Customs Appeals Reports	USA	1910–29
CCPA	Court of Customs and Patent Appeals Reports	USA	1930–82
CCR	Victoria County Court Reports	Australia (Vic)	1962–72
CEC	European Community Cases	EU	1989–
Ch	Law Reports, Chancery Division*	UK	1891–
Ch Cas	Cases in Chancery	England	1660–97
Ch Cas in Ch	Choyce Cases in Chancery	England	1557–1606
Ch Ch	Chancery Chambers Reports, Ontario	Canada	1858–72
Ch D	Law Reports, Chancery Division*	UK	1875–90
Char Cha Cas	Charley's Chamber Cases	UK	1875–76
Char Pr Cas	Charley's Practice Cases	UK	1875–81
Chit	Chitty's Practice Reports, King's Bench	UK	1770–97, 1807–22
CILC	Commonwealth International Law Cases	International	1974–95
Cl & F	Clark and Finnelly's Reports, House of Lords	UK	1831–46
CL (Q)	Crown Lands Law Reports, Queensland Land Court	Australia (Qld)	1859–1973
Cl Ct	United States Claims Court Reporter	USA	1982–92
Clerk Home	Clerk Home Session Cases	Scotland	1735–44
CLR	Commonwealth Law Reports*	Australia	1903–
CLR	Construction Law Reports	Canada	1983–92
CLR (2d)	Construction Law Reports, Second Series	Canada	1993–2000
CLR (3d)	Construction Law Reports, Third Series	Canada	2000–
CLSR	Computer Law and Security Reports	International	1985–
CMLR	Common Market Law Reports	EU	1962–
Co Rep	Coke's Reports, King's Bench	England	1572–1617
Cock & R	Cockburn and Rowe's Election Cases	UK	1833
Coll	Collyer's Reports, Chancery	UK	1844–46
Colles	Colles' Cases in Parliament	UK	1697–1713
Colt	Coltman's Registration Cases	UK	1879–85

Com	Comyn's Reports, King's Bench, Common Pleas and Exchequer	UK	1694–1741
Com Cas	Commercial Cases	UK	1895–1941
Com Law Rep	Common Law Reports	UK	1853–55
Com LR	Commercial Law Reports	UK	1980–92
Comb	Comberbach's Reports, King's Bench	England	1685–98
Con & L	Connor and Lawson's Irish Chancery Reports	Ireland	1841–43
Conn	Connecticut Reports	USA	1814–
Conn App	Connecticut Appellate Reports	USA	1983–
Conn Supp	Connecticut Supplement	USA	1935–
Cooke	Cooke's Practice Reports, Common Pleas	UK	1706–47
Cooke & A	Cooke and Alcock's Reports, King's Bench	Ireland	1833–34
Cooke Pr Reg	Cooke's Practical Register of the Common Pleas	UK	1705–42
Coop Pr Cas	C P Cooper's Chancery Practice Cases	UK	1837–38
Coop t Brough	C P Cooper's Cases tempore Brougham, Chancery	UK	1833–34
Coop t Cott	C P Cooper's Cases tempore Cottenham, Chancery	UK	1846–48
Corb & D	Corbett and Daniell's Election Cases	UK	1819
Coup	Couper's Justiciary Reports	Scotland	1868–85
Cout	Coutlee's Digest of Cases	Canada	1875–1903
Cowp	Cowper's Reports, King's Bench	UK	1774–78
Cox	S C Cox's Equity Cases	UK	1783–96
Cox & A	Cox and Atkinson's Registration Appeal Cases	UK	1843–46
Cox CC	E W Cox's Reports of Cases in Criminal Law	UK	1842–1941
Cox M & H	Cox, Macrae and Hertslet's County Courts Cases and Appeals	UK	1846–52
CP	Common Pleas Reports, Ontario	Canada	1850–82
CPD	Law Reports, Common Pleas Division*	UK	1875–80
CPR	Canadian Patent Reporter	Canada	1941–71
CPR (2d)	Canadian Patent Reporter, Second Series	Canada	1971–84
CPR (3d)	Canadian Patent Reporter, Third Series	Canada	1985–99
CPR (4th)	Canadian Patent Reporter, Fourth Series	Canada	1999–
CPSAR	Commonwealth Public Service Arbitration Reports	Australia	1921–84
CR	Criminal Reports	Canada	1946–67
CR NS	Criminal Reports, New Series	Canada	1967–78
CR (3d)	Criminal Reports, Third Series	Canada	1978–91
CR (4th)	Criminal Reports, Fourth Series	Canada	1991–96
CR (5th)	Criminal Reports, Fifth Series	Canada	1997–2002
CR (6th)	Criminal Reports, Sixth Series	Canada	2002–
Cr & J	Crompton and Jervis' Reports, Exchequer	UK	1830–32
Cr & M	Crompton and Meeson's Reports, Exchequer	UK	1832–34
Cr & Ph	Craig and Phillips' Reports, Chancery	UK	1840–41
Cr App R	Criminal Appeal Reports	UK	1908–
Cr App R (S)	Criminal Appeal Reports (Sentencing)	UK	1979–
Cr M & R	Crompton, Meeson and Roscoe's Reports, Exchequer	UK	1834–35
Cranch	Cranch's Supreme Court Reports	USA	1801–15

Craw & D	Crawford and Dix's Circuit Cases	Ireland	1839–46
Craw & D Abr C	Crawford and Dix's Abridged Cases	Ireland	1837–38
Cress	Cresswell's Insolvency Cases	UK	1827–29
Cripps	Cripps' Church and Clergy Cases	UK	1847–50
Cro Char	Croke's Reports tempore Charles I, King's Bench and Common Pleas	England	1625–41
Cro Eliz	Croke's Reports tempore Elizabeth I, King's Bench and Common Pleas	England	1582–1603
Cro Jac	Croke's Reports tempore James I, King's Bench and Common Pleas	England	1603–25
Crockford	Crockford's Maritime Law Cases	UK, USA	1860–71
CS	Rapports judiciaires officiels de Québec, Cour supérieure*	Canada	1892–1966
CS	Recueils de jurisprudence du Québec, Cour supérieure*	Canada	1967–85
CTB	Decisions of the Board of Review, Commonwealth Taxation Board of Review	Australia	1937–50
CTBR	Decisions of the Income Tax Board of Review, Commonwealth	Australia	1925–37
CTBR NS	Commonwealth Taxation Board of Review Decisions, New Series	Australia	1950–86
CTC	Canada Tax Cases	Canada	1917–71
CTC NS	Canada Tax Cases, New Series	Canada	1972–
Cun	Cunningham's Reports, King's Bench	UK	1734–36
Curt	Curteis' Ecclesiastical Reports	UK	1834–44
D B & M	Dunlop, Bell and Murray's Reports, Session Cases, Second Series	Scotland	1838–62
D Falc	Falconer's Decisions, Court of Session	Scotland	1744–51
Dal	Dalison's Reports, Common Pleas	England	1486–1580
Dall	Dallas' Supreme Court Reports	USA	1790–1800
Dalr	Dalrymple's Decisions, Court of Session	Scotland	1698–1718
Dan	Daniell's Reports, Exchequer in Equity	UK	1817–23
Dan & L	Danson and Lloyd's Mercantile Cases	UK	1828–29
Dav	Davis' Reports, King's Bench	Ireland	1604–12
Dav & Mer	Davison and Merivale's Reports, Queen's Bench	UK	1843–44
Dav Pat Cas	Davies' Patent Cases	UK	1785–1816
Day	Day's Election Cases	UK	1892–95
DCA	Dorion's Queen's Bench Reports	Canada	1880–84
DCR NSW	District Court Reports, New South Wales	Australia (NSW)	1952–75
DDCR	Dust Diseases and Compensation Reports	Australia (NSW)	2003–
De G & J	De Gex and Jones' Reports, Chancery	UK	1857–59
De G & Sm	De Gex and Smale's Reports, Chancery	UK	1846–52
De G Bankr	De Gex's Bankruptcy Reports	UK	1844–48

De G F & J	De Gex, Fisher and Jones' Reports, Chancery	UK	1859–62
De G J & Sm	De Gex, Jones and Smith's Reports, Chancery	UK	1862–66
De G M & G	De Gex, Macnaghten and Gordon's Reports, Chancery	UK	1851–57
Dea & Sw	Deane and Swabey's Ecclesiastical Reports	UK	1855–57
Deac	Deacon's Bankruptcy Reports	UK	1835–40
Deac & Ch	Deacon and Chitty's Bankruptcy Reports	UK	1832–35
Dears	Dearsly's Crown Cases Reserved	UK	1852–56
Dears & B	Dearsly and Bell's Crown Cases Reserved	UK	1856–58
Deas & A	Deas and Anderson's Decisions	Scotland	1829–32
Del	Delane's Decisions, Revision Courts	UK	1832–35
Den	Denison and Pearce's Crown Cases Reserved	UK	1844–52
Dhaka LR	Dhaka Law Reports	Bangladesh	1949–
Dick	Dickens' Reports, Chancery	UK	1559–1798
Dirl	Dirleton's Decisions, Court of Session	Scotland	1665–77
DLR	Dominion Law Reports	Canada	1912–55
DLR (2d)	Dominion Law Reports, Second Series	Canada	1956–68
DLR (3d)	Dominion Law Reports, Third Series	Canada	1969–84
DLR (4th)	Dominion Law Reports, Fourth Series	Canada	1984–
Dowl & L	Dowling & Lowndes' Practice Reports	UK	1843–49
DSR	Dispute Settlement Reports*	WTO	1996–
DTC	Dominion Tax Cases	Canada	1920–
East	East's Term Reports, King's Bench	UK	1800–12
ECR	European Court Reports, Reports of Cases before the Court*	EU	1954–90
ECR	European Court Reports, Reports of Cases before the Court of Justice and the Court of First Instance*	EU	1990–
ECR-SC	European Court Reports, Reports of European Community Staff Cases*	EU	1994–
EGLR	Estates Gazette Law Reports	UK	1985–
EHRR	European Human Rights Reports	Council of Europe	1979–
ELR	Environmental Law Reporter of New South Wales	Australia (NSW)	1981–83
ELR	Environmental Law Reporter	Australia (NSW)	1983–
EMLR	Entertainment and Media Law Reports	UK	1993–
EOC	Equal Opportunity Cases	Australia	1984–
Eq Cas Abr	Equity Cases Abridged	UK	1667–1744
Eq Rep	Equity Reports	UK	1853–55
ER	English Reports	UK	1220–1867
Eur Comm HR	European Commission of Human Rights, Collection of Decisions*	Council of Europe	1960–74
Eur Comm HR	European Commission of Human Rights, Decisions and Reports*	Council of Europe	1974–98

Eur Court HR	Reports of Judgments and Decisions, European Court of Human Rights*	Council of Europe	1996–
Eur Court HR (ser A)	Judgments and Decisions, European Court of Human Rights*	Council of Europe	1960–95
Eur Court HR (ser B)	Pleadings, Oral Arguments and Documents, European Court of Human Rights*	Council of Europe	1960–88
Ex	Exchequer Reports	UK	1847–56
Ex CR	Reports of the Exchequer Court of Canada*	Canada	1875–1922
Ex CR	Canada Law Reports, Exchequer Court of Canada*	Canada	1923–70
Ex D	Law Reports, Exchequer Division*	UK	1875–80
F	Federal Reporter*	USA	1880–1924
F 2d	Federal Reporter, Second Series*	USA	1924–93
F 3d	Federal Reporter, Third Series*	USA	1993–
F Supp	Federal Supplement, District Court Reports*	USA	1932–98
F Supp 2d	Federal Supplement, District Court Reports, Second Series*	USA	1998–
F & F	Foster and Finlason's Reports, Nisi Prius	UK	1856–67
Fac Dec	Faculty Decisions, Octavo Series	Scotland	1825–41
Falc & F	Falconer and Fitzherbert's Election Cases	UK	1835–38
Fam	Law Reports, Family Division*	UK	1972–
Fam LR	Family Law Reports	Australia	1976–
FC	Canada Federal Court Reports*	Canada	1971–
FC	Faculty Collection, New Series	Scotland	1808–25
FC	Faculty Collection, Old Series	Scotland	1752–1808
FCR	Family Court Reporter	UK	1987–1999
FCR	Butterworths' Family Court Reports	UK	2000–
FCR	Federal Court Reports*	Australia	1984–
Fed Cas	Federal Cases	USA	1789–1880
Fed Claims Rep	United States Federal Claims Reporter	USA	1992–
Ferg Cons	Ferguson's Consistorial Decisions	Scotland	1811–17
Fitzg	Fitz-Gibbons' Reports, King's Bench	UK	1728–33
Fl & K	Flanagan and Kelly's Reports, Rolls Court	Ireland	1840–42
Fla R	Florida Reports	USA	1846–48
Fla Supp	Florida Supplement	USA	1952–82
Fla Supp	Florida Supplement, Second Digest	USA	1982–
FLC	Australian Family Law Cases	Australia	1976–
FLR	Family Law Reports	UK	1980–
FLR	Federal Law Reports	Australia	1956–
Fol Dic	Kames and Woodhouselee's Folio Dictionary, Court of Session	Scotland	1540–1796
Fonbl	Fonblanque's Bankruptcy Reports	UK	1849–52
Foord	Foord's Supreme Court Reports, Cape of Good Hope	South Africa	1880
Forbes	Forbes' Decisions	Scotland	1705–13
Forr	Forrest's Reports, Exchequer	UK	1800–01

Fort	Fortescue's Reports	UK	1695–1738
Fost	Foster's Crown Cases	UK	1743–61
Fount	Fountainhall's Decisions, Court of Session	Scotland	1678–1712
Fox & S	M C Fox and T B C Smith's Irish King's Bench Reports	Ireland	1822–24
Fox & S Reg	J S Fox and C L Smith's Registration Cases	UK	1886–95
Fox Pat C	Fox's Patent, Trade Mark, Design and Copyright Cases	Canada	1940–71
Fras	S Fraser's Election Cases	UK	1776–77
Fraser	Fraser's Court of Session Cases, Fifth Series	Scotland	1898–1907
FRD	Federal Rules Decisions	USA	1938–
Freem Ch	Freeman's Reports, Chancery	England	1660–1706
Freem KB	Freeman's Reports, King's Bench and Common Pleas	England	1670–1704
FRNZ	Family Reports of New Zealand	NZ	1984–
FSR	Fleet Street Reports	UK	1963–
FTLR	Financial Times Law Reports	UK	1986–88
FTR	Australian Federal Tax Reporter	Australia	1969–
G Coop	G Cooper's Reports, Chancery	UK	1792–1815
Ga	Georgia Reports	USA	1846–
Ga App	Georgia Appeals Reports	USA	1907–
Gal	Gale's Reports, Exchequer	UK	1835–36
Gal & Dav	Gale and Davison's Reports, Queen's Bench	UK	1841–43
Gaz LR	Gazette Law Reports	NZ	1898–1953
Giff	Giffard's Reports, Chancery	UK	1856–65
Gil & Fal	Gilmour and Falconer's Decisions, Court of Session	Scotland	1661–66, 1681–86
Gilb Ch	Gilbert's Reports, Chancery	UK	1705–26
Gilb KB	Gilbert's Cases, King's Bench	UK	1713–15
Gl & J	Glyn and Jameson's Bankruptcy Cases	UK	1821–28
Glan El Cas	Glanville's Election Cases	England	1623–24
Glas	Glascock's Miscellaneous Reports	Ireland	1831–32
Godb	Godbolt's Reports	England	1575–1638
Gould	Gouldsborough's Reports	England	1586–1602
Gow	Gow's Reports, Nisi Prius	UK	1818–20
Gr	Grant's Upper Canada Chancery Reports	Canada	1849–81
Greg	Gregorowski's Reports of the High Court of the Orange Free State	South Africa	1883–87
Grif Pat Cas	Griffin's Patent Cases	UK	1885–87
Gwill	Gwillim's Tithe Cases	UK	1285–1824
GWLD	Griqualand West Local Division Reports	South Africa	1910–46
GWR	Griqualand West High Court Reports	South Africa	1882–1910
H & Tw	Hall and Twells' Reports, Chancery	UK	1849–50
H Bl	Henry Blackstone's Reports, Common Pleas	UK	1788–96
Hag Adm	Haggard's Admiralty Reports	UK	1822–38
Hag Con	Haggard's Consistorial Reports	UK	1789–1821

Hag Crt Rep	The Hague Court Reports, First Series	International	1902–14
Hag Crt Rep 2d	The Hague Court Reports, Second Series	International	1920–28
Hag Ecc	Haggard's Ecclesiastical Reports	UK	1827–33
Hailes	Hailes' Decisions, Court of Session	Scotland	1766–91
Hale PC	Hale's Pleas of the Crown	UK	1736
Har & Ruth	Harrison and Rutherford's Reports, Common Pleas	UK	1865–66
Har & Woll	Harrison and Wollaston's Reports, King's Bench and Bail Court	UK	1835–36
Harc	Harcarse's Decisions, Court of Session	Scotland	1681–91
Hardres	Hardres' Reports, Exchequer	England	1655–69
Hare	Hare's Reports, Chancery	UK	1841–53
Haw	Hawaii Reports	USA	1847–
Haw App	Hawaii Appellate Reports	USA	1980–94
Hay & Marr	Hay and Marriott's Admiralty Decisions	UK	1776–79
Hayes	Hayes' Irish Exchequer Reports	Ireland	1830–32
Hayes & Jo	Hayes and Jones' Irish Exchequer Reports	Ireland	1832–34
HBR	Hansell's Bankruptcy and Companies (Winding-Up) Cases	UK	1915–17
HEC	Hodgin's Election Reports	Canada	1871–79
Hem & M	Hemming and Miller's Reports, Chancery	UK	1862–65
Hertzog	Hertzog's Cases in the High Court, South African Republic	South Africa	1893
Het	Hetley's Reports	England	1627–32
HKC	Hong Kong Cases	Hong Kong	1946–
HKCFAR	Authorised Hong Kong Court of Final Appeal Reports*	Hong Kong	1997–
HKDCLR	Hong Kong District Court Law Reports	Hong Kong	1953–96
HKLR	Hong Kong Law Reports*	Hong Kong	1905–96
HKLRD	Authorised Hong Kong Law Reports and Digest*	Hong Kong	1997–
HKPLR	Hong Kong Public Law Reports	Hong Kong	1991–97
HL Cas	House of Lords Cases	UK	1847–66
HLR	Housing Law Reports	UK	1982–
Hob	Hobart's Reports, Common Pleas	England	1603–25
Hodges	Hodges' Reports, Common Pleas	UK	1835–37
Hog	Hogan's Reports, Rolls Court	Ireland	1816–34
Holt Adm	W Holt's Admiralty Cases on the Rule of the Road	UK	1863–67
Holt Eq	W Holt's Equity Reports	UK	1845
Holt KB	J Holt's Reports, King's Bench	UK	1688–1710
Holt NP	F Holt's Reports, Nisi Prius	UK	1815–17
Hop & C	Hopwood and Coltman's Registration Cases	UK	1868–78
Hop & Ph	Hopwood and Philbrick's Registration Cases	UK	1863–67
Horn & H	Horn and Hurlstone's Reports, Exchequer	UK	1838–39
Hov Supp	Hoveden's Supplement to Vesey Junior's Reports, Chancery	UK	1789–1817
How	Howard's Supreme Court Reports	USA	1843–60

How Ch Pr	Howard's Chancery Practice	Ireland	1619–1775
How EE	Howard's Equity Practice, Exchequer	Ireland	1760
Hud & B	Hudson and Brooke's Reports, King's Bench	Ireland	1827–31
Hume	Hume's Decisions, Court of Session	Scotland	1781–1822
Hunt	Hunter's Torrens Cases	UK, Australia, Canada, NZ	1865–93
Hurl & C	Hurlstone and Coltman's Reports, Exchequer	UK	1862–66
Hurl & N	Hurlstone and Norman's Reports, Exchequer	UK	1856–62
Hurl & W	Hurlstone and Walmsley's Reports, Exchequer	UK	1840–41
Hut	Hutton's Reports, Common Pleas	England	1612–39
I Ch R	Irish Chancery Reports, Second Series	Ireland	1850–66
I Eq R	Irish Equity Reports, First Series	Ireland	1838–50
ICJ Pleadings	Pleadings, Oral Arguments, Documents, International Court of Justice*	International	1946–
ICJ Rep	Reports of Judgments, Advisory Opinions and Orders, International Court of Justice*	International	1946–
ICLR	Irish Common Law Reports, Second Series	Ireland	1850–66
ICR	Industrial Cases Reports	UK	1972–
ICR	Irish Circuit Reports	Ireland	1841–43
ICSID Rep	International Centre for Settlement of Investment Disputes Reports	International	1975–
Idaho	Idaho Reports	USA	1866–
Ill	Illinois Reports	USA	1849–1952
Ill 2d	Illinois Reports, Second Series	USA	1953–
Ill App	Illinois Appellate Court Reports	USA	1877–1954
Ill App 2d	Illinois Appellate Court Reports, Second Series	USA	1954–72
Ill App 3d	Illinois Appellate Court Reports, Third Series	USA	1973–
Ill Ct C	Illinois Court of Claims Reports	USA	1905–
ILM	International Legal Materials	International	1962–
Insur LR	Canadian Insurance Law Reporter	Canada	1934–
ILR	International Law Reports	International	1950–
ILR	Irish Law Reports, First Series	Ireland	1838–50
ILRM	Irish Law Reports Monthly	Ireland	1981–
ILT	Irish Law Times	Ireland	1867–1980
Imm AR	Immigration Appeal Reports	UK	1972–
Ind App	Indiana Appellate Court Reports	USA	1890–1979
IPR	Intellectual Property Reports	Australia	1982–
IR	Industrial Reports	Australia	1981–2006
IR	Industrial Reports‡	Australia	2006–
IR	Law Reports, Ireland, Fourth Series*	Ireland	1878–93
IR	Irish Reports, Fifth Series*	Ireland	1894–
Ir Cir Rep	Reports of Irish Circuit Cases	Ireland	1841–43

‡ This report series contains the authorised reports of Fair Work Australia and the Australian Industrial Relations Commission.

IR CL	Irish Reports, Common Law, Third Series*	Ireland	1866–78
IR Eq	Irish Reports, Equity, Third Series*	Ireland	1866–78
IR R & L	Irish Reports, Registry Appeals and Land Cases*	Ireland	1868–76
Iran–US CTR	Iran–United States Claims Tribunal Reports	International	1981–
IRLR	Industrial Relations Law Reports	UK	1972–
Irv	Irvine's Justiciary Reports	Scotland	1852–67
ITDA	Income Tax Decisions of Australasia	Australia	1891–1930
ITLR	Irish Times Law Reports	Ireland	1967–
ITR	Industrial Tribunal Reports	UK	1966–78
J Bridg	Sir John Bridgman's Reports, Common Pleas	England	1613–21
J Shaw	J Shaw's Justiciary Reports	Scotland	1848–52
Jac	Jacob's Reports, Chancery	UK	1821–22
Jac & W	Jacob and Walker's Reports, Chancery	UK	1819–21
JDR	Juta's Daily Reporter, Cape Provincial Division	South Africa	1915–26
Jebb	Jebb's Crown Cases Reserved	Ireland	1822–40
Jebb & B	Jebb and Bourke's Reports, Queen's Bench	Ireland	1841–42
Jebb & S	Jebb and Symes' Reports, Queen's Bench and Exchequer	Ireland	1838–41
Jenk	Jenkins' Reports, Exchequer	England	1220–1623
JO	Journal officiel de la République française	France	1881–
John	Johnson's Reports, Chancery	UK	1858–60
John & H	Johnson and Hemming's Reports, Chancery	UK	1859–62
John Ch	Johnson's Chancery Reports, New York	USA	1814–23
Jones	Jones' Reports, Exchequer	Ireland	1834–38
Jones & C	Jones and Carey's Reports, Exchequer	Ireland	1838–39
Jones & La T	T Jones and La Touche's Reports, Chancery	Ireland	1844–46
JP	Justice of the Peace and County Reports	UK	1837–1926
JP	Justice of the Peace and Local Government Review Reports	UK	1927–82
JP	Justice of the Peace Reports	UK	1983–
Jur	Jurist Reports	UK	1838–54
Jur NS	Jurist Reports, New Series	UK	1855–66
K	Kotze's High Court Reports, Transvaal Province	South Africa	1877–81
K & F NSW	Knox and Fitzhardinge's Reports, New South Wales	Australia (NSW)	1879–80
Kames Rem Dec	Kames' Remarkable Decisions, Court of Session	Scotland	1716–28, 1730–52
Kames Sel Dec	Kames' Select Decisions, Court of Session	Scotland	1752–68
Kan	Kansas Reports	USA	1862–
Kan App	Kansas Appeals Reports	USA	1895–1902
Kan App 2d	Kansas Appeals Reports, Second Series	USA	1977–
Kay	Kay's Reports, Chancery	UK	1853–54
Kay & J	Kay and Johnson's Reports, Chancery	UK	1854–58
KB	Law Reports, King's Bench Division*	UK	1901–51
Keane & G	Keane and Grant's Registration Cases	UK	1854–62
Keb	Keble's Reports, King's Bench	England	1661–79

Keen	Keen's Reports, Rolls Court	UK	1836–38
Keil	Keilwey's Reports, King's Bench	England	1496–1531
Kel	Sir John Kelynge's Reports, Crown Cases	England	1662–69
Kel W	W Kelynge's Reports, Chancery and King's Bench	UK	1730–34
Keny	Kenyon's Notes of Cases, King's Bench	UK	1753–59
Kilk	Kilkerran's Decisions, Court of Session	Scotland	1738–52
KILR	Knight's Industrial Law Reports	UK	1975
KIR	Knight's Industrial Reports	UK	1966–74
Kn	Knapp's Reports, Privy Council	UK	1829–36
Kn & O	Knapp and Ombler's Election Cases	UK	1834–35
Knox (NSW)	Knox's Supreme Court Reports	Australia (NSW)	1877
Konst & W	Konstam and Ward's Reports of Rating Appeals	UK	1909–12
Konst Rat App	Konstam's Reports of Rating Appeals	UK	1904–08
L Ed	United States Supreme Court Reports, Lawyer's Edition, First Series	USA	1790–1956
L Ed 2d	United States Supreme Court Reports, Lawyers' Edition, Second Series	USA	1956–
La	Louisiana Reports	USA	1901–72
La App	Louisiana Appeal Reports	USA	1924–32
LACC	Land Appeal Court Cases	Australia (NSW)	1890–1921
Lane	Lane's Reports, Exchequer	England	1605–12
Lat	Latch's Reports, King's Bench	England	1625–28
Law Rec	Law Recorder, Old Series	Ireland	1827–31
Law Rec NS	Law Recorder, New Series	Ireland	1833–38
Laws Reg Cas	Lawson's Registration Cases	UK	1885–1914
LCJ	Lower Canada Jurist	Canada	1857–91
LCR	Lower Canada Reports	Canada	1848–67
Ld Raym	Lord Raymond's Reports, King's Bench and Common Pleas	UK	1694–1732
LDB	Legal Decisions Affecting Bankers	UK	1879–
Le & Ca	Leigh and Cave's Crown Cases Reserved	UK	1861–65
Leach	Leach's Crown Cases, King's Bench	UK	1730–1815
Lee	Sir G Lee's Ecclesiastical Judgments	UK	1752–58
Legge	Legge's Supreme Court Cases	Australia (NSW)	1825–62
Leo	Leonard's Reports, King's Bench, Common Pleas and Exchequer	England	1540–1615
Lev	Levinz's Reports, King's Bench and Common Pleas	England	1660–97
Lewin	Lewin's Crown Cases on the Northern Circuit	UK	1822–38
Ley	Ley's Reports	England	1608–29
LGATR (NSW)	Local Government Appeals Tribunal Reports	Australia (NSW)	1972–80
LGERA	Local Government and Environmental Reports of Australia	Australia	1993–

LGR	Local Government Reports	UK	1903–
LGR (NSW)	Local Government Reports	Australia (NSW)	1913–56
LGRA	Local Government Reports of Australia	Australia	1956–93
Lilly	Lilly's Reports and Pleadings of Cases in Assize	England	1688–93
Litt	Littleton's Reports, Common Pleas	England	1626–32
LJ Adm	Law Journal Reports, Admiralty	UK	1832–46
LJ Bcy	Law Journal Reports, Bankruptcy	UK	1832–46
LJ Ch	Law Journal Reports, Chancery	UK	1832–46
LJ CP	Law Journal Reports, Common Pleas	UK	1832–46
LJ Eccl	Law Journal Reports, Ecclesiastical	UK	1832–46
LJ Ex	Law Journal Reports, Exchequer	UK	1832–46
LJ Ex Eq	Law Journal Reports, Exchequer in Equity	UK	1832–46
LJ KB	Law Journal Reports, King's Bench	UK	1832–46
LJ MC	Law Journal, Magistrates' Cases	UK	1832–46
LJ P	Law Journal, Probate, Divorce and Admiralty	UK	1875–
LJ P M & A	Law Journal Reports, Probate, Matrimonial and Admiralty	UK	1832–46
LJ PC	Law Journal Reports, Privy Council	UK	1832–46
LJ QB	Law Journal Reports, Queen's Bench	UK	1832–46
LJR	Law Journal Reports	UK	1947–49
Ll & G t Plunk	Lloyd and Goold's Reports tempore Plunkett, Chancery	Ireland	1834–39
Ll & G t Sug	Lloyd and Goold's Reports tempore Sugden, Chancery	Ireland	1834–39
Ll & W	Lloyd and Welsby's Mercantile Cases	UK	1829–30
Ll L Rep	Lloyd's List Law Reports	UK	1919–51
Ll Pri Cas	Lloyd's Reports of Prize Cases	UK	1914–24
Lloyd's Rep	Lloyd's Law Reports	UK	1951–
LLR	Leader Law Reports	South Africa	1909–10
Lofft	Lofft's Reports, King's Bench	UK	1772–74
Long & T	Longfield and Townsend's Reports, Exchequer	Ireland	1841–42
Lownd & M	Bail Court Cases	UK	1852–54
Lownd M & P	Lowndes, Maxwell, and Pollock's Reports, Bail Court and Practice	UK	1850–51
LR (NSW)	Law Reports, New South Wales	Australia (NSW)	1880–1900
LR A & E	Law Reports, Admiralty and Ecclesiastical Cases*	UK	1865–75
LR CCR	Law Reports, Crown Cases Reserved*	UK	1865–75
LR Ch App	Law Reports, Chancery Appeal Cases*	UK	1865–75
LR CP	Law Reports, Common Pleas*	UK	1865–75
LR Eq	Law Reports, Equity Cases*	UK	1865–75
LR Ex	Law Reports, Exchequer*	UK	1865–75
LR HL	Law Reports, English and Irish Appeals and Peerage Claims, House of Lords*	UK	1865–75
LR Ind App	Law Reports, Indian Appeals, Privy Council*	UK	1873–1950

LR Ind App Supp	Law Reports, Indian Appeals, Privy Council, Supplement*	UK	1872–73
LR P & D	Law Reports, Probate and Divorce Cases*	UK	1865–75
LR PC	Law Reports, Privy Council Appeals*	UK	1865–75
LR QB	Law Reports, Queen's Bench*	UK	1865–75
LR RP	Law Reports, Restrictive Practices*	UK	1957–72
LR Sc & Div	Law Reports, Scotch and Divorce Appeals, House of Lords*	UK	1865–75
LRC	Law Reports of the Commonwealth	Commonwealth	1980–
LSJS	Law Society Judgment Scheme	Australia (SA)	1948–
LT	Law Times Reports, Old Series	UK	1843–59
LT NS	Law Times Reports, New Series	UK	1859–1947
Lud El Cas	Luder's Election Cases	UK	1784–87
Lumley PL Cas	Lumley's Poor Law Cases	UK	1834–42
Lush	Lushington's Admiralty Reports	UK	1859–1962
Lut	Lutwyche's Entries and Reports, Common Pleas	England	1682–1704
Lut Reg Cas	Lutwyche's Registration Cases	UK	1843–53
LVR	Land and Valuation Court Reports, New South Wales	Australia (NSW)	1922–70
M & S	Maule and Selwyn's Reports, King's Bench	UK	1813–17
M & W	Meeson and Welsby's Reports, Exchequer	UK	1835–47
M'Cle	M'Cleland's Reports, Exchequer	UK	1824
M'Cle & Yo	M'Cleland and Younge's Reports, Exchequer	UK	1824–25
Mac	Macassey's New Zealand Reports	NZ	1861–72
Mac & G	Macnaghten and Gordon's Reports, Chancery	UK	1849–51
MacF	MacFarlane's Jury Trials, Court of Session	Scotland	1838–39
MacG	MacGillivray's Copyright Cases	UK	1901–49
Macl & R	Maclean and Robinson's Appeals, House of Lords	UK	1839
Macpherson	Macpherson's Court of Session Cases	Scotland	1862–73
Macq	Macqueen's Reports, Scotch Appeals, House of Lords	UK	1847–65
Macr & H	Macrae and Hertslet's Insolvency Cases	UK	1847–52
Macr Pat Cas	Macrory's Patent Cases	UK	1841–56
Madd	Maddock's Reports, Chancery	UK	1815–22
Man & G	Manning and Granger's Reports, Common Pleas	UK	1840–44
Man & Ry KB	Manning and Ryland's Reports, King's Bench	UK	1827–30
Man & Ry MC	Manning and Ryland's Magistrates' Cases	UK	1827–30
Man LR	Manitoba Law Reports*	Canada	1884–90
Man R	Manitoba Reports*	Canada	1883–1961
Man R (2d)	Manitoba Reports, Second Series*	Canada	1979–
Man R t Wood	Manitoba Reports tempore Wood	Canada	1875–83
Mans	Manson's Bankruptcy and Companies (Winding-Up) Cases	UK	1894–1914
March NC	March's New Cases, King's Bench	England	1639–42
Marsh	Marshall's Common Pleas Reports	UK	1813–16

Mass	Massachusetts Reports	USA	1804–
Mass App Ct	Massachusetts Appeals Court Reports	USA	1972–
Mass App Div	Massachusetts Appellate Division Reports	USA	1936–50, 1980–
Mayn	Maynard's Reports	England	1273–1326
MCC	Mining Commissioner's Cases, Ontario	Canada	1906–17
MCD	Magistrates' Court Decisions	NZ	1939–80
MCR	Montreal Condensed Reports	Canada	1853–4
Md	Maryland Reports	USA	1851–
Md App	Maryland Appellate Reports	USA	1967–
Meg	Megone's Companies Acts Cases	UK	1888–91
Menz	Menzies' Supreme Court Reports, Cape of Good Hope	South Africa	1828–49
Mer	Merivale's Reports, Chancery	UK	1815–17
Mich	Michigan Reports	USA	1847–
Mich App	Michigan Appeals Reports	USA	1965–
Milw	Milward's Ecclesiastical Reports	Ireland	1819–43
Minn	Minnesota Reports	USA	1851–1977
Misc	New York Miscellaneous Reports	USA	1892–1942
Misc 2d	New York Miscellaneous Reports, Second Series	USA	1955–2003
Misc 3d	New York Miscellaneous Reports, Third Series	USA	2003–
Miss	Mississippi Reports	USA	1818–1965
MJ	Military Justice Reporter	USA	1975–
MLJ	Malayan Law Journal	Malaysia	1932–42, 1946–
MLR QB	Montreal Law Reports, Queen's Bench	Canada	1884–91
MLR SC	Montreal Law Reports, Superior Court	Canada	1885–91
MMC	Martin's Mining Cases	Canada	1853–1907
Mo	Missouri Reports	USA	1821–1956
Mod	Modern Reports	UK	1669–1755
Mol	Molloy's Reports, Chancery	Ireland	1827–31
Mont	Montana Reports	USA	1868–
Mont & A	Montagu and Ayrton's Bankruptcy Reports	UK	1833–38
Mont & B	Montagu and Bligh's Bankruptcy Reports	UK	1832–33
Mont & Ch	Montagu and Chitty's Bankruptcy Reports	UK	1838–40
Mont & M	Montagu and MacArthur's Bankruptcy Reports	UK	1828–29
Mont BC	Montagu's Bankruptcy Reports	UK	1829–32
Mont D & De G	Montagu, Deacon, and De Gex's Bankruptcy Reports	UK	1840–44
Moo	Moore's Reports, Common Pleas and Exchequer	UK	1817–27
Moo & P	Moore and Payne's Reports, Common Pleas and Exchequer	UK	1827–31
Moo & S	Moore and Scott's Reports, Common Pleas and Exchequer	UK	1831–34
Moo Ind App	Moore's Indian Appeal Cases, Privy Council	UK	1836–72
Moo KB	Sir F Moore's Reports, King's Bench	England	1519–1621

Moo PC	Moore's Privy Council Cases	UK	1836–62
Moo PC NS	Moore's Privy Council Cases, New Series	UK	1862–73
Mood & M	Moody and Malkin's Reports, Nisi Prius	UK	1826–30
Mood & R	Moody and Robinson's Reports, Nisi Prius	UK	1830–44
Mood CC	Moody's Crown Cases Reserved	UK	1824–44
Mor	Morison's Dictionary of Decisions, Court of Session	Scotland	1540–1808
Morr	Morrell's Bankruptcy Reports	UK	1884–93
Mos	Mosely's Reports, Chancery	UK	1726–31
MPR	Maritime Provinces Reports	Canada	1929–68
Mun Rep	Municipal Reports	Canada	1845–52
Mur	Murray's Reports, Jury Court	Scotland	1815–30
Mur & H	Murphy and Hurlstone's Reports, Exchequer	UK	1836–37
MVR	Motor Vehicle Reports	Australia	1983–
My & Cr	Mylne and Craig's Reports, Chancery	UK	1835–41
My & K	Mylne and Keen's Reports, Chancery	UK	1832–35
N & S	Nicholls and Stops' Reports	Australia	1897–1904
NAC	Native Appeal Cases	South Africa	1894–1929
NBER	New Brunswick Equity Reports	Canada	1894–1911
NBR	New Brunswick Reports*	Canada	1825–1928
NBR (2d)	New Brunswick Reports, Second Series*	Canada	1968–
NC	North Carolina Reports	USA	1868–
NC App	North Carolina Court of Appeals Reports	USA	1968–
ND	North Dakota Reports	USA	1890–1953
NE	North Eastern Reporter*	USA	1885–1936
NE 2d	North Eastern Reporter, Second Series*	USA	1936–
Neb	Nebraska Reports	USA	1860–
Nels	Nelson's Reports, Chancery	England	1625–93
Nev	Nevada Reports	USA	1865–
Nev & M KB	Nevile and Manning's Reports, King's Bench	UK	1832–36
Nev & M MC	Nevile and Manning's Magistrates' Cases	UK	1832–36
Nev & P KB	Nevile and Perry's Reports, King's Bench	UK	1836–38
Nev & P MC	Nevile and Perry's Magistrates' Cases	UK	1836–37
New Mag Cas	Reports of New Magistrates' Cases	UK	1844–51
New Pract Cas	Reports of New Practice Cases	UK	1844–48
New Rep	New Reports	UK	1862–65
Nfld & PEIR	Newfoundland & Prince Edward Island Reports*	Canada	1970–
Nfld LR	Newfoundland Law Reports*	Canada	1817–1949
NH	New Hampshire Reports	USA	1816–
NI	Northern Ireland Law Reports*	UK	1925–
NJ	New Jersey Reports	USA	1948–
NJS	New Jersey Superior Court Reports	USA	1948–
NLR	Natal Law Reports, Old Series	South Africa	1867–72
NLR NS	Natal Law Reports, New Series	South Africa	1879–1932
NM	New Mexico Reports	USA	1888–
Nolan	Nolan's Magistrates' Cases	UK	1791–92

Noy	Noy's Reports, King's Bench	England	1559–1649
NPD	Natal Provincial Division Reports	South Africa	1933–46
NSC	New Sessions Cases	UK	1844–51
NSR	Nova Scotia Reports*	Canada	1834–1929, 1965–69
NSR (2d)	Nova Scotia Reports, Second Series*	Canada	1969–
NSW Bktcy	New South Wales Bankruptcy Cases	Australia (NSW)	1890–91
NSW Bky & C	New South Wales Bankruptcy and Company Cases	Australia (NSW)	1891–93
NSW Bky C & P	New South Wales Bankruptcy, Company and Probate Cases	Australia (NSW)	1893–99
NSW CCR	New South Wales Compensation Court Reports	Australia (NSW)	1984–2003
NSW Conv R	New South Wales Conveyancing Reports	Australia (NSW)	1980–
NSW Land App Cts	New South Wales Land Appeal Court Cases	Australia (NSW)	1890–1921
NSW Sel Cas (Dowling)	Dowling's Select Cases, New South Wales	Australia (NSW)	1828–44
NSWLR (Adm)	New South Wales Law Reports, Vice-Admiralty	Australia (NSW)	1879–1900
NSWLR (Bky)	New South Wales Law Reports, Bankruptcy	Australia (NSW)	1893–1900
NSWLR (D)	New South Wales Law Reports, Divorce and Matrimonial Causes	Australia (NSW)	1880–1900
NSWLR (Eq)	New South Wales Law Reports, Equity	Australia (NSW)	1879–1900
NSWLR	New South Wales Law Reports, Law	Australia (NSW)	1879–1900
NSWLR	New South Wales Law Reports*	Australia (NSW)	1971–
NSWR	New South Wales Reports*	Australia (NSW)	1960–70
NSWSCR (Eq)	New South Wales Supreme Court Reports, Equity	Australia (NSW)	1862–76
NSWSCR (L)	New South Wales Supreme Court Reports, Law	Australia (NSW)	1862–76
NSWSCR NS	New South Wales Supreme Court Reports, New Series	Australia (NSW)	1878–79
NTJ	Northern Territory Supreme Court Judgments	Australia (NT)	1951–76
NTLR	Northern Territory Law Reports*	Australia (NT)	1990–
NTR	Northern Territory Reports*	Australia (NT)	1979–91
NTR	Northern Territory Reports	Australia (NT)	1991–
NW	North Western Reporter*	USA	1879–1941
NW 2d	North Western Reporter, Second Series*	USA	1941–

NWTR	Northwest Territories Reports*	Canada	1983–98
NY	New York Reports	USA	1847–1956
NY 2d	New York Reports, Second Series	USA	1956–
NYS	New York Supplement	USA	1888–1938
NYS 2d	New York Supplement, Second Series	USA	1938–
NZ Jur	New Zealand Jurist Reports	NZ	1873–75
NZ Jur NS	New Zealand Jurist Reports, New Series	NZ	1875–79
NZAR	New Zealand Administrative Reports	NZ	1976–
NZBLC	New Zealand Business Law Cases	NZ	1984–
NZCA	New Zealand Court of Appeal Reports	NZ	1867–77
NZCLC	New Zealand Company Law Cases	NZ	1981–
NZFLR	New Zealand Family Law Reports	NZ	1981–
NZLR	New Zealand Law Reports*	NZ	1880–
NZPCC	New Zealand Privy Council Cases	NZ	1840–1932
O Bridg	Sir Orlando Bridgman's Reports, Common Pleas	England	1660–67
O'M & H	O'Malley and Hardcastle's Election Petitions	UK	1869–1929
OAC	Ontario Appeal Cases	Canada	1983–
OB & F	Ollivier, Bell and Fitzgerald's Reports	NZ	1878–80
OBSP	Old Bailey Sessions Papers	UK	1683–1834
OFS	Orange Free State High Court Reports	South Africa	1879–83
Ohio	Ohio Reports	USA	1821–51
Ohio B	Ohio Bar Reports	USA	1981–
Ohio St	Ohio State Reports	USA	1852–1964
Ohio St 2d	Ohio State Reports, Second Series	USA	1964–82
Ohio St 3d	Ohio State Reports, Third Series	USA	1991–
Okla	Oklahoma Reports	USA	1890–1953
OLR	Ontario Law Reports*	Canada	1901–31
OPD	Orange Free State Provincial Division Reports	South Africa	1910–46
OR	Official Reports of the South African Republic	South Africa	1894–99
OR	Ontario Reports	Canada	1882–1900
OR	Ontario Reports*	Canada	1931–73
OR (2d)	Ontario Reports, Second Series*	Canada	1973–90
OR (3d)	Ontario Reports, Third Series*	Canada	1990–
Or	Oregon Reports	USA	1853–
Or App	Oregon Reports, Court of Appeals	USA	1969–
ORC	Orange River Colony Reports	South Africa	1903–09
Ow	Owen's Reports, King's Bench and Common Pleas	England	1556–1615
OWN	Ontario Weekly Notes*	Canada	1909–62
OWR	Ontario Weekly Reporter	Canada	1902–16
P	Law Reports, Probate*	UK	1891–1971
P	Pacific Reporter*	USA	1883–1931
P 2d	Pacific Reporter, Second Series*	USA	1931–2000
P 3d	Pacific Reporter, Third Series*	USA	2000–
P & CR	Property, Planning and Compensation Reports	UK	1949–
P Wms	Peere Williams' Reports, Chancery and King's Bench	UK	1695–1735

Pa	Pennsylvania State Reports	USA	1845–
Paige Ch	Paige's Chancery Reports, New York	USA	1828–45
Palm	Palmer's Reports, King's Bench	England	1619–29
Park	Parker's Reports, Exchequer	UK	1743–67
Pat	Paton's Scotch Appeals, House of Lords	UK	1726–1821
Pater	Paterson's Scotch Appeals, House of Lords	UK	1851–73
PCC	Palmer's Company Cases	UK	1985–89
PCIJ (ser A)	Publications of the Permanent Court of International Justice, Series A*	International	1923–30
PCIJ (ser B)	Publications of the Permanent Court of International Justice, Series B*	International	1922–30
PCIJ (ser A/B)	Publications of the Permanent Court of International Justice, Series A/B*	International	1931–40
PD	Law Reports, Probate Division*	UK	1875–90
Peake	Peake's Reports, Nisi Prius	UK	1790–94
Peake Add Cas	Peake's Additional Cases, Nisi Prius	UK	1795–1812
Peck	Peckwell's Election Cases	UK	1802–06
PEIR	Prince Edward Island Reports	Canada	1850–72
Pelham	Pelham's Reports, South Australia	Australia (SA)	1865–66
Per & Dav	Perry and Davison's Reports, Queen's Bench	UK	1838–41
Per & Kn	Perry and Knapp's Election Cases	UK	1833
Per P	Perrault's Prévosté de Québec	Canada	1726–59
Pet	Peters' Supreme Court Reports	USA	1828–42
Petty SR	Petty Sessions Review	Australia (NSW)	1967–93
Ph	Phillips' Chancery Reports	UK	1841–49
Phil Ecc	J Phillimore's Ecclesiastical Reports	UK	1809–21
Phil El Cas	Phillips' Election Cases	UK	1780–81
Phil Judg	Phillimore's Principal Ecclesiastical Judgments	UK	1867–75
Pig & R	Pigott and Rodwell's Reports, Common Pleas	UK	1843–45
Pitc	Pitcairn's Criminal Trials	Scotland	1488–1624
Plow	Plowden's Reports	England	1550–80
PNGLR	Papua New Guinea Law Reports*	PNG	1971–
Pollex	Pollexfen's Reports, King's Bench	England	1669–85
Pop	Popham's Reports, King's Bench	England	1592–1627
Pow R & D	Power, Rodwell and Dew's Election Cases	UK	1848–56
Prec Ch	Precedents in Chancery	UK	1689–1722
Price	Price's Reports, Exchequer	UK	1814–24
Price Min Cas	Price's Mining Commissioner's Cases	Canada	1906–10
PRNZ	Procedure Reports of New Zealand	NZ	1983–
Pyke	Pyke's Lower Canada Reports, King's Bench	Canada	1809–10
Q Conv R	Queensland Conveyancing Reports	Australia (Qld)	1982–
QAR	Queensland Administrative Reports	Australia (Qld)	1992–2004
QB	Law Reports, Queen's Bench Division*	UK	1891–1900, 1952–
QBD	Law Reports, Queen's Bench Division*	UK	1875–90

QCR	Queensland Criminal Reports	Australia (Qld)	1860–1907
Qd R	Queensland Reports*	Australia (Qld)	1958–
QJPR	Queensland Justice of the Peace Journal	Australia (Qld)	1907–72
QLCR	Queensland Land Court Reports	Australia (Qld)	1974–
Qld Lawyer	Queensland Lawyer	Australia (Qld)	1973–
QLJR	Queensland Law Journal Reports	Australia (Qld)	1881–1901
QLR	Québec Law Reports	Canada	1874–91
QLR	Queensland Law Reporter	Australia (Qld)	1972–76
QLR (Beor)	Beor's Queensland Law Reports	Australia (Qld)	1876–78
QPELR	Queensland Planning and Environmental Law Reports	Australia (Qld)	1996–
QPLR	Queensland Planning Law Reports	Australia (Qld)	1981–95
QPR	Québec Practice Reports	Canada	1897–1982
QSCR	Queensland Supreme Court Reports	Australia (Qld)	1860–81
QSR	State Reports, Queensland*	Australia (Qld)	1902–57
QWN	Queensland Weekly Notes	Australia (Qld)	1902–72
R	The Reports	UK	1892–95
R & IT	Rating and Income Tax Reports	UK	1924–60
RA	Ratings Appeals	UK	1962–
RAC	Ramsay's Appeal Cases	Canada	1874–86
Rast	Rastell's Entries	UK	1566
Rayn	Rayner's Tithes Cases	UK	1575–1782
Real Prop Cas	Real Property Cases	UK	1843–48
Rec Lebon	Recueil des arrêts du Conseil d'État statuant au contentieux	France	1848–
Rep Ch	Reports in Chancery	UK	1625–1712
Res Cas	Reserved Cases	Ireland	1860–64
Rett	Rettie's Court of Session, Justiciary and House of Lords Cases, Fourth Series	UK	1873–98
RFL	Reports of Family Law	Canada	1971–78
RFL (2d)	Reports of Family Law, Second Series	Canada	1978–86
RFL (3d)	Reports of Family Law, Third Series	Canada	1986–94
RFL (4th)	Reports of Family Law, Fourth Series	Canada	1994–2000
RFL (5th)	Reports of Family Law, Fifth Series	Canada	2000–04
RFL (6th)	Reports of Family Law, Sixth Series	Canada	2004–
RI	Rhode Island Reports	USA	1828–1980
RIAA	United Nations Reports of International Arbitral Awards	International	1948–
Rick & M	Rickards and Michael's Locus Standi Reports	UK	1885–89
Rick & S	Rickards and Saunders' Locus Standi Reports	UK	1890–94
Ridg L & S	Ridgeway, Lapp and Schoales's Reports	Ireland	1793–95
Ridg PC	Ridgeway's Parliamentary Cases	Ireland	1784–96
Ridg t H	Ridgeway's Reports tempore Hardwicke, King's Bench and Chancery	UK	1733–45
Ritch Eq Rep	Ritchie's Equity Reports, Nova Scotia	Canada	1873–82
RJQ	Recueils de jurisprudence du Québec*	Canada	1975–

RJRQ	Rapports judiciaries revises de la Province de Québec	Canada	1726–1879
RL	Revue Légale, Old Series	Canada	1869–92
RL NS	Revue Légale, New Series	Canada	1895–
Rob Ecc	Robertson's Ecclesiastical Reports	UK	1844–53
Rob L & W	Roberts, Leeming and Wallis's New County Court Cases	UK	1849–51
Robert	Robertson's Scotch Appeals, House of Lords	UK	1707–27
Robin	Robinson's Scotch Appeals, House of Lords	UK	1840–41
Rolle	Rolle's Reports, King's Bench	England	1614–25
Rosc	Roscoe's Supreme Court Reports, Cape of Good Hope	South Africa	1861–78
Rose	Rose's Bankruptcy Cases	UK	1810–16
Ross LC	Ross's Leading Cases in Commercial Law	UK	1853–57
Rowe	Rowe's Reports of Interesting Cases	UK	1798–1824
RPC	Reports of Patent, Design and Trade Mark Cases	UK	1884–
RPD	Repatriation Pension Decisions	Australia	1933–85
RR	Revised Reports	UK	1785–1866
RRC	Ryde's Rating Cases	UK	1956–79
RTR	Road Traffic Reports	UK	1970–
Rus EC	Russell's Election Cases, Nova Scotia	Canada	1874
Russ	Russell's Reports, Chancery	UK	1826–29
Russ & My	Russell and Mylne's Reports, Chancery	UK	1829–31
Russ & Ry	Russell and Ryan's Crown Cases Reserved	UK	1799–1824
RVR	Rating and Valuation Reporter	UK	1961–
Ry & Can Cas	Railway and Canal Cases	UK	1835–54
Ry & Can Tr Cas	Railway and Canal Traffic Cases	UK	1855–1950
Ry & M	Ryan and Moody's Reports, Nisi Prius	UK	1823–26
Ryde & K Rat App	Ryde and Konstam's Reports, Rating Appeals	UK	1894–1904
Ryde Rat App	Ryde's Rating Appeals	UK	1886–93
S Ct	Supreme Court Reporter	USA	1882–
SA	South African Law Reports*	South Africa	1947–
SAIR	South Australian Industrial Reports	Australia (SA)	1916–
SALCR	South Australian Licensing Court Reports	Australia (SA)	1967–78
Salk	Salkeld's Reports, King's Bench	UK	1689–1712
SALR	South Australian Law Reports*	Australia (SA)	1865–92, 1899–1920
SAPR	South Australian Planning Reports	Australia (SA)	1967–81
Sask LR	Saskatchewan Law Reports*	Canada	1907–31
Sask R	Saskatchewan Reports*	Canada	1979–
SASR	South Australian State Reports*	Australia (SA)	1921–
Sau & Sc	Sausse and Scully's Reports, Rolls Court	Ireland	1837–40
Saund & A	Saunders and Austin's Reports, Locus Standi	UK	1895–1904
Saund & B	Saunders and Bidder's Reports, Locus Standi	UK	1905–19

Saund & C	Saunders and Cole's Reports, Bail Court	UK	1846–48
Saund & M	Saunders and Macrae's County Courts and Insolvency Cases	UK	1852–58
Sav	Savile's Reports, Common Pleas	UK	1580–94
Say	Sayer's Reports, King's Bench	UK	1751–56
SC	Supreme Court Reports, Cape of Good Hope	South Africa	1880–1909
SC	South Carolina Reports	USA	1868–
SC	Session Cases, Court of Sessions*	Scotland	1906–
SC (HL)	Session Cases, House of Lords*	Scotland	1906–
SC (J)	Session Cases, Court of Justiciary*	Scotland	1906–
SC (PC)	Session Cases, Privy Council*	Scotland	2000–
Sc NR	Scott's New Reports, Common Pleas and Exchequer	UK	1840–45
Sc RR	Scots Revised Reports, House of Lords Series	UK	1707–1865, 1898–1908
Sch & Lef	Schoales and Lefroy's Reports, Chancery	Ireland	1802–06
Scott	Scott's Cases, Common Pleas and Exchequer	UK	1834–40
SCR	Canada Supreme Court Reports*	Canada	1876–1922
SCR	Canada Law Reports, Supreme Court of Canada*	Canada	1923–69
SCR	Canada Supreme Court Reports*	Canada	1970–
SCR	Supreme Court Reports, Supreme Court of India*	India	1950–
SD	South Dakota Reports	USA	1890–1976
SE	South Eastern Reporter*	USA	1887–1939
SE 2d	South Eastern Reporter, Second Series*	USA	1939–
Sea & Sm	Searle and Smith's Reports, Probate, Divorce and Matrimonial Causes	UK	1859–60
Searle	Searle's Supreme Court Reports	South Africa	1850–67
Sel Cas Ev	Strange's Select Cases in Evidence	UK	1698–1732
Shaw & M	Shaw and Maclean's Scotch Appeals, House of Lords	UK	1835–38
Shaw App	Shaw's Scotch Appeals, House of Lords	UK	1821–24
Shaw Just	Shaw's Cases, Court of Justiciary	Scotland	1819–31
Shaw Teind	Shaw's Teind Court Decisions	Scotland	1821–31
Show KB	Shower's Reports, King's Bench	England	1678–95
Show Parl Cas	Shower's Parliamentary Cases	England	1677–98
Sid	Siderfin's Reports, King's Bench, Common Pleas and Exchequer	England	1657–70
Sim	Simons' Reports, Chancery	UK	1826–50
Sim & St	Simons and Stuart's Reports, Chancery	UK	1822–26
Sim NS	Simons' Reports, Chancery, New Series	UK	1850–52
Skin	Skinner's Reports, King's Bench	England	1681–98
SLR	Scottish Law Reporter	Scotland	1865–1924
SLR	Singapore Law Reports	Singapore	1965–2009
SLR	Singapore Law Reports*	Singapore	2010–
SLR(R)	Singapore Law Reports (Reissue)*	Singapore	1965–2009
SLT	Scots Law Times	Scotland	1893–

Sm & G	Smale and Giffard's Reports, Chancery	UK	1852–57
Smith & B	Smith and Batty's Reports, King's Bench	Ireland	1824–25
Smith KB	J P Smith's Reports, King's Bench	UK	1803–06
Smith LC	Smith's Leading Cases	UK	1837
Smith Reg Cas	C L Smith's Registration Cases	UK	1895–1914
So	Southern Reporter*	USA	1886–1941
So 2d	Southern Reporter, Second Series*	USA	1941–2009
So 3d	Southern Reporter, Third Series*	USA	2009–
SR (NSW)	State Reports, New South Wales*	Australia (NSW)	1901–59
SR (NSW)	State Reports, New South Wales	Australia (NSW)	1960–70
SR (WA)	State Reports, Western Australia	Australia (WA)	1979–
STC	Simon's Tax Cases	UK	1973–
Stew N Sc	Stewart's Nova Scotia Reports, Vice-Admiralty	Canada	1803–13
Stock Adm	Stockton's Vice-Admiralty Reports and Digest, Court of New Brunswick	Canada	1879–91
Str	Strange's Reports	UK	1716–49
Stu M & P	Stuart, Milne and Peddie's Reports, Court of Session	Scotland	1851–53
Stuart	Stuart's Lower Canada Vice-Admiralty Cases	Canada	1836–74
Stuart KB	Stuart's Lower Canada Reports, King's Bench	Canada	1810–35
Style	Style's Modern Reports, King's Bench	England	1646–55
SW	South Western Reporter*	USA	1886–1928
SW 2d	South Western Reporter, Second Series*	USA	1928–99
SW 3d	South Western Reporter, Third Series*	USA	1999–
Sw & Tr	Swabey and Tristram's Reports, Probate, Divorce and Matrimonial Causes	UK	1858–65
Swab	Swabey's Admiralty Reports	UK	1855–59
Swans	Swanston's Reports, Chancery	UK	1818–19
Swin	Swinton's Reports, High Court and Circuit Courts of Justiciary	Scotland	1835–41
Syme	Syme's Reports, High Court of Justiciary	Scotland	1826–29
T & M	Temple and Mew's Criminal Appeal Cases	UK	1848–51
T Jones	Sir T Jones' Reports, King's Bench and Common Pleas	England	1667–85
T Raym	Sir T Raymond's Reports, King's Bench, Common Pleas and Exchequer	England	1660–84
Taml	Tamlyn's Reports, Rolls Court	UK	1829–30
Tarl	Tarleton's Term Reports	Australia (NSW)	1881–83
Tas LR	Tasmanian Law Reports	Australia (Tas)	1897–1904
Tas LR	Tasmanian Law Reports*	Australia (Tas)	1904–40
Tas R	Tasmanian Reports*	Australia (Tas)	1979–
Tas SR	Tasmanian State Reports*	Australia (Tas)	1941–78
Taunt	Taunton's Reports, Common Pleas	UK	1807–19

Tay	Taylor's Upper Canada Reports, King's Bench	Canada	1823–27
TC	Reports of Tax Cases	UK	1875–
TCM	Tax Court Memorandum Decisions	USA	1942–
Tenn	Tennessee Reports	USA	1871–1971
Tenn App	Tennessee Appeals Reports	USA	1925–72
Term R	Term Reports, King's Bench	UK	1785–1800
Terr LR	Territories Law Reports*	Canada	1885–1907
TH	Transvaal Law Reports, Witwatersrand High Court	South Africa	1902–09
TLR	Times Law Reports	UK	1884–1952
Toth	Tothill's Transactions, Chancery	England	1559–1646
Town St Tr	Townsend's Modern State Trials	UK	1850
TPC	Trade Practices Cases	Australia	1975–81
TPD	Transvaal Provincial Division Reports	South Africa	1910–46
TPR	Trade Practices Reports	Australia	1975–83
TPRS	Trade Practices Reporting Service	Australia	1974–
TR	Taxation Reports	UK	1939–81
Tr L	Trading Law	UK	1981–93
Tr Law	Trading Law and Trading Law Reports	UK	1994–
Tr LR	Trading Law Reports	UK	1983–93
Traff Cas	Traffic Cases	UK	1951–76
Trem PC	Tremaine's Pleas of the Crown	England	1723
Trist	Tristram's Consistory Judgments	UK	1872–90
TS	Transvaal Supreme Court Reports	South Africa	1902–10
Tudor LC Merc Law	Tudor's Leading Cases on Mercantile and Maritime Law	UK	1884
Turn & R	Turner and Russell's Reports, Chancery	UK	1822–24
Tyr	Tyrwhitt's Reports, Exchequer	UK	1830–35
Tyr & Gr	Tyrwhitt and Granger's Reports, Exchequer	UK	1835–36
US	United States Supreme Court Reports*	USA	1790–
UCCP	Upper Canada Common Pleas Reports	Canada	1850–82
UCQB	Upper Canada Reports, Queen's Bench	Canada	1844–82
US App DC	United States Court of Appeals Reports, District of Columbia	USA	1941–
USTC	United States Tax Court Reports	USA	1942–
Utah	Utah Reports	USA	1855–1953
Utah 2d	Utah Reports, Second Series	USA	1953–74
V Conv R	Victorian Conveyancing Reports	Australia (Vic)	1981–
Va	Virginia Reports	USA	1790–
Va App	Virginia Court of Appeals Reports	USA	1985–
VACR	Victorian Accident Compensation Reports	Australia (Vic)	1990–97
VAR	Victorian Administrative Reports	Australia (Vic)	1985–
VATTR	Value Added Tax Tribunals Reports	UK	1973–
Vaugh	Vaughan's Reports, Common Pleas	England	1665–73
Vent	Ventris' Reports, King's Bench and Common Pleas	England	1668–88
Vern	Vernon's Reports, Chancery	UK	1680–1719
Vern & S	Vernon and Scriven's Reports, King's Bench	Ireland	1786–88

Ves & B	Vesey and Beames' Reports, Chancery	UK	1812–14
Ves Jr	Vesey Junior's Reports, Chancery	UK	1789–1817
Ves Sen	Vesey Senior's Reports, Chancery	UK	1746–55
VIR	Victorian Industrial Reports	Australia (Vic)	1982–
VLR	Victorian Law Reports*	Australia (Vic)	1885–1956
VLR (Eq)	Victorian Law Reports, Equity*	Australia (Vic)	1875–84
VLR (IP & M)	Victorian Law Reports, Insolvency, Probate and Matrimonial Causes*	Australia (Vic)	1875–84
VLR (L)	Victorian Law Reports, Law*	Australia (Vic)	1875–84
VLR (M)	Victorian Law Reports, Mining*	Australia (Vic)	1875–84
VPA	Victorian Planning Appeal Decisions	Australia (Vic)	1969–81
VR	Victorian Reports*	Australia (Vic)	1957–
VR (Adm)	Victorian Reports, Vice-Admiralty	Australia (Vic)	1872–73
VR (Eq)	Victorian Reports, Equity	Australia (Vic)	1867–72
VR (IE & M)	Victorian Reports, Insolvency, Ecclesiastical and Matrimonial Cases	Australia (Vic)	1869–72
VR (L)	Victorian Reports, Law	Australia (Vic)	1866–72
VR (M)	Victorian Reports, Mining	Australia (Vic)	1870–72
W & W	Wyatt and Webb's Victorian Reports	Australia (Vic)	1861–63
W Jones	Sir W Jones' Reports, King's Bench and Common Pleas	England	1620–41
W Rob	W Robinson's Admiralty Reports	UK	1838–52
W Va	West Virginia Reports	USA	1864–
W W & A'B	Wyatt, Webb and A'Beckett's Victorian Reports	Australia (Vic)	1864–69
W W & A'B (Eq)	Wyatt, Webb and A'Beckett's Victorian Reports, Equity	Australia (Vic)	1864–69
W W & A'B (IE & M)	Wyatt, Webb and A'Beckett's Victorian Reports, Insolvency, Ecclesiastical and Matrimonial Cases	Australia (Vic)	1864–69
W W & A'B (M)	Wyatt, Webb and A'Beckett's Victorian Reports, Mining Cases	Australia (Vic)	1864–69
WAAR	Western Australian Arbitration Reports	Australia (WA)	1901–20
Wal by L	Wallis' Irish Chancery Reports by Lyne	Ireland	1766–91
Wall	Wallace's Supreme Court Reports	USA	1863–74
WALR	Western Australian Law Reports*	Australia (WA)	1898–1958
WAR	Western Australian Reports*	Australia (WA)	1958–
Wash	Washington Reports	USA	1889–1939
Wash 2d	Washington Reports, Second Series	USA	1939–
Wash App	Washington Appellate Reports	USA	1969–
WCATR	Workers Compensation Appeal Tribunal Reports, South Australia	Australia (SA)	1988–97
WCBD (Vic)	Workers Compensation Board Decisions, Victoria	Australia (Vic)	1938–78
WCBD (WA)	Workers' Compensation Board Decisions, Western Australia	Australia (WA)	1949–65
WCC	Workmen's Compensation Cases	UK	1898–1907
WCR (NSW)	Workers' Compensation Reports, New South Wales	Australia (NSW)	1926–84

WCR (Q)	Workers' Compensation Reports, Queensland	Australia (Qld)	1919–
WCR (WA)	Workers' Compensation Reports, Western Australia	Australia (WA)	1979–90
WCTR	Workers Compensation Tribunal Reports, South Australia	Australia (SA)	1997–
Web Pat Cas	Webster's Patent Cases	UK	1601–1855
Welsh Reg Cas	Welsh's Registry Cases	Ireland	1832–40
West HL	West's Reports, House of Lords	UK	1839–41
West t Hard	West's Reports tempore Hardwicke, Chancery	UK	1736–39
West Ti Cas	Western's London Tithe Cases	UK	1535–1822
Wheat	Wheaton's Supreme Court Reports	USA	1816–27
White	White's Justiciary Reports	Scotland	1885–93
Wight	Wightwick's Reports, Exchequer	UK	1810–11
Will PCs	Williams' Practice Cases, District of Port Phillip, New South Wales	Australia (NSW)	1846
Will Woll & D	Willmore, Wollaston and Davison's Reports, King's Bench and Bail Court	UK	1837
Will Woll & H	Willmore, Wollaston, and Hodges' Reports, Queen's Bench and Bail Court	UK	1838–39
Willes	Willes' Common Pleas Reports	UK	1737–58
Wils & S	Wilson and Shaw's Scotch Appeals, House of Lords	UK	1825–34
Wils Ch	Wilson's Reports, Chancery	UK	1818–19
Wils Ex	Wilson's Reports, Exchequer	UK	1805–17
Wils KB	Wilson's Reports, King's Bench and Common Pleas	UK	1742–74
Winch	Winch's Reports, Common Pleas	England	1621–25
Wis	Wisconsin Reports	USA	1853–1957
Wis 2d	Wisconsin Reports, Second Series	USA	1957–
WLD	Witwatersrand Local Division Reports	South Africa	1910–46
WLR	Weekly Law Reports	UK	1953–
WLR	Western Law Reporter	Canada	1905–16
WN	Weekly Notes	UK	1866–1952
WN (NSW)	Weekly Notes, New South Wales	Australia (NSW)	1884–1970
Wolf & B	Wolferstan and Bristowe's Election Cases	UK	1859–64
Wolf & D	Wolferstan and Dew's Election Cases	UK	1856–58
Woll	Wollaston's Reports, Bail Court	UK	1840–41
Wood	Wood's Tithe Cases, Exchequer	UK	1650–1798
WR	Weekly Reporter	UK	1852–1906
WWR	Western Weekly Reports	Canada	1911–
Wyo	Wyoming Reports	USA	1870–1959
Y & C Ch	Younge and Collyer's Reports, Chancery	UK	1841–43
Y & C Ex	Younge and Collyer's Reports, Exchequer	UK	1834–42
Y & J	Younge and Jervis' Reports, Exchequer	UK	1826–30
YAD	Young's Admiralty Decisions	Canada	1865–80
Yel	Yelverton's Reports, King's Bench	England	1602–13

Yo	Younge's Reports, Exchequer	UK	1830–32
YR	Yukon Reports*	Canada	1987–89

Table A: Australian Medium Neutral Unique Court (and Tribunal) Identifiers

In accordance with rule 2.8.1, medium neutral citations should only be used where a court or tribunal itself allocates the medium neutral citation. In general, this means that medium neutral citations should be used from approximately 1999 onwards. Specific dates for Australian superior and appellate courts are indicated in rule 2.8.1.

The table below sets out the current, preferred medium neutral unique court identifiers for some Australian courts and tribunals. Where a body is not listed below but allocates a unique court identifier to its decisions, that unique court identifier should be used.

Unique Court Identifier	Court or Tribunal
AATA	Administrative Appeals Tribunal of Australia
ACompT	Australian Competition Tribunal
ACopyT	Australian Copyright Tribunal
ACTAAT	Australian Capital Territory Administrative Appeals Tribunal
ACTCA	Australian Capital Territory Court of Appeal
ACTSC	Supreme Court of the Australian Capital Territory (including Full Court)
ADFDAT	Defence Force Discipline Appeal Tribunal
ADO	Australian Designs Office
AIRC	Australian Industrial Relations Commission
AIRCFB	Australian Industrial Relations Commission — Full Bench
ATP	Australian Takeovers Panel
FamCA	Family Court of Australia
FamCAFC	Family Court of Australia — Full Court
FCA	Federal Court of Australia
FCAFC	Federal Court of Australia — Full Court
FMCA	Federal Magistrates' Court of Australia
FMCAfam	Federal Magistrates' Court of Australia — Family Law
FWA	Fair Work Australia
FWAFB	Fair Work Australia — Full Bench
HCA	High Court of Australia
HCASL	High Court of Australia — Special Leave Dispositions
HCATrans	High Court of Australia — Transcripts
IRCA	Industrial Relations Court of Australia

MRTA	Migration Review Tribunal of Australia
NFSC	Supreme Court of Norfolk Island
NNTTA	National Native Title Tribunal
NSWADT	New South Wales Administrative Decisions Tribunal
NSWADTAP	New South Wales Administrative Decisions Tribunal — Appeal Panel
NSWCA	New South Wales Court of Appeal
NSWCC	Compensation Court of New South Wales
NSWCCA	New South Wales Court of Criminal Appeal
NSWCSAT	Community Services Appeals Tribunal of New South Wales
NSWDC	District Court of New South Wales
NSWDRGC	Drug Court of New South Wales
NSWFTT	Fair Trading Tribunal of New South Wales
NSWIRComm	Industrial Court of New South Wales
NSWLEC	Land and Environment Court of New South Wales
NSWSC	Supreme Court of New South Wales (including Full Court)
NTCA	Northern Territory Court of Appeal
NTCCA	Northern Territory Court of Criminal Appeal
NTSC	Supreme Court of the Northern Territory
QADT	Queensland Anti-Discrimination Tribunal
QCA	Queensland Court of Appeal
QCAT	Queensland Civil and Administrative Tribunal
QDC	District Court of Queensland
QLAC	Land Appeal Court of Queensland
QLAT	Queensland Liquor Appeals Tribunal
QLRT	Queensland Land and Resources Tribunal
QLC	Land Court of Queensland
QPEC	Planning and Environment Court of Queensland
QSC	Supreme Court of Queensland
RRTA	Refugee Review Tribunal of Australia
SADC	District Court of South Australia
SAEOT	Equal Opportunity Tribunal of South Australia
SAERDC	Environment, Resources and Development Court of South Australia
SAIRC	Industrial Relations Court of South Australia
SAIRComm	Industrial Relations Commission of South Australia
SASC	Supreme Court of South Australia (including Full Court until end of 2009)

SASCFC	Supreme Court of South Australia — Full Court
SAWCAT	Workers Compensation Appeal Tribunal of South Australia
SAWCT	Workers Compensation Tribunal of South Australia
TASADT	Anti-Discrimination Tribunal of Tasmania
TASRMPAT	Resources Management and Planning Appeal Tribunal of Tasmania
TASSC	Supreme Court of Tasmania (including Full Court until end of 2009)
TASCCA	Tasmanian Court of Criminal Appeal
TASFC	Supreme Court of Tasmania — Full Court
VCAT	Victorian Civil and Administrative Tribunal
VCC	County Court of Victoria
VMHRB	Mental Health Review Board of Victoria
VSC	Supreme Court of Victoria
VSCA	Victorian Court of Appeal
WADC	District Court of Western Australia
WASAT	Western Australia State Administrative Tribunal
WASC	Supreme Court of Western Australia
WASCA	Western Australia Court of Appeal (including Full Court)

Table B: Pinpoint Abbreviations

The table below lists abbreviations used for pinpoint references in citations of legislation. Where nothing is indicated in the 'use' column, the abbreviation is used generally (including for Australian legislation and delegated legislation).

Descriptor	Abbreviation	Plural	Abbreviation	Use
Amendment	amend	Amendments	amends	United States legislation
Appendix	app	Appendices	apps	
Article	art	Articles	arts	
Chapter	ch	Chapters	chs	
	c			United Kingdom and Canadian legislation
	cap			Hong Kong and Singaporean legislation
Clause	cl	Clauses	cls	
Division	div	Divisions	divs	
Order	O	Orders	OO	
Paragraph	para	Paragraphs	paras	
Part	pt	Parts	pts	
Regulation	reg	Regulations	regs	
Rule	r	Rules	rr	
Schedule	sch	Schedules	schs	
Section	s	Sections	ss	
	§		§§	United States legislation
Sub-clause	sub-cl	Sub-clauses	sub-cls	
Subdivision	sub-div	Subdivisions	sub-divs	
Sub-paragraph	sub-para	Sub-paragraphs	sub-paras	
Sub-regulation	sub-reg	Sub-regulations	sub-regs	
Sub-rule	sub-rule	Sub-rules	sub-rules	
Subsection	sub-s	Subsections	sub-ss	
Title	tit	Titles	tits	United States legislation

Bibliography

Australasian Legal Information Institute (10 January 2010) <http://www.austlii.edu.au>

The Bluebook: A Uniform System of Citation (Harvard Law Review Association, 18th ed, 2005)

British and Irish Legal Information Institute <http://www.bailii.org>

Chinese University Hong Kong, *Citation Styles* (August 2008) <http://www.cuhk.edu.hk/policy/academichonesty/p03_4_4a.htm>

Dickerson, Darby, *ALWD Citation Manual: A Professional System of Citation* (Aspen Publishers, 3rd ed, 2006)

French, Derek, *How to Cite Legal Authorities* (Oxford University Press, 2nd ed, 2003)

McGill Law Journal, *Canadian Guide to Uniform Legal Citation* (Carswell, 6th ed, 2006)

McLay, Geoff, Christopher Murray and Jonathan Orpin, *New Zealand Law Style Guide* (Thomson Reuters, 2009)

New York University School of Law Journal of International Law and Politics, *Guide to Foreign and International Legal Citations* (Wolters Kluwer, 2nd ed, 2009)

Nygh, Peter E and Peter Butt (eds), *Butterworths Concise Australian Legal Dictionary* (LexisNexis Butterworths, 3rd ed, 2004)

Prince, Mary Miles, *Prince's Bieber Dictionary of Legal Abbreviations: A Reference Guide for Attorneys, Legal Secretaries, Paralegals, and Law Students* (WS Hein, 6th ed, 2009)

Publications Department and Law Reporting Department, Singapore Academy of Law, *The Singapore Academy of Law Style Guide* (2004)

Raistrick, Donald, *Index to Legal Citations and Abbreviations* (Sweet and Maxwell, 3rd ed, 2008)

United Nations Documentation: Research Guide (10 February 2010) <http://www.un.org/Depts/dhl/resguide>

Woodley, Mick (ed), *Osborn's Concise Law Dictionary* (Sweet and Maxwell, 11th ed, 2009)

Example text and citations are taken in some cases from (2009) 33 *Melbourne University Law Review* and (2009) 10 *Melbourne Journal of International Law*.

Suggestion Form

When using the *AGLC*, you may become aware of instances where it does not adequately address a citation issue. Please take the time to complete and return this suggestion form with details of the issues you have encountered so that they can be addressed in the next edition of the *AGLC*.

Description of Problem (Include Reference to Relevant Rules)

Suggested Solution or Rule

Name	Contact Number	Email Address

If mailing this form, please address it to:

AGLC Committee
c/- The Editors
Melbourne University Law Review
Melbourne Law School
The University of Melbourne Victoria 3010
Australia

Alternatively, this form may be faxed to (+61 3) 9347 8087 or suggestions (including a reference to the relevant rules) may be emailed to law-mulr@unimelb.edu.au.

Index

D

E

F

G

H

I

J

L

M

Q

R

S

T

U

V

W

NOTES

NOTES

Full Citation	Subsequent References*
AUSTRALIAN CASES	
Tame v New South Wales (2002) 211 CLR 317.	*Tame* (2002) 211 CLR 317.
Andrew Shelton & Co Pty Ltd v Alpha Healthcare Ltd (2002) 5 VR 577.	*Alpha Healthcare Ltd* (2002) 5 VR 577.
Nydam v The Queen [1977] VR 430.	*Nydam* [1977] VR 430.
DPP (Vic) v Finn (2008) 186 A Crim R 235.	*Finn* (2008) 186 A Crim R 235.
Minister for Immigration and Citizenship v SZIAI [2009] HCA 39 (23 September 2009).	*SZIAI* [2009] HCA 39 (23 September 2009).
Barton v Chibber (Unreported, Supreme Court of Victoria, Hampel J, 29 June 1989).	*Barton* (Unreported, Supreme Court of Victoria, Hampel J, 29 June 1989).
AUSTRALIAN LEGISLATION	
Australian Constitution s 19.	
Corporations Act 2001 (Cth).	*Corporations Act* s 9.
Charter of Human Rights and Responsibilities Act 2006 (Vic).	*Charter* s 7.
Police Regulations 2003 (Vic).	*Police Regulations* reg 6.
Australian Securities Exchange, *Listing Rules* (at 11 January 2010).	*Listing Rules* r 1.3.1.
Carbon Pollution Reduction Scheme Bill 2009 (Cth).	CPRS Bill 2009 cl 83.

* Where there is no text in this column, subsequent references should appear in full. Examples of subsequent references using short titles assume that a short title is included in the first reference to the source in accordance with rule 1.4.3.

Full Citation	Subsequent References*
JOURNAL ARTICLES	
Helen Rhoades, 'The Dangers of Shared Care Legislation: Why Australia Needs (Yet More) Family Law Reform' (2008) 36 *Federal Law Review* 279.	Rhoades, above n 3, 281.
Jeremy Masters, 'Easing the Parting' (2008) 82(11) *Law Institute Journal* 68.	Masters, above n 7, 69–71.
BOOKS	
R G Frey (ed), *Utility and Rights* (Basil Blackwell, 1985).	Frey, above n 92.
Meg Russel, 'Reform of the House of Lords: Lessons for Bicameralism' in Nicolas Aroney, Scott Prasser and J R Nethercote (eds), *Restraining Elective Dictatorship: The Upper House Solution?* (University of Western Australia Press, 2008) 119.	Russel, above n 17, 122.
Jean-Paul Sartre, *Being and Nothingness: An Essay on Phenomenological Ontology* (Hazel E Barnes trans, Methuen, 1958) 151 [trans of: *L'Etre et le Néant* (first published 1943)].	Sartre, above n 2, 151.
GOVERNMENT DOCUMENTS	
Commonwealth, *Parliamentary Debates*, Senate, 18 June 2008, 2642–4 (Bob Brown).	
Law Reform Committee, Parliament of Victoria, *Inquiry into Alternative Dispute Resolution and Restorative Justice* (2009).	Law Reform Committee, Parliament of Victoria, above n 1, 26.

Full Citation	Subsequent References*
NEWSPAPER ARTICLES	
Elenor Laise, 'TCW Slam Gundlach in Lawsuit over His Exit', *The Wall Street Journal* (New York), 8 January 2010, C1.	Laise, above n 7, C1.
Editorial, 'Medicare by Name, No Longer by Nature', *News*, *The Age* (Melbourne), 12 March 2004, 12.	'Medicare by Name', above n 18, 12.
Farrah Tomazin, 'Kinder Wage Breakthrough', *The Age* (online), 19 May 2009, <http://www.theage.com.au/national/education/kinder-wages-breakthrough-20090519-bcwh.html>.	Tomazin, above n 82.
WORKING, RESEARCH AND DISCUSSION PAPERS	
Paul Memmott and Peter Blackwood, 'Holding Title and Managing Land in Cape York — Two Case Studies' (Research Discussion Paper No 21, Australian Institute of Aboriginal and Torres Strait Islander Studies, 2008).	Memmott and Blackwood, above n 41, 37.
CONFERENCE PAPERS	
Anne Orford, 'Roman Law and the Godly Imperium in England's New Worlds' (Paper presented at the Workshop on the Theo-Political Renaissance, Department of English, Cornell University, 25 April 2008).	Orford, above n 16, 2.
INTERNET MATERIALS	
World Health Organization, *Violence against Women: A Priority Health Issue* (1997) <http://www.who.int/gender/violence/prioreng/en>.	World Health Organization, above n 7.

Full Citation	Subsequent References*
Khalid al Nur, 'Politics of Rage, Politics of Change' on *Making Sense of Sudan* (25 September 2009) <http://blogs.ssrn.org/sudan/2009/09/25/politics-of-rage-politics-of-change>.	al Nur, above n 3.
TREATIES	
Treaty on the Non-Proliferation of Nuclear Weapons, opened for signature 1 July 1968, 729 UNTS 161 (entered into force 5 March 1970).	*NPT* art 3.
Agreement Relating to Co-operation on Antitrust Matters, Australia–United States of America, 1369 UNTS 43 (signed and entered into force 29 June 1982).	*Antitrust Agreement* art 1.
UNITED NATIONS MATERIALS	
Universal Declaration on Human Rights, GA Res 217A (III), UN GAOR, 3rd sess, 183rd plen mtg, UN Doc A/810 (10 December 1948).	*UDHR*, UN Doc A/810, art 9.
Giorgio Gaja, Special Rapporteur, *Second Report on the Responsibility of International Organizations*, UN Doc A/CN.4/651 (2 April 2004).	Gaja, above n 12, 1.
Human Rights Committee, *Views: Communication No 1011/2001*, 81st sess, UN Doc CCPR/C/81/D/1011/2001 (26 August 2004) ('*Madafferi v Australia*').	*Madafferi v Australia*, UN Doc CCPR/C/81/D/1011/2001, 22.
INTERNATIONAL JUDICIAL DECISIONS	
Avena and Other Mexican Nationals (Mexico v United States of America) (Judgment) [2004] ICJ Rep 12.	*Avena (Judgment)* [2004] ICJ Rep 12.

Full Citation	Subsequent References*
Western Sahara (Advisory Opinion) [1975] ICJ Rep 12.	*Western Sahara* [1975] ICJ Rep 12, 17.
Southern Bluefin Tuna (Australia v Japan) (Jurisdiction and Admissibility) (2000) 39 ILM 1359.	*Southern Bluefin Tuna* (2000) 39 ILM 1359, 1370.
Re Polystyrene and Impact Crystal from the United States of America (United States of America v Mexico) (Panel Decision) (North American Free Trade Agreement Chapter 19 Panel, Case No MEX-94-1904-03, 12 September 1996).	*Polystyrene Decision* (North American Free Trade Agreement Chapter 19 Panel, Case No MEX-94-1904-03, 12 September 1996) 8.
Prosecutor v Ntaganda (Warrant of Arrest) (International Criminal Court, Pre-Trial Chamber I, Case No ICC-01/04-02/06-18, 22 August 2006).	*Ntaganda (Arrest Warrant)* (International Criminal Court, Pre-Trial Chamber I, Case No ICC-01/04-02/06-18, 22 August 2006) 4.
INTERNATIONAL ECONOMIC MATERIALS	
Marrakesh Agreement Establishing the World Trade Organization, opened for signature 15 April 1994, 1867 UNTS 3 (entered into force 1 January 1995) annex 2 ('*DSU*').	*DSU* art 4.
Preferential Tariff Treatment for Least-Developed Countries, WTO Doc WT/L/304 (17 June 1999, adopted 15 June 1999) (Decision on Waiver).	*Waiver Decision*, WTO Doc WT/L/304, paras 1–2.
Appellate Body Report, *Australia — Measures Affecting Importation of Salmon*, WTO Doc WT/DS18/AB/R, AB-1998-5 (20 October 1998) [105].	Appellate Body Report, *Australia — Salmon*, WTO Doc WT/DS18/AB/R, [100].

Full Citation	Subsequent References*
EUROPEAN SUPRANATIONAL MATERIALS	
Regulation (EC) No 2037/2000 of the European Parliament and of the Council of 29 June 2000 on Substances That Deplete the Ozone Layer [2000] OJ L 244/1, art 3(1).	*Regulation (EC) No 2037/2000* [2000] OJ L 244/1, art 4(2).
Treaty on the Functioning of the European Union, opened for signature 7 February 1992, [2009] OJ C 115/199 (entered into force 1 November 1993) ('*FEU*').	*FEU* art 1.
O'Casey v Commission of the European Communities (T-184/94) [1998] ECR-SC II-565, II-577–8.	*O'Casey* (T-184/94) [1998] ECR-SC II-565, II-572.
Campbell v United Kingdom (1992) 233 Eur Court HR (ser A).	*Campbell* (1992) 233 Eur Court HR (ser A) 17.
CANADA	
Eli Lilly Canada Inc v Apotex Inc [2008] 2 FC 3.	*Apotex* [2008] 2 FC 3, 4.
Controlled Drugs and Substances Act, SC 1996, c 19, s 4.	*CDS Act* s 4.
CHINA	
«施忠荣受贿案» [Shi Zhong Rong — Case of Taking Bribes] [2009] 4 中华人民共和国最高人民检察院公报 [Gazette of the Supreme People's Procuratorate of the People's Republic of China] 28, 29.	
«著作權法» [Copyright Act] (Republic of China) Legislative Yuan, 10 February 2010.	*Taiwan Copyright Act* art 10.

Full Citation	Subsequent References*
GERMANY	
Bundesverfassungsgericht [German Constitutional Court], 1 BvR 131/96, 24 March 1998 reported in (1998) 97 BVerfGE 391.	
Bürgerliches Gesetzbuch [Civil Code] (Germany) § 823(1).	
FRANCE	
Cour de cassation [French Court of Cassation], 06-81968, 5 December 2006 reported in [2006] Bull crim n° 304, 1095.	
Code de procédure pénale [Code of Criminal Procedure] (France).	
HONG KONG	
Ng Ka Ling v Director of Immigration [1999] 1 HKLRD 337.	*Ng Ka Ling* [1999] 1 HKLRD 337.
Dogs and Cats Regulations (Hong Kong) cap 167A, reg 22.	*Cats and Dogs Regulations* reg 21.
MALAYSIA	
Achieva Technology Sdn Bhd v Lam Yen Ling [2009] 8 MJL 625 (High Court).	*Achieva Technology* [2009] 8 MJL 625.
Digital Signature Regulations 1998 (Malaysia).	*DSR* reg 58(a).
NEW ZEALAND	
Haylock v Patek [2009] 1 NZLR 351.	*Haylock* [2009] 1 NZLR 351.
Habeas Corpus Act 2001 (NZ).	*Habeas Corpus Act* s 3.

Full Citation	Subsequent References*
SINGAPORE	
Virtual Map (Singapore) Pte Ltd v Singapore Land Authority [2009] 2 SLR 558 (Court of Appeal).	*Virtual Map* [2009] 2 SLR 558, 563.
Land Titles Act (Singapore, cap 157, 1994 rev ed) pt III.	*Land Titles Act* s 7.
SOUTH AFRICA	
Christian Education South Africa v Minister of Education [1999] 2 SA 83 (Constitutional Court).	*Christian Education* [1999] 2 SA 83, 84.
Local Government Transition Act 1993 (South Africa).	*LGT Act* s 9.
UNITED KINGDOM	
R (Amin) v Secretary of State for the Home Department [2004] 1 AC 653.	*Amin* [2004] 1 AC 653, 673–4 [39].
Cavell USA Inc v Seaton Insurance Co [2009] EWCA Civ 1363 (16 December 2009).	*Cavell USA* [2009] EWCA Civ 1363 (16 December 2009) [24].
Workmen's Compensation Act 1906, 6 Edw 7, c 58.	*Workmen's Compensation Act* s 2.
Human Rights Act 1998 (UK) c 42, s 6(1).	*HRA* s 12.
UNITED STATES OF AMERICA	
Kansas v Hendricks, 521 US 346 (1996).	*Hendricks*, 521 US 346, 356–7 (1996).
Tracy v Beaufort County Board of Education, 335 F Supp 2d 675 (D SC, 2004).	*Tracy*, 335 F Supp 2d 675 (D SC, 2004).